Morin's Book 21

Of the Active Determination of
the Celestial Bodies & the Passive
Determination of Sublunary Things

Jean Baptiste Morin
Physician and Royal Professor
in Mathematics born at Villefranche
in Beaujolais and died at Paris November 9,*
1656 aged 73.

Engraved by E. Desrochers in Paris rue du Foin near rue St Jacque.

Morin strongly resisted
those who move the earth:
But this astronomical war
does not destroy its movement.

*Morin is known to have died on November 6.

Morin's Book 21

Of the Active Determination of the Celestial Bodies & the Passive Determination of Sublunary Things

Jean-Baptiste Morin de Villefranche

Translated from Latin
by Penelope Sitter

THE WESSEX ASTROLOGER

Published in 2024 by The Wessex Astrologer Ltd
PO Box 9307
Swanage
BH19 9BF
England

For a full list of our titles go to www.wessexastrologer.com

© Penelope Sitter 2024
Penelope Sitter asserts her moral right to be recognised as the translator of this work

ISBN 9781916625112

Cover design by Fiona Bowring at Bowring Creative
Typeset by Kevin Moore

A catalogue record for this book is available at The British Library

No part of this book may be reproduced or used in any form or by any means without the written permission of the publisher.
A reviewer may quote brief passages.

Table of Contents

Foreword — ix
Translator's Introduction — xv

Astrologia Gallica, Book Twenty-One

Preface — 1

Section I

1. Of the formal, or essential, determination of the *Primum Caelum* — 7
2. Of the formal, or essential, determination of the Planets & fixed Stars — 10
3. Of a certain especially important & excessively inveterate error of Astrologers — 14
4. Of the accidental determination of the *Primum Caelum* — 21
5. Of the accidental determination of the Planets & fixed stars taken collectively — 29
6. Are the Celestial Bodies universal causes only? — 33
7. Are the Celestial Bodies only causes of Sublunary effects, or only signs, or both, & in what way? — 37
8. Does the whole *Caelum* concur in any & all Sublunary effects? — 45

Section II

Of the various kinds of accidental determination of the Planets with respect to particular Sublunary things

1. Of the accidental determination of the Planets by location of the body or by rulership in the houses of a figure — 49
2. Of a single Planet in any house of a figure — 56
3. Of several Planets in any house of a figure — 68
4. Of the ruler of one house of a figure in another house. And first, does it always combine the significations of the two houses? — 73
5. In what way a Planet ruling one house & in another combines the significations of the two houses — 82
6. Of several Planets ruling the same house, or one Planet ruling several houses — 91
7. Of the accidental determination of the Planets by reason of exaltation & Triplicity — 93
8. Whether the Planets are efficaciously determined in the figure for the native by their essential debilities (as they call them), namely, exile & fall — 99
9. Of the accidental determination of the Planets by aspect, & in what way this is to be understood — 103
10. That by their aspects the Planets cause benefit & misfortune, & in what way — 105
11. Of the connections, or aspects, of the Planets compared to each other in diverse ways — 111
12. Which things about any Planet & its aspects are principally to be looked at so that a truer judgment of them may be composed — 119

13.	Of the accidental determination of the Planets of one natal figure when they are found in the places of the Planets or of the principal significators of another figure	126
14.	Whether by reason of their essential significations the houses of the natal figure determine the celestial bodies with respect to the native alone, or in truth also with respect to other persons	130
15.	Of the double determination of the essential significations of each house of the figure: of course, intrinsic & extrinsic	138
16.	That nothing among Physical causes more perfectly imitates God's way of acting than the celestial bodies	140

Appendix of Charts	145
Notes	158
Bibliography	187
Index of Persons	192
Subject Index	196

Foreword

With this publication of Book 21, the crown jewel from Morin de Villefranche's 26-volume *Astrologia Gallica*, we have finally a definitive English-language translation available to dedicated students of this perennial art.

Book 21 is drawn from Morin's *magnum opus*, composed over a thirty-year period and written in Latin in a folio volume of 784 pages. The work was a defense of astrology at a time during the early to mid-seventeenth century when modern science was separating itself from the ideas and values of antiquity and the Middle Ages, a time when modern science was actively divorcing itself from philosophy. Morin's goal was very ambitious. His intent was to present astrology as a practical discipline based on a solid classical philosophical foundation. Morin wanted to provide the *Astrologia Gallica* to those who already were professionals; it was to be used as a reference that would serve for astrologers as the *Physician's Desk Reference* does for physicians. It was not intended originally for a beginner.

Section 1 of the text must be deeply appreciated in the context of the times it was written. Morin examines and then logically dismisses various prevailing theories on the influence of the sky that had been held from ancient times. Those theories were from his astrological colleagues as well as from those brought against astrology by the emerging sciences. Most of the arguments are now outdated. Morin was born and lived during the last decades of the Renaissance. From the Age of Reason, through the century of the Enlightenment up to and including our times, astrology, a time-honored discipline, was dismissed, discredited and regarded as a relic. For centuries, astronomy and astrology had been synonymous. Matter and spirit were one; the world was "sensible" and spiritual at one and the same time. Descartes, a leading figure in the emergence of modern philosophy and science, with his materialistic approach considered spirit and matter to be two completely separate realities. He, along with a number of others, provided the ideological thrust to discredit astrology.

Rejection of ancient ideas and world views were expressed by the motto, *Sapere Aude*! Dare to know! "Have the courage to use your own understanding!" This was the motto of Enlightenment used by Immanuel Kant when he defined "tutelage" as "man's inability to use his understanding without direction from another." Think for yourself was the drumbeat.

Writing during this period, Morin was caught up in the whirlwind of dramatic and fundamental changes in philosophy and science in the Western World. He was forced to straddle the past and present, to reconcile the ideas of Ficino, Pico della Mirandola and Giordano Bruno and address the ideas of early precursors of the Enlightenment like Galilei, Kepler and Leibniz. He had one foot placed firmly in the past, defending a geocentric world view, and the other foot contending with the development and acceptance of Copernicus's heliocentric world view. The emergence of the nascent forms of modern science eventually and most assuredly dealt the death knell to the study of astrology in European universities. The birth of modern science saw the schism of art from science, the divorce of astrology from astronomy.

Morin's approach is not a "coffee-table book" approach with pictures or, as is common today, a "cookbook" with recipes. Its study necessitates an unbiased and disciplined frame of mind. James H. Holden said: "To be faithful to the spirit of scientific inquiry, preconceptions must be set aside and the inquirer's mind must draw its own conclusions based on the evidence." As the Scottish poet William Drummond of Hawthornden, a contemporary of Morin, wrote, "He who will not reason is a bigot; he who cannot is a fool; and he who dares not is a slave." We must think for ourselves. This was the siren call of the Age of Reason.

Today's most highly regarded researchers in the field of astrology credit Morin as the last great apologist of astrology in the West. While this discipline has gained ever increasing acceptance in the eyes of the public, it remains a pseudo-science in the eyes of most academics. As recently as 1974 in the September/October 1975 issue of *The Humanist*, the voice of 186 leading academically trained scientists signed a statement, authored by Bart J. Bock, a distinguished astronomer, to declare astrology unscientific. Reading the article, you immediately see that signing the declaration demonstrated a complete lack of understanding of *the most* fundamental consideration in natal astrology, viz: how to enter the chart to begin its study. All who signed the statement committed the most basic mistake made by an uninformed person who lacks knowledge. They all signed a statement that disregarded the singularly most important consideration in a horoscope: the Ascendant.

The tremendous value of Book 21 for the modern practitioner is its *instructional value*. As the late Zoltan Mason of New York, the preeminent practitioner of Morin's tradition for almost seventy years, wrote of the book: "[Morin's] method necessitates that the Horoscope be taken as a unit. Without the ability to synthesize, no person can truly interpret a Horoscope." And: "...both the student and the teacher of Astrology have at last the opportunity to study the pure form of the Celestial Art, free from fatalism and superstition."

Section 2 of Book 21 can arguably be said to provide the foundation stone, the indispensable primer, a gateway to all further efforts that lead to the practice of this perennial tradition. In Section 2, Morin unfolds the rules for a rational approach to horoscope interpretation according to his approach to delineation, which he summarizes in two compact phrases that encapsulate his entire tradition: "Of the Active Determination of the Celestial Bodies & the Passive Determination of Sublunary Things." His "Theory of Determination" rests on an extensive and detailed explanation of three principles: Determinations, Planetary States, and Accidental Significators.

These principles form the basis that encourages chart synthesis in which one sees the chart as an integrated whole. Morin's approach necessitates the study of the chart's structural elements in a prioritized and organized fashion. In this approach, what you mention first is more important than what you mention next, and so on. Every chart has twelve signs, ten planets (if you include the so-called modern planets, Neptune, Uranus, and Pluto) and twelve houses. What varies from one chart to the next and gives rise to limitless possibilities is conditioned by careful measurement of the two metrics: Quantity and Quality. That is, by measurement of "How much?" and "Of what?" For example, every chart has Jupiter, but one must measure how great is its influence in the particular chart – Quantity-wise. This is critical and pivotal. Similarly, every chart has planets posited in one sign or another, but planets posited in some signs have a greater constructive value than in other signs. That is a Qualitative measure. Although the measurement of the quantity and quality of influence has been discussed by other earlier gifted astrologers, it is Morin's orderly unfolding that gives the reader the experience of being instructed by a talented and gifted teacher.

Morin's tradition was introduced relatively recently to English-speaking audiences under the title *Cornerstones of Astrology*, a highly paraphrased and incomplete version of Book 21 by Schwickert and Weiss published in 1972. Two additional translations followed, both in 1974. Those are *The Morinus System of Horoscope Interpretation*, by Richard Baldwin, and *Astrosynthesis*, translated by Lucy Little under the guidance of Zoltan Mason from Henri Selva's 1897 abridged French paraphrase. These two volumes, though more faithful to Morin's text than *Cornerstones of Astrology*, are also highly paraphrased and omit important portions of the text of the Latin original.

Penelope Sitter's translation makes available a faithful rendering of the full text and brings Morin's voice to life. The translation also provides to current and future generations of practitioners a useful set of detailed endnotes, an appendix of charts, a comprehensive and detailed subject index, and a separate index of persons. Altogether this translation of Book 21 is assured to be the authoritative and complete English-language text for contemporary students and a foundation for future university-level programs on our enduring art.

With the availability of this reliable translation of Morin's text, the attentive and patient reader will quickly appreciate the great gift that Morin handed down to posterity in one slim volume. That gift is to teach us how to think as an astrologer.

Robert M. Corre
New York 2024

Translator's Introduction

Jean-Baptiste Morin de Villefranche (1583–1656), often known by the Latinized name Morinus, was a French physician, mathematician, natural philosopher, astronomer and astrologer. He studied medicine at the University of Avignon, and in 1615 received the doctor of medicine degree. In 1629, after serving for more than a decade as a personal physician, he was appointed Regius Professor of Mathematics at the Collège Royal in Paris, a position he held until his death. By the time of that appointment, Morin, who had taken up the study and practice of astrology after he completed his formal education, had become the leading 17th century French astrologer.

Morin wrote several astrological works, and wrote on astronomy and on philosophical, scientific, and technical subjects.[1] His most important publication by far is his masterwork, the 26-volume treatise, whose translated title is *French Astrology established with its own principles and methods and divided into 26 books*. This work, completed a few years before Morin's death and published posthumously in 1661, was some thirty years in the making.

The foundational volume of *Astrologia Gallica*, as the work is generally known, and the one translated here, is Book 21: *Of the active determination of the Celestial Bodies and the passive determination of Sublunary Things*. The work focuses on natal astrology, though many of its principles apply to other branches of astrology. In it, Morin states a theory of astrological signification and sets out the method of determination that he considers to be proper horoscopic method. In the first of the two sections of Book 21, he treats these and other theoretical matters. Though he includes some theory in the second and longer section, Morin devotes Section 2 for the most part to the indispensable essentials for use of the method to delineate natal charts. Section 2 also includes a chapter on how to compare, or rather to combine, two nativities.

For any serious English-speaking student of Morin, an English language translation of Book 21 is very much needed. Morin's greatest gift to students and practitioners of horoscopic astrology is the theory and method he explains. Book 21 is their main source. Yet the perhaps surprising truth is that, in fact, this volume has never been given an actual translation into English, or even a complete and true paraphrase.

Astrosynthesis: The Rational System of Horoscope Interpretation according to Morin de Villefranche, published in 1974, is Lucy Little's translation of Henri Selva's 1897 abridged French paraphrase and partial summary of Book 21. Richard S. Baldwin's *Book Twenty-One: The Morinus System of Horoscope Interpretation*, also published in 1974, paraphrases most of the volume. Like *Astrosynthesis*, Baldwin's version of the book has been valuable to English-speaking astrologers. But neither work actually translates Book 21, and both, especially *Astrosynthesis*, omit parts of Morin's text. Baldwin's version, moreover, adds a few things Morin did not say, gets some simply wrong, and misstates others in a way that obscures or confuses important concepts. We have not had a translation into English that Morin's Book 21 needs and deserves.

One sometimes hears it said that Morin's Latin is difficult to follow. In Book 21, Morin is almost invariably clear and exact. His sentences are often long, sometimes very long. Because they are often complex, they require focus. Because they are well structured and well reasoned, a careful reader can track their progress. Some sentences, once the reader reaches their end, require review from the top. Some arguments, and some ideas that may be unfamiliar, require study. But, with the necessary review and study, and with reflection, an attentive reader who knows astrological

Translator's Introduction

basics will be able to follow the developing flow of the exposition and argument, and can move along with the train of Morin's thought.

Morin's voice is sorely missing from the existing incomplete English-language paraphrases and summaries of Book 21. When he is allowed to speak in his own voice, the text, even in translation, becomes engaging and, though dense and sometimes demanding, enjoyable to read and study. Book 21 has a beauty that only lucid reasoning, stated in a direct and honest voice, can bring to human thought and argument. In the Latin text, and I hope as far as possible in this translation, Morin's voice comes through to give the sense that he is talking directly to the reader with a great desire to explain his meaning. He wants to reach us, an objective not always easily realized when the thing to be reached is human understanding. From the time I have spent with Morin's voice and reasoning, I feel that, if we met, we could take up our conversation where it left off at the close of the book.

Morin usually begins a chapter with the exposition of his view on a topic, and frequently sets out a numbered series of related points, or of arguments in support of his position. He often sets up a contrast of his views with the ideas of others, particularly ones with which his contemporaries would have been familiar. Where he sees faulty thinking on a consequential matter, Morin seeks to bring clarity. He seeks to clarify the fundamentals astrologers need to understand to formulate sound astrological theory and to work most effectively with horoscopic charts.

Although with the necessary attention a reader can follow Morin's reasoning, it is one thing to follow statements of principles and rules and the arguments made to support them. It is another to truly see the power of the method that constitutes a complex art, and still another to use the method in practice. We see the truth of horoscopic astrology in demonstrations of its use. It requires more than explanation or study of rules and arguments to recognize the uniquely revealing power of the method Morin sets out. At least for most, it will require observation of skillful demonstrations of the method's use with enough focus and learning to actually see and understand its power. The efficacy of the method becomes even more apparent as one's skill in its use develops.

Morin's theory of astrological signification states that a celestial body signifies and effects no earthly thing except as its significations are determined through its placement among the houses of a horoscopic figure. According to the method Morin states, the houses a celestial body influences by location, rulership or aspect determine its particular significations and effects.

Rather than simply accept and repeat doctrine, Morin questions traditional authorities. To do so, he relies, as he often says, on reason and experience. It is sometimes said by those who hold tradition in high regard that "the old ways are the good ways." Morin seeks the oldest ways. He wants to reach back to his idea of the earliest authority to restore astrological method to its origins. He wants to discover the true foundations of the method and the true reasons for them. He draws doctrines and techniques from first principles and sets them in a system in which each factor plays its proper part. From his reasoned inquiry into foundational principles, and from keen observation, Morin established a reliable system whose skillful use reveals defining realities of human lives.

Morin teaches, in Book 21 and more fully also in the other specifically astrological volumes of *Astrologica Gallica*, how to use horoscopic method in practice. In Book 21, he teaches how to assess a planet's effects based on its nature and its condition and placement in a horoscopic figure. He explains a systematic, succinct and exceptionally clarifying way to delineate a planet's effects on matters of the houses through its location, rulership and aspects. Further, he shows in Book 21 the power of analogies between celestial bodies and earthly things, and teaches how to use those analogies to great effect in practice.

In Book 21 and elsewhere, Morin sets out other techniques for use of horoscopic method that are similarly invaluable. Those include especially, for example, the fundamental and illuminating techniques of house

Translator's Introduction

As astrologers continue the valuable work, begun some years ago, of translating traditional astrological texts, many definitions, doctrines and techniques that had been for centuries largely lost are becoming available. Such an abundance can result in overwhelm. To avoid confusion, and to make techniques and definitions readily available to memory and therefore usable in practice, astrologers need to systematically organize the wealth of material now offered. To do that, we need astrological theory that keeps pace with ongoing discoveries. Above all, we need, and the integrity of the horoscopic art requires, a stable and reliable method by which to guide practice.

With his penetrating inquiry into astrological method and his questioning of authority, Morin rejects a number of definitions and techniques on which other astrologers rely. One, of course, may disagree with Morin on certain matters and still find great and unique value in his work. In fact, with the necessary investigation, astrologers might find that the method Morin states is the foundational method of horoscopic astrology. With that foundation, definitions, doctrines and techniques, including some Morin rejects, might find their most effective place in theory and practice.

Morin made discoveries on foundational matters given little or no attention in the tradition with which he was familiar. Whether or not one ultimately agrees with him on any given matter, one who wishes to truly understand the horoscopic art should undertake the work needed to understand the import of what Morin teaches. His work is of a quality and importance, and has an intellectual stature, that, at the very least, defines the terms of questions that anyone who seeks to understand the true art must engage. One who fails to stand on the shoulders of a giant of Morin's stature loses a stellar opportunity to see far and wide, and deeply, into the great art.

An art *is* its method; it is a way of practice. Morin saw into the heart of the demanding art of horoscopic astrology, and discovered there an extraordinarily effective and revealing method. From his work, Morin offers great gifts of understanding to his successors.

The following Aphorism 25, Segment 1, from Cardanus is given at the close of George Wharton's 17th century "Teaching how Astrology may be restored; from Morinus."

Difficile est Judicare, per ea quae scripta sunt; longè difficilius artem ipsam tradere: Difficillimum autem artem ipsam invenire:

"It is difficult to Judge by means of what is written; by far more difficult to hand down the art: but the Most Difficult is to discover the art itself."

Notes on the Translation

This translation aims to be a literal one. Square brackets indicate occasional small additions or other insertions made for the sake of English-language clarity. Several endnotes explain terms that may be unfamiliar. A few show choices made in the translation, including choices of words that translate less directly than most to contemporary English. A number of endnotes refer to parts of other books of *Astrologia Gallica* relevant to topics Morin takes up in Book 21. Some give historical information that may be of interest to readers. That information is about the time and place in which Morin lived, or about people to whom he refers, especially those on whose nativities he comments. Corrections of typographical errors that do not spell out an actual word are not given endnotes; errors that form an actual word, number or glyph in the Latin original are noted. In view of the much more seldom use of the subjunctive mood in English than in Latin, and to avoid a stilted English text, the translation often uses the indicative where Morin's Latin text uses the subjunctive. In some places, to produce a text that is easier to read, and where nothing is lost in significance, the translation may simplify the verb tense. So, in some places, instead of using, for example, the future perfect, it may use the present or present perfect. In a few places, when it is grammatically permissible and seems to make a sentence easier to follow, I insert a semicolon where Morin uses a comma.

Charts to which Morin refers in Book 21 are found in the Appendix of Charts. Nativities found in other volumes of *Astrologia Gallica* are cast for the same date and place Morin uses. They are cast here to reproduce the Ascendant degree and, in all except one chart, the minute of arc that Morin gives the chart. The exception is the nativity of the Duke of Montmorency, for which Morin gives only the rising degree, without minutes. To match with modern software the Ascendant degree, in some charts the time used here varies by some minutes from the time Morin gives. The resulting figures match quite closely those from Morin. The other nativities in the Appendix are approximations drawn from Morin's descriptions of them, and are identified as such. In Section 2, Chapter 7, Morin comments on Abû 'Ali al-Khayyât's use of the triplicity rulers of the sect light in two figures. Although given by Abû 'Ali as though they are actual nativities, these are hypothetical figures that cannot be reproduced for any time during the relevant time period. You will find figures that match these descriptions in the Appendix of Charts drawn in whole sign format.[2]

Astrologia Gallica
Book 21

Of the Active Determination of
the Celestial Bodies & the Passive
Determination of Sublunary Things

Preface

Ancient Astrologers judged of the effects of the Celestial Bodies on Sublunary things for the most part from fictions wholly alien to nature, or from certain natural foundations that were only confusedly perceived and then worse applied. Of the former kind are the terms, decans, faces, the various parts, annual, monthly, and daily progressions,[3] and other groundless figments[4] introduced by the Arabs, Chaldeans, and Egyptians.[5] The latter kind are the universal significators,[6] which Cardanus[7] in various places calls significators according to substance, and about which the minds of all Astrologers up to now have been principally occupied. And certainly it is natural that the Sun should have a greater Analogy with honors, Kings, the Father, &c than with dishonor, peasants, children, &c. And the reasoning is the same about Jupiter for wealth, Venus for the wife, Mercury for inborn talent,[8] and so of others, as explained by us in Book 13, Section 3, Chapter 3.[9] But what Astrologers have deduced from this is incongruous. Doubtless the Sun is the universal significator of the Father or honors, so [it was supposed] that in any geniture the honors or dignities of the native and (at least in a diurnal nativity) the Father are to be judged principally from the Sun, whichever house he occupies or over whichever he rules, and, above all, that the Sun is to be directed[10] for the state of the Father and honors; and so of the rest. But the celestial bodies are universal causes, in themselves indifferent with respect to individual sublunary things, and therefore determinable by these. And there are various modes of determination with respect to the influxes, which are reduced to two primary kinds—namely, location and rulership in the celestial figure; therefore the celestial bodies act on sublunary births, at least through their influxes, only according to the mode by which they are particularly determined; that is, as they are, at the time the native emerges into this light, by body or by aspect in any house of the figure, or preside over any, or are connected to the ruler of any house. Nor does any Planet cause or signify anything in the natal figure except that to which it is determined by this method, as will be sufficiently apparent below.

And the compelling truth of this doctrine is interspersed in the Aphorisms of ancient Astrologers, who often judge the effects of the stars as they are in this or that house, or preside over this or that, or are connected with the rulers of the houses; but this is so confused and intermingled with figments or fictions that until now it has not been able to shine forth in its simplicity, as if it had been neglected. In fact, it is apparent from Ptolemy's *Quadripartite*,[11] Book 3, Chapter 1, that the method of divination by the combination of the stars with each other and with the signs and houses of the celestial figure (which are nothing other than those determinations that we will advance here) is ancient. And, as Cardanus explains in the *Commentary*, it was common among his Predecessors, the Egyptians, Chaldeans and Arabs, from whom the Greeks took the Astrology[12] handed down from Adam and Noah, though already then impure and corrupted.[13] But Ptolemy rejects this method, not because he says that it is itself false, but only confused, difficult, and nearly infinite, and belongs more to one-by-one conjectures than to universal precepts;[14] yet Cardanus admits in the *Commentary* that, if it could be conveyed, it would be far easier. And so Ptolemy turned to the general precepts he thought out for himself, such as, according to Cardanus in the *Commentary*, taking the place of the Sun for life in the natal figure, and comparing the whole *Caelum*[15] to it; and he does the same with his other general significators. Ptolemy, however, is frequently compelled to use that Ancient method,[16] as when he compares the Sun or the Moon with the ruler of the Midheaven or of the Horoscope;[17] and the confusion, or difficulty or infinity, is much greater in bringing together the place of the Sun with the whole *Caelum* for life—as Cardanus wants in the *Commentary* on Chapter 7, Book 2 of the *Quadripartite*—than in judging of the life from the state of the Horoscope and its ruler. And so that ancient method must be completely restored if we want to follow the true Astrology and its own consistent principles, handed down to posterity from Adam and Noah. And I, with the nod of God,[18] having at last discerned and purged the figments from the primary foundation of judicial Astrology in its purity, hand down the same to posterity. Doing this in this Book on the various determinations of the Celestial Bodies, of which the Ancients did not even dream, yet in which the whole natural science[19] of judging or predicting consists, as will appear plainly in a new Physical light from what follows.

SECTION I

Chapter I

Of the formal, or essential, determination of the *Primum Caelum*

All Philosophers acknowledge that the Celestial Bodies are universal causes, and the reason, according to our definition of universal causes in Book 7, Chapter 8, is because they produce Physical[20] effects with the principal agents inferior[21] to themselves. But certainly these effects are accidental[22] to those bodies, for it is accidental to the *Caelum* and the Sun that they produce a human being, a horse, an apple, &c, over which flows the formal effect[23] of those bodies; as when the Sun pours out a Solar influence,[24] which certainly is not accidental to the Sun but is present in him from his essence,[25] as a person sees; and so the Sun, even placed in imaginary spaces outside the *Caelum*, could not but pour out his influence and heat, even though it should be received in no subject of inherence.[26] Therefore the Sun is not a universal cause of this effect, but a particular one, inasmuch as he himself produces the effect without the concurrence of an inferior agent, whether his heat or influence is received by nothing or by some subject of inherence.

From this surely it is apparent that every universal cause is intrinsically indifferent to its accidental effects, and so is determinable to these, but not to its formal effect, for it is essentially determined to the latter by the Author of nature, inasmuch as it is a certain kind of Physical thing endowed with a certain kind of active virtue.[27] Accordingly, we first take up here this formal determination,[28] beginning with the *Primum Caelum*,[29] and from there we will proceed to the Planets and fixed stars.

And so the *Primum Caelum* is intrinsically, or essentially, determined to the virtue, most universal and proper[30] to itself, of producing, together with whatsoever other Physical causes, any and all possible natural effects in each of the regions of the World—Celestial, Ethereal, and Elemental[31] — for which reason it eminently[32] contains all other Physical virtues, as is proved by us in Book 14, Section 1, Chapter 1.[33] Therefore the *Caelum* itself is the first Physical cause, of which see Chapter 1, Section 3, Book 20.

You will object. If the *Primum Caelum* and all other bodies except the Sun and the Earth were annihilated, the Sun, nevertheless, would pour out his light, and his heat and influence, and would illuminate and warm the Earth, and flow into it, or onto an animal born on it, independently of the *Primum Caelum*; so the Sun even now confers the same independently of the *Primum Caelum*, for the *Caelum* does not confer by its presence or existence that which it does not take away by its absence or annihilation; therefore the *Primum Caelum* is not the first Physical cause.

I reply. Certainly it is true that if such a hypothesis is admitted the Sun would pour out the qualities mentioned above, as we have shown in Book 8, Chapter 8. For they are formal to the Sun and active at a distance; indeed, he would illuminate and warm the Earth because these effects are not formally celestial, for they are Elemental and agree with fire. But they would not flow onto the Earth, or, from the hypothesis, onto an animal born on it, except in a very general way; but not in a particular way, as with respect to life, honors, &c, because there is no particular actual influx except through house placement[34] in the celestial figure, on which all the particular reasons of influencing are founded. But with the Sun and the Earth alone existing, even though the movement of the Sun in his own orbit around the Earth would continue, there would be no celestial figure, because, of course, the houses of the figure are not divided along the Ecliptic, or the path of the Sun or of another Planet—and especially of the Moon, a primary Planet,[35] of which the same can be said of the Sun— but rather along the Equator, the circle proper to the *Primum Caelum*,[36] as we have proved in Book 17,[37] Section 2, Chapter 5. And the Stars *per se* are observed to influence by reason of these houses only, and not of others.

You will press on. The primary houses,[38] on which the reckoning of influencing is primarily founded, are nothing but the division of the entire surrounding space; and on Earth it is, or can be conceived as, the poles and axis, and therefore the Equator, by which space itself is divided; so certainly the influx of the Sun or of the other Planets would have to be admitted.

But I reply. There is no active influx from the primary houses, which are nothing but empty space, not intrinsically active, but only determinative, as we explained in Book 17, Section 3, Chapters 3 and 4. And yet we experience that the Dodecatemoria[39] actively influence with the Planets, and by themselves when they are present alone in the Horoscope or in other houses; but the Dodecatemoria are not parts of immobile space in that they are themselves mobile through the primary houses, or spaces; neither are they parts of the Earth, which also is immobile, and so in itself is without the poles, axis, &c of the Equator. They are, therefore, parts of the *Primum Caelum* that were determined from the Planets at the beginning of creation—that is, first causes from second ones—and so they now together simultaneously influence as the first and second causes of the same effect, which is necessarily dependent on both. From this it follows that the stars cannot influence particularly without the concurrence of the *Primum Caelum*, even though they may illuminate and warm.

From what has been said it is certainly apparent first: It is one thing to pour out heat or influence but another to heat and influence. For the latter requires a subject receptive to heat and influence; the former assuredly not; for the outpouring can occur in the absence of a subject, as if in imaginary spaces where the power of the *primum mobile*[40] is likely to be poured out, if around it those spaces are granted. Further, the *Primum Caelum* is the first unique cause of all actual celestial influx but the first common cause of illumination and heating, inasmuch as it eminently contains light, heat, and the other elemental qualities; otherwise, the elements of diverse natures would not be differentiable in the Dodecatemoria.

Chapter II

Of the formal, or essential, determination of the Planets & fixed Stars

Not unlike the *Primum Caelum*, which is determined by the Author of nature to its proper nature[41] and active virtue, so the seven Planets (which in Book 9, Section 2,[42] Chapter 2, and in Theorem 2 of *The Elements of Astrology*,[43] we proved to differ from each other in nature and virtue) were essentially determined to their proper natures and formal virtues. The Sun, of course, to acting in a solar manner—that is, to illuminate, to heat and to influence with a solar virtue; the Moon to acting with a lunar virtue, and so of the rest of the Planets, and also the fixed stars of diverse kinds.

But how difficult it is to define the proper nature and formal virtue of each Planet is already said in Book 13, Section 3, Chapters 1 and 2. And the difficulty of acquiring this knowledge arises from the fact that the same simple virtue causes one thing in metal, another in plants, another in brutes, and another in human beings; indeed, it causes different things in different persons, and in the same individual. And, moreover, it causes one thing with one sign, and another thing with another. Likewise, one thing connected with one Planet, and another thing connected with another, and also connected in different ways to the same other Planet; and finally, one thing in one house, and another in another, and different things with the rulers of different houses, as is established from *The Elements of Astrology*. For that reason, the way of discovering a Planet's simple nature and formal virtue in so many and innumerable combinations cannot but be extremely difficult. But, because the same simple virtue acts in whatsoever class of things and in all things at the same time, if that virtue in any class or kind[44] of things is attended to by a person with foresight and diligence, it nevertheless will be possible to have from that a knowledge of it not at all mediocre, and this way will be the surest of all.

When a Planet occupies its own domicile, as the Sun in Leo, the nature of the Planet is unmixed with another, especially if he is not connected to another Planet by body or aspect, because Leo is of a solar nature. Then, therefore, it is to be observed what he does in each of the houses of the figure with respect to human births (which, indeed, in Paris, where people are born every hour, can be observed on a single day, so long as the state of the Sun will have remained such); for though in each of the houses he produces different kinds of effects, yet all are solar in the investigation of the lives of natives; therefore that solar effect, which will be common to all, may justly best be said to be the proper nature of the Sun. And the reasoning is the same about the other Planets.

And no force is more certain than that one. With foresight of the time of such a state of the Sun or of another Planet more midwives would be preferred, for on any day they would diligently note the significations of the hours of births. But if the Sun should be considered while he is connected by body or aspect with other Planets, a composite influx would emerge from that connection, for which reason the Sun's distinct virtue would be unknown because this knowledge depends on distinct knowledge of the simple influx that we seek. Similarly, if the Sun should be seen in different signs of the Zodiac, it would be the same as if he were connected to different Planets because the signs repeat the natures of the Planets; and so the same difficulty would recur; the way set out by us, therefore, is more certain and easier than all others. For the primary houses, or spaces or places, of the celestial figure neither influence nor actively concur in the effect; but they only determine the influx of the celestial bodies, which suffer no mixture from those places. And as in this way the nature of the Sun is laid bare, the nature of Leo is laid bare in entirely the same way, for they are of the same unique and simple nature—the Sun indeed formally, but Leo determinatively, from Book 14, Section 1, Chapter 6. In this way, therefore, the nature of each Planet, both celestial, or influential, and Elemental, can be ascertained.

Further, with respect to the Sun and the Moon, each of which has a single domicile, no difficulty presents itself in this place. But for Saturn, Jupiter, Mars, Venus, and Mercury, to each of which a duplex domicile is assigned, no mediocre difficulty emerges in distinguishing their Elemental nature, especially because the two domiciles in the pair that is assigned to each of these Planets was determined at the beginning of the World to contrary elemental natures; for example, the domiciles of Saturn are Capricorn and Aquarius, one of which is hot and moist, the other cold and dry. And Astrologers are accustomed in general to say, both of the universal constitutions of the air and of the particular temperaments of natives,[45] that Saturn in Capricorn is cold and dry—that is, cooling and drying—but in Aquarius hot and humid; and, in sum, that he is, at least in effect, of such quality as is the nature of the sign he occupies. And their reasoning is the same about the rest of the Planets. How, then, will it be known that Saturn is by his nature cold and dry if he cools only in a cold sign, dries in a dry one, warms in a warm one, and moistens in a humid one?[46]

But here assuredly the difficulty is to be freed from knots. I say first: Astrologers err when in determining the air and the temperaments of natives they have no account of the proper, or formal, Elemental nature of the Planets placed in the signs, but want Saturn and Mars in Aries to be effectively warm to the same degree—as is seen in Origanus,[47] Part 3, Chapter 5, and in others—which, however, is contrary to Theorem 9 of *The Elements of Astrology*.

I say Second: A sign by itself—that is, one empty of Planets—located in the Horoscope or elsewhere, also acts; and indeed, it acts Elementally in accord with the nature to which it was determined at the beginning of the

World, but influentially in accord with the nature of its rulers. So, because Saturn has two domiciles, Capricorn and Aquarius, their Elemental natures are contrary to each other, yet each of them influences in a Saturnine way; therefore, from Saturn found in them, the influential nature of Saturn is first discovered, because from Saturn in either sign that nature is effectively doubled. The formal Elemental nature also is ascertained in that way, because with Capricorn he will cool and dry intensely, but not with Aquarius for, on the contrary, there his cold and dryness will be remitted, which cannot be done except by the contrary qualities of heat and moistness; for this reason Saturn is said to be extrinsically, or manifestly, formally cold and dry; but intrinsically, or latently, he is eminently warm and moist.[48]

From this, certainly, it is deduced that, although Saturn by his celestial or influential nature is hot, cold, moist, and dry, yet Elementally he is formally only cold and dry.[49] And therefore Aquarius refers only to his influential nature, but Capricorn also to his formal elemental nature; and so Capricorn contains more of the nature of Saturn than Aquarius, and therefore Saturn in Aquarius is less malefic than in Capricorn. For in Capricorn the harmful Elemental qualities certainly come out excessively, but in Aquarius they mix in due proportion, because Aquarius is determined to the airy elemental nature.[50] And the reasoning is the same about the other minor Planets.

Chapter III

Of a certain especially important & excessively inveterate error of Astrologers

The essential determination of the Planets pertains to something that until now is assumed by all Astrologers; namely, that the Sun (for example) signifies *per se* the Father, Husband, Kings, Magnates, Fame, Dignities, Life, &c, which Cardanus in various places calls to signify according to substance; and similarly that the Moon signifies the Mother, Queens, the People, &c; Jupiter, wealth; Mercury, inborn talent, and so of the rest—as is seen in the Books of the old Astrologers who call such Planets in themselves the general significators of things; and they make this essential signification the principal foundation of their prediction, so that they even direct those Planets for such significations. On that account, Ptolemy, in *Quadripartite*, Book 3, Chapter 4, says about Parents: *The Sun and Saturn agree with the Father according to nature, the Moon and Venus with the Mother; the position of these stars, among themselves and in relation to others, signifies the accidents of the parents.*[51] Similarly, Book 4, Chapter 3, where, concerning marriages, he regards it as correct to look at the Moon for the wife and the Sun for the Husband, and at their state, and from that to predict about the wife and the Husband. Then, Book 3, Chapter 18, where of the qualities of the soul[52] he says: *The qualities of the soul that are proper to the mind and reasoning are taken in each from the condition of Mercury; but then those proper to the moral parts and inferior powers are taken from the lights of solid body—that is, from the Moon and from the stars that are configured with her by conjunction or aspect.*[53] Therefore, according to this doctrine, all Astrologers up to the present pass judgment on the father in any geniture from the Sun or Saturn, on the mother from the Moon or Venus, on character[54] from the Moon, on inborn talent from Mercury, whatever house of the figure they occupy or over whichever they rule, looking only at their celestial state and how they are related to the rest of the Planets, according to the texts of Ptolemy mentioned above, and taking no account of the houses of the figure and their rulers.

But that this doctrine strays greatly from the truth, and that in its transmission the Ancients abused the Analogical virtue of the Planets, is shown First: Because, although the individual Planets differ among themselves in nature and powers, they have the virtue, common to all of them without distinction, of signifying something, from Theorem 19 of *The Elements of Astrology*; they also have an essential Analogy with the various classes and kinds[55] of Sublunary things that are more congruent with the nature of the individual Planets, as has been set forth by us in Book 13, Section 3, Chapter 3, as the Sun with life, the Father, honors, &c. Yet because this Analogical virtue is the same as the influential, or essential, virtue of the Sun, and that influence of the Sun is most universal and indifferent, as is said in the same chapter, therefore from this Analogy the Sun *per se* can no more signify life than the Father, the Husband, or the King and Honors, although by reason of that Analogy he signifies illustrious, public and visible things and persons rather than mean and obscure ones. Accordingly, in this indifference he cannot be taken for one more than for another. But if he were taken for all these—and so, Father, Husband, life, Honors, &c—or if the same were taken as signified about these things for the Native, no one will assert this would not be most incongruous and contrary to experience. In fact, Cardanus himself is seen to ridicule this doctrine in the sixth chapter of the *Book of Revolutions* where he says that Ptolemy imposed a new confusion when he gave many significations to one significator, and posited the Moon as signifying the body, then the habits of mind,[56] then life, and wife, and mother, and maidservants, and daughters, and sisters: *How then* (says Cardanus) *will the*

Moon be disposed for him whose wife dies in childbirth and he himself of long life? and his many daughters unharmed? and the maidservants fugitives? and the mother soon dead, and the body healthy, and the understanding inconstant and bad?[57]

Second: When Ptolemy, Cardanus, and others want judgment of the native's father to be from the celestial state of the Sun in every diurnal geniture, and in a nocturnal geniture from the state of Saturn, they do not see that it is incongruous to judge that, from the Sun still passing through and surrounded by Leo, as Ptolemy wants, or either conjunct or trine Jupiter or Venus, no child is born during the day throughout the whole circuit of the Earth whose father from this birth will not be fortunate and long-lived, or, on the contrary, unfortunate and soon ready to die if the Sun is badly conditioned.[58] Above all, is not that state of the Sun able to last for several days with the same particular virtue? In fact, is it not foolish to suppose that in that time each father is signified as of the same kind, or that the same is signified for each native regarding his own father? This certainly is not only repugnant to experience, but in addition it would make the essential significations of the houses pointless, and hence the construction of houses pointless. And the same is to be said of Mercury for inborn talent as long as his celestial state is favorable or unfavorable, and of Jupiter for wealth, &c.

And so, it is to be said that certainly the individual Planets are essentially determined to those individual things with which they have an Analogy, and which, owing to that Analogy, they especially promote or signify, according to Chapter 3, Section 3, Book 13; but this determination (which is essential) is, of course, intrinsically universal and indifferent, so that it signifies a human being no more than a brute because they draw their Analogies as much from the things of brutes as of human beings, and, among multiple persons born at the same time throughout the whole Earthly Orb, no more from one than from another; and none of these can signify *per se* life more than death, Father than Husband, friends than enemies, unless they are particularly determined to this by their location or rulership in the houses of the figure, or by their connection with house rulers, as will be explained below. But when they are determined, if it happens that they are determined to that to which they have an Analogy—as the Sun to the Parents during the day or at night by location or rulership in the fourth, or to honors by location or rulership in the tenth, or Mercury to the qualities of inborn talent by his location or rulership in the first—then, because the universal determination through Analogy concurs with the particular through the houses, they work efficaciously in full measure by reason of that particular determination in accordance with their benefic or malefic state. And because it often happens that such significators are particularly determined in accord with their Analogies, ancient Astrologers were deceived, supposing that is a perpetual truth which is only temporary and accidental.

Their doctrine about the father certainly was false for me, who was born during the day and had the Sun and Moon excellently surrounded by Mercury, Venus, Jupiter and Saturn in conjunction, and in trine[59] to Mars, ruler of the Horoscope, but in the twelfth house. This Moon was the significator of my parents because she is the ruler of the fourth, and above all of my Mother owing to the feminine Moon in the feminine sign of Pisces. And because the Moon was closely conjunct Saturn, departing from him and applying to no other, therefore she also signified undeserved hatred and harm to me from my Parents, but especially from my Mother.[60] But the Sun in partile[61] conjunction with Jupiter made Bishop and Cardinal Richelieu my hidden enemy,[62] owing to the Sun in the twelfth with Saturn. Therefore, the Sun was for me only a significator of such enemy Magnates and of injury from them, but, although it was a diurnal birth, not of my Father, for my Father never hated me nor did he, at least voluntarily, harm me. On account of which those celestial causes, so long universally esteemed, and used as if to signify something particular—though of course seen universally they are able to signify only universally, but not something particular to Peter or John—are hooted offstage.

You will object first. It is doubtless true that the Sun, seen alone, is too universal to be the significator of the Father, as also the Moon of character, Mercury of inborn talent, &c; but the Moon, intrinsically indifferent to signifying this or that character, is determined by the sign in which she is and by her ruler, and according to the diversity of the sign and the ruler she signifies a diversity of characters. And so Ptolemy, Cardanus, and others instruct that the Moon should be taken for the character, but more completely [also] her ruler; and so of Mercury for inborn talent, &c.

But I reply. In this also ancient Astrologers went astray. For of course it can be said that the Moon influences and signifies differently according to the different signs she passes through and the ruler to which she is subject; but this influence and these significations are still universal throughout the whole World, and the Moon, seen only in her celestial state, signifies the character no more than the Mother, the wife, &c; therefore, so that she can signify one of these rather than another, a particular determination is required, especially location and rulership[63] in the natal figure, or connection with the rulers of the houses to which these things belong. For in the truth of the matter, and in accord with principles, the ruler of the Horoscope applying, especially with a benefic aspect, to the Sun, Analogous to Honors, signifies Honors for the native; Jupiter, Analogous to wealth, applying signifies wealth; Venus, Analogous to the wife, applying, a wife, and she will signify a wife more strongly if Venus is in the seventh or the ruler of the seventh. And the reasoning is the same in the others; for which reason the greatest attention is to be given to the Planets in or ruling any house, and to whether they apply fortunately or unfortunately to a Planet Analogous to the significations of that house, and to [the Analogous Planet's] celestial state and determination in the figure. For from this, very true Prognostications are derived, and here an outstanding concealed treasure[64] of Astrology takes its place. Moreover, when the Moon occupies Cancer the Objection will be of no importance because Cancer and the Moon are of the same nature, and the Moon will not then be subject to the rulership of another Planet. Add to this that as long as Mercury remains in the same sign inborn talent would be alike throughout the Orb of Earth, contrary to the experience that with every hour, and even at the same moment of time, it may be very dissimilar. And so if Mercury, the general significator of inborn talent because of the Analogy mentioned above, is also its particular significator in a geniture through location or rulership in the first house—to which the signification of inborn talent and of the whole state of the body and mind[65] belong—the influx of Mercury will be most efficacious for inborn talent; or if Mercury is connected to the Horoscope or to its ruler by rulership or aspect, for in this way also he is determined to inborn talent. And the more ways and more strongly he is determined, the more efficaciously he will influence inborn talent; but if not at all, consideration of Mercury for inborn talent will be groundless. And the reasoning is the same with the rest.

You will object second. In several places Ptolemy attends to the location of the general significators with respect to the angles of the figure, and he regards them, in consequence of that determination, as particularly determined.

I reply first. That determination, with only four angles in the figure, is still too general and cannot be particular as it can through each of the twelve houses. But unless it is particular the Moon will not signify the character more than the Mother or the Spouse. I reply second: This was not always done by Ptolemy, as is established from the passages cited above, nor was it observed by other Astrologers, for in their judgment of inborn talent Mercury and his ruler are immediately and primarily attended to, whatever Mercury's location in the figure might be; that is, without taking into account any particular determination of him, which may be with respect to children, wife, or death, an approach rejected above, and not undeservedly. As for the supposed division and signification of the houses, when the Moon was in the seventh at night the same was said of the Mother and the Spouse, which certainly should not be done even if the Moon, ruler of the fourth and therefore the significator of the parents, especially of the Mother, is found in the seventh, because, of course, the Moon is more efficaciously determined by her bodily location in the seventh to signification of the wife than of the Mother; and so of the rest. Now with so great an error exposed in the Ancients, we proceed to the accidental determinations of the celestial bodies.

Chapter IV

Of the accidental determination of the *Primum Caelum*

After having said enough above about the active essential determination of the Celestial Bodies, we treat here of their accidental determination, starting again with the *Primum Caelum*, or the first Physical cause. As we have pointed out here before, Sublunary bodies actively determine the celestial bodies, as explained in Book 7, Chapter 10, but the latter can determine Sublunary bodies only passively, because, of course, Sublunary bodies receive from celestial bodies, not the other way around. Though on account of the impression they receive, Sublunary bodies themselves then act and in that way are said to be actively determined, at least secondarily, and so become the particular causes of their own effects.[66]

And so the *Primum Caelum* is accidentally determined in every way by reason of efficient causes. First, to the nature of the Planets, both influential and Elemental, through the signs of the Zodiac. This determination is taken up in Book 14, Section 1. But this determination is common to the whole Earth and to each kind of Sublunary thing, and is perpetual and unchangeable from the beginning of the World all the way to the end when this state of nature shall cease, the burning Heavens will be dissolved and the Elements will melt in the heat of fire, and a new Heaven and Earth will be made, as is foretold in the Scriptures, and then another state of the World will follow, not so greatly subject to disturbance or to change.

Second, [the *Primum Caelum* is accidentally determined] to the nature of each of the Planets and fixed stars by the motion of the Stars under the *primum mobile*; for, as from the birth of the World the determination of the *Caelum* is common to the whole Earth and is of perpetual strength, so in like manner when a human being is born, or a brute, that part of the *Primum Caelum* under which the Sun is seen, and which is called the apparent place of the Sun, is determined to the Solar nature by the Sun viewed under that part for the native as long as he lives; and so the place of Saturn is determined at that time for the same native to the nature of Saturn, the place of Jupiter to the nature of Jupiter, and so for the rest of the Planets and the fixed stars. And throughout his life these places function for that native in place of the determining Planets, not unlike the way the signs function for the whole Earth in place of the ruling Planets as long as this state of the Earth endures. Indeed, the first Physical cause is in every way determinable, both universally and particularly, as befits such a cause; not only is the place of Saturn determined to the nature of Saturn, but also his antiscion, his opposition, and all the other aspects, both dexter and sinister, as was explained by us in Book 14, Section 1, Chapter 4, then in Book 16,[67] in all of which [places] the Saturnine virtue remains with respect to the native, as is evident both from the directions of these places or to them[68] and from the revolutions and transits of the Planets through the same places, which certainly is most worthy of admiration.

But it appears to be very difficult to define by what means this is done. Lucio Bellantius,[69] against Pico,[70] in Complaint 16, Article 1, supposes that the force of the Planets is impressed upon parts of the *primum mobile* and preserved there for a long time. But he is deceived. First, because the *Caelum* is the first Physical cause, but the Planets are second causes. And a first cause suffers nothing and receives nothing formally from a second one. Second, the *Caelum* would be continually altered formally, although it is unalterable. Third, the power of Saturn remains in his radical place during the whole life of the native, but whenever other Planets, especially the Moon, pass through the place of Saturn during the life of the native they, by impressing their own virtues on the same place, would efface the force that Saturn has impressed; and so they would make it weak with respect to the native, or at least confuse and distort it by such a mixture of virtues so that it would be redolent of the natures, not of Saturn, but rather of other Planets, which, however, is contrary to experience even in a native who should die at 100 or 500 years. Fourth, by their motion under the signs the Planets would destroy the proper forces of the signs through such an impression, or would entirely distort them. But the part of a sign on the Horoscope that is empty of Planets and without aspects acts on the native purely according to the nature of that sign. Therefore, the force of the Planets does not remain in a part of a sign through an impression.

Kepler's *Book on the Fiery Triangle*,[71] Chapter 10, denies, owing to the immense distance, that the conjunctions of the Planets impress any force on the part of the sphere of the fixed stars under which the Planets come together, which force would remain in that part for some time; but he says that the whole force of a conjunction consists in an impression on Sublunary nature and its Divine faculties, the *Caelum* conferring nothing but a bare object. Accordingly, in Chapter 8 he says: *The work of conjunction is not the work of the conjoined Planets, from which* (he says) *there is only illumination and heating, but rather it is the work of sublunary nature itself. For although the Planets in conjunction move sublunary nature, they do not do so as natural agents that pour out some considerable virtue; they only move nature here as objects move the senses, as, of course, light or color the eyes, sound, the ears; and as the kind of object is, such is the nature of the sublunary thing and the sense.* And therefore he attributes, not only to animals but also to plants and to Earth itself, a sense that perceives only intelligible things (such as are the conjunction, opposition, trine and square of the Planets), and when a conjunction, opposition, square or another figure between Planets is perceived, sublunary things will be aroused to movement and activities, which are called the effects of such figures. *However, the sublunary faculties do not love promiscuously any and all figures* (he says in Chapter 9), *but they have among these a selection of harmonious proportions by which even the Earth is stimulated and excited to the release of ripened exhalations, with a pleasure similar to that which an animal feels in the ejaculation of the seed*, as he says in the book *Of the new star*,[72] Chapter 20. And in Chapter 10 of the *Fiery Triangle*, he says: *Whenever the Planets come to those places that at the birth of a person either were rising or had received the Sun or Moon, then the person's nature is roused so that he may apply himself more eagerly to all the works that, in accord with the condition of place and time, are in the hands of that person. But this could not be done otherwise than by the impression of the imprint*[73] *of the whole* Caelum *placed on that person's generative, sustaining, sensitive, and animal faculty*. And therefore he supposes that it should happen, while everything else in the *Caelum* is moving rapidly, that the position of that imprint as it was at birth still remains. And that which is done in every person he believes also to be done in the faculty with which the Globe of the Earth is endowed. This, then, is Kepler's opinion concerning the positions of the celestial bodies in the *primum mobile* and their configurations.

But this has not a little affinity with that dream of Kepler about the Moon,[74] and it is rejected by us. First, because Kepler does not prove anything of what he here asserts, and above all that in the body of all Sublunary things, and indeed of Earth itself, is a Divine faculty that senses and discerns the presence of a celestial object, and that in its body [that faculty] works in accord with the perception of the object by the senses, the celestial cause doing nothing. Second, Kepler not only makes that faculty rational in perceiving and distinguishing the celestial figures[75] and their times, but also, from the many figures possible in the circle, he allows it the choice of figures under which it moves its body, which is the work of a free agent and for that reason intrinsically indifferent to act or not, contrary to his Hypothesis. Nor does he give a reason why the faculty chooses one figure rather than another. Or if he should say that it is necessarily aroused only by harmonious figures, this then would be proved false because if harmonious figures alone were sufficient to move Sublunary things the same effects would always proceed from the same configuration, nor would it matter which Planets were configured with the same aspect of square, opposition, &c; but the square of Jupiter and Mars does one thing, and the square of Saturn and Mars another. Theorem 15, *The Elements of Astrology*. And diversity of effects cannot be from a figure that is the same; therefore it will be from the different power of the Planets, Saturn and Jupiter, squared with Mars. Third: The perception of an object by the faculty cannot be without some attention of the faculty, as is apparent in sensations. But on what account do the faculties of peasants pay attention to such objects when they are ignorant of these things and do not know what a conjunction, opposition or trine, &c is, or a harmonious figure? Indeed, on what account do the blind and the deaf pay attention to the same, or even others when conjunctions, oppositions and squares are made under the Horizon? If the faculty, even without attention, is aroused to anger, lust, murder, pilgrimages, &c, why not more efficaciously aroused from attending? But the soul[76] of an Astronomer endowed with senses and intellect certainly perceives with his eyes and instruments the conjunctions and aspects of the celestial bodies and yet is not stimulated and moved by them, as Astronomers experience and as Kepler himself could have known from experience; otherwise the observation of the Stars would be dangerous. Moreover, two vital forces, or faculties, that perceive the same objects would be admitted in human beings, one of which, attending to the objects, would perceive the same and not be stimulated, but the other, not attending, would perceive and be stimulated, which is incongruous and unheard of in the perception of objects. Add that this second faculty would be other than the intellect in human beings, and far more excellent and more divine, yet Kepler nevertheless locates that in the Earth itself and in the Planets. Fourth: If the *Caelum* confers nothing on the native, whence, why, and how is it that Peter has one nature[77] actually and formally, and Paul another? For it is not from the faculty alone, which is the same in both, nor from the diversity of the seeds alone, as we have proved in Book 12, Section 1. And nature always conforms to the celestial figure of the nativity; therefore it is impressed by the outpouring of real virtue from the celestial bodies that is formally received in the native. Finally, it could be denied in exactly the same way that the Sun or fire warms the Earth and human beings, and that the heating is from that intrinsic Divine faculty of the Sublunary body which in the presence of the Sun or fire would work as an object in the body in accord with this [faculty]. For why will not that faculty move the body in the presence of the Sun equally for heat as for another effect attributed to the influence of the Sun? Indeed, in that way no external efficient cause would be granted in Physics, which is plainly incongruous. Therefore, what Kepler says—that the stars do not pour out any force—is incongruous, for if none were poured out there would be in the native no impression of the active quality that we call nature. And because when the Planets come to the radical places of the Sun, Moon, or Saturn they arouse the native in accord with the nature of the Sun, Moon, or Saturn, it is necessary that in those places the force of such Planets survives the birth, contrary to Kepler's opinion.

So then, the opinions of Bellantius and Kepler banished, we say that in the radical place of the Sun the solar force remains with respect to the native, but certainly not by an impression, as Bellantius has proposed, but in fact by a determination, and by virtue of that determination that part acts upon that native in a solar manner, and the same is to be said of any other Planet. Nor do we say anything new here, but we stand firm in the same simple doctrine of the determination of the *Primum Caelum*, or of the first cause, which is determinable in every way, and which is in harmony with itself everywhere.

Furthermore, the two determinations of the *Primum Caelum* set forth above happen from the Planets and the fixed stars, by which the stars determine the *Caelum* itself to special ways of acting in accord with the nature of the determining star, but only universally. For in this way the part of the *Primum Caelum* under which Saturn moves is indeed determined to act in a Saturnine manner, but no more for a human being than for a brute, and no more for John than for Peter. Moreover—and this is worthy of admiration—this determination neither destroys nor weakens the accidental determination of the *Primum Caelum* into signs, but the two are compatible with each other; for example, when Saturn passes through Leo he neither removes nor suppresses the Sun, who flourishes throughout the sign of Leo; but in the very place of Saturn, the forces of the Sun and Saturn, then also of several Planets if several are found in the same place, flourish and stand simultaneously. And hence it is that the position of the Sun in Leo, and the position of Saturn in Aquarius, and also Jupiter in Sagittarius, &c, are so very effective; because, namely, in Leo the Solar force is doubled; in Aquarius, the Saturnine, &c; on the other hand, because certainly the natures and forces of the Sun and Saturn are most adverse to each other, hence it is that from Saturn in Leo both forces are hindered and distorted; and so, owing to the malignity of the encounter, an unfortunate effect is produced. Then in other, non-hostile associations, such as Saturn in Sagittarius or Gemini, middling influxes come out, as is proved by experiences of each. Further, this temporary determination of the *Caelum* by the Planets is to be understood not only through the body of the Planet but also through its aspects.

Third, therefore, the *Caelum* is determined by sublunary subjects to the kind of substantive effects undergone—as from the seed of a man received in a congruent womb begetting a human being and influencing him in accord with the capacity of the human species, or from the seed of a horse bringing forth a horse. And so also for plants and minerals.

Fourth and finally, the *Caelum* is determined to the kind of accidents congruent with the subject who undergoes them that are produced according to the location of its parts in the genethliacal figure of that subject. By reason of its location, it makes that subject susceptible in diverse ways to accidents congruent with his own nature; indeed, Aries in the first house makes [him] bilious,[78] audacious, generous, &c; Taurus, lustful; Gemini, talented, and so of the rest of the signs, as much in the Horoscope as in the Midheaven and other places. From this it is evident that the celestial bodies are actively determined to a kind of substantive effect by those subject to them, but the latter are passively determined by the former to the kinds and qualities of accidents congruent with themselves. For a person is subject to the *Caelum*, and receives an impression by which he becomes more liable to these than to those accidents, at one time by acting, at another by undergoing. And in the last two ways the *Caelum* is determined particularly but in the former two only universally.[79]

Furthermore, it is to be noted that the signs signify more, and more efficaciously, than the Planets; for, speaking universally, Cancer signifies in accord with the Moon's rulership in Cancer, then in accord with Jupiter's exaltation in Cancer, and in accord with Mars in triplicity and fallen[80] in Cancer; and the reasoning is the same about the rest. In particular, certainly the degree of the sign on the Horoscope signifies the native more efficaciously than the ruler of the Horoscope or than a Planet in the first house, as is apparent from the directions of the Horoscope; in like manner, aspects to the Horoscope are more efficacious than to the ruler of the Horoscope, and the same is to be said of the Midheaven; and this surely very much agrees with the dignity of the first cause.

Chapter V

Of the accidental determination of the Planets & fixed stars taken collectively

The Planets and the fixed stars, as efficient causes, are determined accidentally in various ways.

First, of course, by the signs of the Zodiac. For, although the Sun must necessarily act with some sign because he cannot but be under some sign, and the Sun and the sign act as partners, he is, however, indifferent to acting with one or another. Therefore, by his position under one, as under Aries, he is determined to act with it, and so Aries and the Sun determine each other, as two men steering the same ship.[81] And the assessment of the ruler of a sign and a sign is the same. For a sign acts in accord with the nature of its ruler because they are of the same nature. And on this are founded all those Aphorisms of Maternus, Stofler, Rantzau,[82] and other Astrologers when they affirm what each Planet does in the domicile of another Planet through the combination of their virtues. But as has been noted, the Planets Saturn, Jupiter, Mars, Venus, and Mercury have two domiciles, nor does the Sun cause the same thing with Aquarius as he causes with Capricorn.

Second, a Planet is determined in its action by coming together with other Planets or fixed stars. Saturn certainly is intrinsically indifferent to acting with Mars or Venus, or with the Eye of the Bull or the Heart of the Scorpion.[83] But when two stars come together as partners in the same action they determine each other. Furthermore, this determination is to be understood both by bodily conjunction and by aspect, and the reasoning is the same for both. These two modes of determination above are merely universal, from which alone nothing particular can be concluded, for they pertain only to the celestial state of the Planet, which is common to all Sublunary things and indifferent with respect to each individual thing. But yet in these two ways the Planets, in acting both universally and particularly, are either helped, or weakened or corrupted,[84] of which more will be said below. And on this are founded all those Aphorisms of ancient Astrologers when they asserted what any Planet causes in conjunction, sextile, square, trine and opposition with another Planet; but they erred in this, for from celestial state seen unconditionally, which is universal over the whole Earth and indifferent, they have predicted specific or particular effects; but this prediction will be deceptive unless the receiving subject and the terrestrial state of the Planets by their location or rulership in the houses of the figure are taken into account.

Third, the Planets are determined to kinds of substantive effects by the Sublunary subjects undergoing them, as is said [also] of the *Primum Caelum*, and from which comes the celebrated saying of Aristotle: *The Sun and man beget man.*[85] And the Son of a King is something different from the Son of a Peasant.

Fourth, they are determined, in accord with the kinds of accidents congruent with the subjects undergoing them, by the houses of the figure or in other ways by which they are applied to those subjects. And these last two modes of determination are particular in that they are related to something particular, such as John or Peter in their geniture.

Moreover, the Planets are determined in four ways by the houses of the figure. Namely, by their bodily location in those houses and by their dignity, aspect and antiscion. The dignity certainly is threefold—of course, of domicile in the house, of exaltation and of Triangle.[86] And a Planet determined by its rulership or bodily location is again determined under this principle in two ways. First, by another Planet seen in itself according to a simple Analogy, as, if the ruler of the Horoscope is with the Sun, from this cause that ruler is determined to the honors of the native.

Second, by another Planet seen as it is determined in the figure. And so the ruler of the first together with the Sun, ruler of the twelfth, portends illnesses and powerful hidden enemies for the native. All of this now will be discussed one by one and it will be shown which determinations are stronger than the others, for in these [determinations] principal concealed treasures of Astrology take their place, which were all alike unknown to the Ancients.

Furthermore, in Astrology it is to be seen first what a Planet signifies for anyone by reason of its nature and celestial state; that is, in accord with the sign it occupies, the ruler to which it is subject, and its connection with other [Planets] by body or aspect; then what it signifies by reason of its terrestrial state; that is, as it is in this or that house of the figure or as it presides over this or that. For the former [or celestial] state is universal to the whole inferior World[87] or common to all Sublunary individuals, and therefore it signifies in itself nothing particular for Peter rather than for John. Yet as the same Planet is seen on account of its latter [or terrestrial] state in the Genethliacal figure of Peter, what it means in particular to Peter himself cannot be defined by reason of the house it occupies or over which it rules unless it is known beforehand what it means by reason of its former [or celestial] state. Accordingly, from the nature of the Planet and its celestial state a mixture of virtues arises in which that Planet's own virtue prevails but is affected well or badly by others; and in accord with this mixture the Planet acts on Peter in a particular way as determined in his figure. Therefore, for the particular effects of the Planets their universal virtue is first to be known from their own nature and from their helping or hindering celestial state. And indeed the Sun in Leo blessed by the trine of Jupiter, and in the absence of malefics, moves all solar things remarkably well with the help of Jovial things in the whole sublunary World, and not only in the nativity of Peter as determined with respect to him. But badly conditioned in Aquarius and square or opposite malefics, both a universal and a particular corruption occur in the Sun's effects. And the reasoning is the same about the rest, as we already have noted in Chapter 3, Section 3 of Book 20; but [now] it seems necessary for us to dispatch in advance, and elucidate in the following [three chapters,] three much-visited questions.

Chapter VI

Are the Celestial Bodies universal causes only?

This [idea that the celestial bodies are only universal causes] is commonly asserted by many Philosophers. And it has especially crept into Astrology, which has been deceived by false definitions of universal and particular causes that have become customary in the Scholastic tradition. But we have dismissed such definitions with valid reasons and have applied genuine ones in Book 7, Chapter 8. Therefore, in accord with the definitions handed down by us, we unravel a knot of questions about both the *Caelum* and the stars, as follows.

If the *Primum Caelum* is seen as a whole in itself it is only a universal cause; because it is seen in this way only as the first and most universal Physical cause, concurring with its own virtue in all the effects of secondary or inferior causes, as is said in [Book 7,] Chapter 10. And, according to our definition, a cause concurring with its inferiors and subordinates is universal.

If, however, the *Primum Caelum* is seen according to its parts, or the Dodecatemoria, then every sign, such as Aries, will be considered either as belonging to the *Caelum*'s material nature, insofar, of course, as it is a part of the *Primum Caelum*, or according to its own formal nature, insofar, of course, as it is such a sign—that is, one determined to the nature of Mars. In the former way it is still, like the *Primum Caelum* itself, a universal cause. But in the latter way it again must be seen in two ways. First, as it concurs in its action with the principal sublunary agents inferior to it, as with a procreating human being or horse. And then, as by its eminent virtue it produces the same effect with a procreating human being or horse, it is by definition [the effect's] universal cause. But according to the effect—that is, a procreated human being or horse—it confers particular qualities that neither a human nor a horse confers, which, of course, are those proper to the influence of the sign, such as an ill-willed character from Scorpio in the Horoscope; then the sign is, according to the definition, the particular cause of such character. Because, as should be known, the *Caelum* and the stars, besides containing in their eminent virtue the powers and effects of sublunary bodies, have something peculiar to themselves that cannot be conferred by sublunary causes. And so, sublunary things need celestial ones, so that they may be perfected and governed by them, as Aristotle himself also acknowledges. Second, a sign, insofar as it is a sign, must be seen as acting universally[88] with the Planets or stars, but only insofar as it is pouring out its forces into the whole universe, taking no account, of course, of particular effects in these sublunary things. And in that pact [between a sign and the Planets or stars with which it acts], a sign is not *per se* a universal cause [as it is when] it acts with causes inferior to itself, for [it acts] only with partners, from Chapters 4 and 5, Section 2, Book 20.[89] Accordingly. it acts as a particular cause, pouring out its own form and virtue into the whole universe. Nor does it matter that from that virtue innumerable and very diverse effects are produced at the same time, for this does not make a cause formally universal, but only accidentally, as we noted in the definitions of universal and particular causes.

Someone will object that every particular cause is subject to some universal one. But a sign, as a sign, is subject to no universal cause, unless you say that the *Primum Caelum* is a universal cause with respect to its parts, which seems incongruous; therefore a sign is not a particular cause.

But I reply first. The antecedent[90] is utterly false; otherwise God, as the particular cause of grace, would be subject to some prior cause. And the *Primum Caelum*, as the particular cause of its own influx, yet would be subject to some superior Physical cause, so that an infinite regress of Physical causes would be given, contrary to our hypothesis of some first

Physical cause, which necessarily must be admitted. I reply second: A sign, as a sign, is a second cause—from Chapter 5, Section 2, Book 20—and therefore subordinate to the first, which is universal. Nor does it matter that a sign seen materially is a part of the *Primum Caelum*, because it is not part of it seen formally, or insofar as it is a sign.

But as regards the Planets, the reasoning is as that of the signs seen formally because, of course, the signs as signs, and the Planets as their rulers, are of the same nature or Planetary virtue. Therefore, a Planet concurring in the effect of any sublunary cause, insofar as by its eminent virtue it produces the same effect as [the sublunary cause]—as the Sun with a man begetting or with a Mother giving birth—is its universal cause because the Sun concurs with a cause inferior to himself. But as he confers a solar character on the native, or makes him fortunate for fame and honors (which undoubtedly cannot be conferred by parents, especially by peasants or indigents, or by giving birth), the Sun is said to be their particular cause; for indeed he alone accomplishes these things by his own virtue or influence. Similarly, seen as acting universally and only pouring out his forces into the whole universe, he must be said to be the particular cause of his effects through light, heat, and influence when, for the production of these effects, no inferior cause subordinate to the Sun concurs with him. Certainly when the Moon, this Earth, or these walls are illuminated or heated by the Sun, these are particular effects for which, therefore, some particular cause is to be assigned. But none other than the Sun appears, the *per se* and principal cause of them, and so he will be their particular cause. The reasoning is the same about influence,[91] and the same is to be said of the other Planets and fixed stars. And that which is asserted here about the Sun acting alone also is to be asserted about him acting together with other Planets or signs, because doubtless the Planets are the Governors of the World, distinguished by their powers and authority, and therefore partners in the government of the World and not subordinated to each other in acting, just as neither are the four Elements, and therefore not inferior or superior among themselves, although the Sun illuminates all others and excels them.

It will be objected. At least when the Sun is in Leo, he acts with Leo as a universal cause; for Leo is inferior to its ruler, the Sun—from Chapter 7, Section 2, Book 20, near the end—whether the Sun is seen as acting universally in the World, or as acting in a particular sublunary body or with a particular sublunary agent.

But I reply. Leo is inferior to the Sun not by reason of the solar influential nature, which is the same in Leo and the Sun, but only insofar as Leo has this from the Sun through a determination. Now certainly the superiority of a universal efficient cause is understood to proceed from superiority of nature, as, without doubt, superior and inferior causes are of different natures, subordinated and at the same time concurring. From this certainly it is inferred that the Sun and Leo act together as partners of the same nature, but the Sun and Cancer as partners of diverse natures, although Leo, by reason of the solar virtue received by determination from the Sun, depends on him essentially, as an inferior on his superior.

Accordingly, the *Caelum* and the stars are sometimes universal causes and sometimes particular, but not always universal, as has been thought by many. Lucio Bellantius against Pico, Article 6, says the *Caelum* acts as a universal cause inasmuch as it produces many and diverse effects at the same time with causes inferior to itself, as with a human being, a human being, and with a dog, a dog. But certainly [it acts as a] particular [cause] when it produces certain effects that are left without their own particular cause, as in births from decayed matter, he says; but a seed, a particular cause endowed with an active force, is in decayed matter, as we said in Book 20, Section 2, Chapters 5 and 6. And a multitude and diversity of simultaneous effects does not make a cause *per se* universal, as said above.

Chapter VII

Are the Celestial Bodies only causes of Sublunary effects, or only signs, or both, & in what way?

To unfold these questions, the definitions of cause and sign are set out to be seen first. And these are to be understood as of a cause *per se* and as of a sensible sign.

Accordingly, a cause *per se* is that which in itself produces an effect; and this either through its own virtue, as the Sun illuminating the Earth, or through another's virtue, as the aspect of a Planet, which acts *per se* but by virtue of the Planet from which that aspect flows, as in Chapter 9, Section 2 will be said. A sensible sign, of course, is that which presents itself to a sense, and also presents what is not apparent to the sense to be known to the understanding. Like hanging ivy, which presents itself to a sense, and in addition discloses, according to popular custom, wine in the cellar for sale. But the formal reason of a sign does not consist in the fact that it presents itself to a sense (for a sign is not a sign of itself), but in the fact that, in addition, something unknown to the senses reveals itself to the understanding, of which it is said to be the sign. Furthermore, a sensible sign is threefold: diagnostic, prognostic, and recollective. A diagnostic is a sign of a present thing, such as are those by which Physicians diagnose the appearance of a present illness. A prognostic is a sign of things to come, such as are those by which Physicians conjecture the health or death of a patient. Then those by which Sailors and Farmers foretell storms to come on the Sea and barrenness or fertility on the Earth. A recollective is, of course, a sign of a past thing, as ash is a sign of a past burning, the track of a Wolf a sign that a Wolf has passed and where it went; and so of others.

This surely understood, I say that some supposed that the celestial bodies are not to be signs of future sublunary events, but that they are nothing but perhaps groundless things and a fallacy because of that passage in *Jeremiah*, Chapter 10: *Do not fear the signs of Heaven.* But by the signs of Heaven the Prophet does not understand the celestial bodies, but only their wooden or golden idols held in high esteem by the Babylonians, as is apparent from what follows in the text, which indeed fits with idols but not with celestial bodies. On the other hand, others are of the contrary opinion, that the celestial bodies are only signs and not causes of sublunary effects because of the words of *Genesis*, Chapter 1, where God said: *Let there be lights in the firmament of Heaven to divide day and night, and let them be for signs and seasons, and for days and years,* &c. And it seems that Kepler (above, Chapter 4) was entirely of this refuted opinion when he says that Planets conjunct, square, or opposite do not move sublunary nature as natural agents pouring out a measure of virtue, but only move the vegetable and animal faculties of sublunary things and of the Earth itself as objects move the senses. Besides what already has been said against Kepler, it is certain that the Sun is a sign neither of the day nor of the year, but a cause, for he makes a day and a year. Nor does the account of the Sun as a sign fit with respect to the day he makes. For from what is said above, the reason of a sign consists in the fact that the sign reveals to the understanding something beyond itself that is unknown to the senses and of which it is said to be the sign; but the day is apparent to the senses, and therefore the Sun is not a sign of the day, nor consequently of the year, which consists of 365 days, but is only a cause of them.

Accordingly, it is necessary that when the holy Scripture says the Sun and Moon are for signs, we understand that they are signs of things other than days and years or seasons; it remains, therefore, that they are signs of other effects that happen in sublunary things. And Kepler indeed would have granted this, provided that there were no causes of such effects except the very nature of the sublunary things objectively stimulated by the celestial signs. In truth, he partly contradicts himself in this respect; for it is admitted that the imprint of the whole constitution of the celestial bodies is made in the generative, sustaining, sensitive animal faculty of a human being or of the Earth, which imprint remains, and by which the nature of a human being and of the Earth is roused to action. Therefore, it is necessary for that imprint to have a permanent power of arousing, at least whenever the Planets come by direction or transit to the main places of the impressed constitution. And in consequence, when that imprint flows from the *Caelum* and is imprinted on that faculty, then its power of arousing also will flow or be poured out from the *Caelum*, contrary to Kepler's opinion. And so the *Caelum* will be a natural cause of these sublunary effects. For the *Caelum* is the cause of the imprint, and therefore of these effects, for the cause of a cause is a cause of what is [later] caused.[92] Nor will it help to say that the *Caelum* is indeed an objective cause but not an effective one, or that it does not efficiently concur, but is only a power, for this is neither able to do everything nor whatever you will, but only that for which it is powerful; but that by which it is powerful is necessarily something effective, otherwise its power would not be effective; and according to Kepler it is powerful through an impressed imprint; therefore the imprint pouring from the *Caelum* will be effective. Add to this that a person's faculty must be stimulated and aroused by that imprint impressed on him, not only to act or to devote himself eagerly to all external works that are in his hands, as Kepler claims, but also to generate passions, and illnesses or downfalls, from which the person himself and that faculty are destroyed; because certainly this insane, cruel, and treacherously murderous faculty internal to us, which perceives celestial objects with or without attention, most diligently pursues its end, with the *Caelum* or the stars causing nothing, nor a person feeling it, nor understanding it with foresight, nor strongly preventing it with reason; because it is posited that this faculty is superior to intellect and reason, independent of these and absolute, all of which is utterly alien to the dignity of intellect and reason.

Therefore, it is evident from what is said above that celestial bodies are signs and causes of sublunary effects, against Cardanus who in the *Book of Interrogations*,[93] Question 13, wants the stars to be only causes but not signs; and what kind of things they truly are, it seems to us to be here discerned.

The celestial constitution when a person is born is a recollective sign of the temperament and the conformation[94] of the body. For, of course, these things precede birth, and the infant is born into the light in a state of the *Caelum* and a location most congruent with his temperament and bodily constitution, as we have said elsewhere. Therefore, from the present celestial figure the quality of the texture of temperament and conformation that preceded it can be judged; and so it will be their recollective sign, but not their cause for the reason that they have preceded.

Furthermore, the same celestial figure is a diagnostic sign of the temperament and conformation of the native insofar as these are perfected and finished, and of the character, inborn talent, and general disposition of the native impressed by the *Caelum* and by which he is exposed to the various accidents of life and death. The reason is that the texture of temperament and conformation preceding birth is most efficaciously completed and determined by the constitution of the *Caelum*, which brings the fetus into the light from the womb at the most congruent time and subjects it to its fate; and from the same, the propensities of the sensitive appetite, the qualities of inborn talent, and the impressed character of the whole fated subjection are imprinted like a seal on that native, in accord with the nature, state, and placement, or particular determination, of the celestial bodies, as daily experience proves. For that reason, the celestial figure at the moment of birth is not only their sign, by which they are known, but also the same is their cause *per se*, inasmuch as the temperament and conformation of the body are perfected and determined by that celestial constitution. But in addition, the character, the qualities of inborn talent, and the state of subjection to fate are themselves newly impressed on the body being born as a kind of celestial form by which individual persons are distinguished from each other in the dispositions of body, mind, character, and inborn talent, both to act and to undergo.

Finally, the same celestial figure is a prognostic sign of the accidents that will be for the person born from the fatal subjection mentioned above; for, indeed, that celestial constitution, subjecting the native to itself, contains the power of his accidents, to be produced at congruent times through directions, transits, and revolutions, as will be sufficiently explained in its proper place.[95] And from this it is apparent that the celestial figure is not only a diagnostic and prognostic sign, but also the cause of that of which it is a diagnostic and prognostic sign, so that if it were not a cause it would not be a sign, and precisely to the extent it is a sign, to that extent it is a cause. For if it were not an efficient cause, from where and by what virtue would the exact conformity to the celestial constitution be effectively caused? But for the very fact that it is a cause, and therefore as a cause acts in accord with the disposition of the subject, from this it follows that the celestial constitution can be resisted, as Ptolemy would have it when he said in *Centiloquy*, Aphorism 5: *One who is skilled*[96] *can avert many of the effects of the stars when he knows their nature and prepares himself before their occurrence*. And therefore such a sign and such a cause are by no means of unavoidable necessity, as many have thought, whose error is also condemned by the Church. It is apparent also that the same celestial figure is at the same time an actual cause of that of which it is a diagnostic sign, and a potential one of that of which it is a prognostic sign, as will be explained along with directions and transits; but from the foregoing it is also deduced that if the stars do what they signify, therefore those Planets that are significators of death must cause and bring it about, either by direction or by revolution; and the same is true of the rest.

You will object: Mars, ruler of the Horoscope, badly conditioned in the eighth, signifies a violent death for the native; but, as is apparent, Mars does not kill the native; therefore he is only a sign and not a cause.

I reply: Mars does not kill the native directly, but indirectly, for by his influx impressed on the native he renders the latter subject to the violent death into which that native falls through that influx; therefore Mars is the cause of the cause of the native's death.

Moreover, that no one should be frightened by the fatal subjection here set forth by us, read Chapter 24, Section 2, Book 12, where fate is treated. And what is asserted here about the *Caelum* and the stars in a particular figure, and also in a universal figure[97] and revolutions, is to be understood to be asserted at least about diagnostic and prognostic signs, as will be explained in its proper place.

But it also can be asked: Do the stars signify any and all things that will happen to a person after his birth?

To which I reply, no. Otherwise, a fatal necessity would be introduced, and what we quoted above from Ptolemy would not be true. And therefore the stars do not signify opposition to the force of the stars by human foresight and divinely illumined reason; for if the stars signify an illness or duel to any one at some time, they will not at the same time signify that there will be no duel or illness through the person's foresight by avoiding the occasions or consulting about remedies suitable to his health. For which reason it is said of the things that happen to a person after birth that some are not in his power, such as siblings, enemies, death, fortune; but others are in his power, such as wealth, children, servants, spouses, disputes,[98] wars, journeys, dignities, undertakings. For about all these things extrinsic to the native, he determines freely for himself with his actions, and can simply and completely either spit them out or avoid them, even if he is very much inclined to some of them by the influx of the stars.

Now certainly whatever things are signified by the stars to be for the native, they strongly incline or dispose that native, both actively and passively, to carry out those things, so that such a disposition most certainly can be firmly asserted. And of those effects that are congruent with such a disposition, those that are not in the power of the native can be asserted more certainly; but, of course, the occurrence of those that depend on his volition is more doubtful. As for most things, however, they usually follow the disposition of the stars; then also a person is usually ignorant of himself—that is, of his disposition and of what is to be for him—and therefore he will not do enough to meet misfortunes[99] that are to be. And it is arduous, and beyond nature, to resist natural inclinations, and therefore very few undertake this struggle and persevere in it resolutely. And from this it is that Astrological predictions are so frequently discovered to be true; inferior and particular causes, of course, yield to the virtue of the superior and universal ones, according to the law of nature, although predictions themselves are only conjectural; nor is it lawful to predict anything about them with certainty.

Therefore, from what has been said in all of this Chapter 7, we conclude that the force of the seed affected by the celestial influx at the moment of conception is the efficient cause of the actual temperament and conformation of the native, initiated at that very moment. But the celestial figure at the moment of birth is a recollective sign of the temperament and conformation first introduced, diagnostic of the present and perfected, but prognostic of things to come from such a constitution of the body. It is not, however, a cause of the past, or of the figure of those who preceded, as of the Father, Mother, Elder Siblings, &c, but only of the present and the future. And certainly of those things that are present—such as the completed temperament and conformation, inborn talent, character, &c—it is an actual cause; but of what is to be—as of children, and of those things that happen to the native with respect to parents, siblings, children, servants, spouse, dignities, wealth, &c—a potential cause, in its time reducible to an act by actual causes, which, if absent, or if contrary ones are present (as when a signified illness is prevented by suitable remedies), that cause will not be reduced to an act and will be frustrated in its effect. Yet it will be said of the cause—because the celestial stimulus to the signified effect was not lacking at the time in the native or with respect to his affairs—that the cause lacked actual concurrence or was hindered; entirely, as is said in the case of preventative grace. And so the natal constitution is a prognostic sign of the accidents that will be for the native unless they are prevented; then also a cause if they will have happened.

Chapter VIII

Does the whole *Caelum* concur in any & all Sublunary effects?

We have already written [on this question] in Book 10, Chapter 3 against the false opinions of Pico Mirandola, Sixtus ab Hemminga,[100] Alexander De Angelis,[101] and other ignorant haters of Astrology, but the matter is easily untangled by making distinctions in the consideration of effect.

For if the effect is considered as a whole in itself—that is, both according to those things that are actually in it, as in a person, temperament, bodily form, inborn talent, &c, and according to those that are within his power, such as actions, religion, illnesses, &c, or both according to those things that are intrinsic to him, such as character, inborn talent, temperament, &c, and according to those things that are extrinsic[102] to him, such as wealth, siblings, parents, children, and other significations of the houses excepting the first—then it is certain that the whole of the *Caelum* concurs with that effect seen in its totality, in that the whole *Caelum* is divided for its effect into twelve parts, or houses, for its substance and for each kind of accident of which it may be capable.

But if the effect is considered only according to some part of itself that pertains to the same act or power, whether it is intrinsic or extrinsic—for example, if a person is considered only with respect to inborn talent, or wealth, or honors, or children, or death, &c—then the whole *Caelum* does not concur effectively with that part; but only the signs, Planets and stars are considered that, by body, rulership or aspect, take possession of the house to which, in accord with the essential significations of the houses, that part of the effect belongs, and also Analogous Planets joined[103] to that part; as, if a person is seen with respect to marriage, only the parts of the *Caelum* and the stars determined to marriage by bodily location, rulership, or aspect effectively concur with this, but not all of the *Caelum* or all the stars, as will be sufficiently explained in the following Section.

SECTION II

Of the various kinds of accidental determination of the
Planets with respect to particular Sublunary things

Chapter I

Of the accidental determination of the Planets by location of the body or by rulership in the houses of a figure

These two modes of determination are more efficacious than the others, but the most efficacious of all is that through the bodily location of a Planet in any house of a celestial figure. Therefore, these are to be taken up first, and afterwards the rest.

What happens in these inferior regions is caused by the superior ones; the *Caelum* and the stars are indeed Aristotle's witnesses when he says: *This inferior world is contiguous with the superior regions, so that all its power is governed from there*; and elsewhere: *The Sun and man beget man*.[104] But this posited, and because the state of the celestial bodies is laid out before the eyes and minds of human beings to be contemplated, it will be possible to have from knowledge of it foresight of what will be; for if past celestial causes and their effects have been closely observed, such as Eclipses or the conjunctions of Planets in the same sign, what will be done by the recurrence of the same now or in the future can be correctly foretold. And those causes will be said to signify that such things will be because such are their effects. For they are said to signify only from their effects; and so if they cause nothing, from what and in what way are they said to signify? See Chapter 7, Section 1.

Moreover, although each Planet has a unique and simple essential virtue, effectively diffused through the whole World, by which it does whatever it does, yet this virtue is to be viewed in two ways. First, as it is intrinsic and unqualified, and thus universally and indifferently affects all kinds of Sublunary things and individual ones, and can do something in each. Theorem 22, *The Elements of Astrology*. Second, as it is received in some subject and is referred to it, and is determined by that subject; so that, although the Sun acts with the same virtue in a human being and a plant when each is generated, it does not cause the same in a human being and a plant on account of the diverse nature and disposition of the subjects receiving the same virtue because, received in the manner of the receiver in diverse kinds of subjects, it produces diverse effects though it be applied to each in the same manner.

Again, although certainly that universal virtue is determined by the person being born, it does not affect each person, even those born at the same instant of time, in the same way because it is not determined in the same way by each individual, or the Planet is not applied in the same way to each individual; but for one it is in the first house, for another in the second, for another in the third, &c, or in one it is the ruler of the first, in another the ruler of the second, in another of the third, &c, from which various effects are produced in each individual at the same instant of time from the same Planet, as experience everywhere proves.

From this certainly it is to be deduced that the Sun, determined by the birth of Peter, cannot be the cause of all the present or future accidents of Peter's birth, for all those accidents belong not to a single house of the celestial figure, but to all twelve, to which the Sun, neither by bodily location nor by rulership, can be determined at the same time with respect to Peter. The Sun, therefore, causes only that to which he is determined, but the rest is done by the other Planets in accord with the determination of each. And so on that account the whole figure of the *Caelum* acts upon the native in accord with how he is subject to the accidents essential to the twelve places of the figure, and by the impressions of its influence it affects him with respect to those accidents. Not, however, by the whole causing any and all kinds of accident, as Pico and De Angelis would have it; but by each part of it causing a kind of accident as each part of the *Caelum* is determined to this or that kind in the figure itself. As, if in some geniture the Sun is in the first house or is its ruler, he will act on the native with respect to life, character and inborn talent. And then if Jupiter is in the tenth or is its ruler, he will act with respect to actions and dignities; if Mars is in the eighth or is its ruler, he will act with respect to the death of that native; and so of the rest. And though the death of siblings, children, spouses, or other accidents signified for them in the geniture of the native pertain more to them than to the native, yet, as they are in the geniture of the native, they also pertain to him because, of course, as persons who affect the native die or are themselves affected, so also are they his good fortune,[105] such as children, or his misfortune, such as enemies.

Now with these premises, it is to be said that the primary houses, which are only parts of mundane space divided by a Physical method for the body being born, are themselves neither the causes nor, properly speaking, the significators of the accidents that are essentially attributed to them (for space is not active in itself, because it is only something empty), but they are only determinants, either of the signs or the Planets or of the fixed stars, to these or those kinds of accidents that are suitable to the native and are in accord with the essential significations of the houses set forth by us in Chapter 3, Section 1, Book [17]. For in those spaces, by reason of their position in relation to the Horizon or to the person born in it, there is a kind of determinative virtue, which we call the virtue of the houses. The first space, therefore, is not properly said to signify life, but only to determine with respect to life, and therefore to be of life, as the second is, of course, the space of wealth, and so of the rest—namely, [they are] determinative.

But neither are the secondary houses[106]—that is, the parts of the *Caelum*, or signs, occupying the primary houses—properly significators of the accidents attributed to the primary houses, nor are the Planets placed in them or ruling those signs. For the celestial bodies do not in any other way signify things present or that will be except as they cause what they are said to signify, from Chapter 7, Section 1. But Capricorn or Saturn in the first space, or the same Saturn as ruler of the first, does not always cause life or maintain it, but sometimes destroys or denies it. And the same Saturn in or ruling the tenth house sometimes brings and sometimes denies honors or dignities. For that reason, generally speaking, the celestial bodies located in the first space are properly said to signify only with respect to life, character, and inborn talent; in the tenth space, with respect to actions, profession, dignities; and so of the rest. Because what they first signify is not simply and without qualification that the native will have such things, but only whether or not he will have such things, and this is able to be signified first from the Planets in or ruling the house and their state; then if he is going to have it, its quality and quantity.

First, therefore, the Planets signify with respect to some kind of accident by reason of their determination. Second, whether such an accident is inherent in the birth, or whether it will happen. Third, what its quality and quantity is or will be; and defining these belongs to the nature and state of the Planets that are in the houses of the accident or preside over them; aspects, which act in accord with the nature of the aspecting Planet, also belong to that state. For the Sun signifying friends by bodily location, rulership, or aspect, will signify these as Kings, Princes, or Magnates; Saturn signifying illnesses will signify these as Saturnine; and so of the rest, according to the table of the rulerships of the Planets placed in Book 13, Section 3, Chapter 3. The same is to be said of the rulers of the first, tenth, and other houses, which, by virtue of their rulership, signify the same thing as if they were in those houses, for, of course, a sign acts with the virtue of its ruler, as is said elsewhere.

Now it is true that a Planet in the seventh house signifies with respect to the spouse, enemies and disputes; that is common to all Planets from what is proper to the seventh house or to the kind of determination; but whether such a native is to have success or not, and of what kind, that is particular to each Planet, either by its own nature (as Jupiter and Venus in the seventh give spouses and happy marriages; Saturn and Mars deny, or take away, or hinder or impose misfortunes on marriages) or by accident from the sign of the seventh and its ruler, from [the Planet's] position in relation to the Sun, and its connection with other Planets, especially with the ruler of the seventh or the first; then also from the rulership over other houses of the Planet located in the seventh. For if a Planet in the seventh is the ruler of the twelfth, it will signify something different about marriage, enemies, and disputes than if it were the ruler of the tenth; and the reasoning is the same about the rest of the houses. And the ruler of the seventh comes to be judged in a similar way as a Planet in the seventh, though that ruler may not be in the seventh; for the Planets always act in accord with their proper nature and their particular determination, especially, of course, through their bodily location and rulership; for Mars in or ruling the eleventh[107] gives noble and military friends, or disturbs friendships by quarrels, according to whether his celestial state is fortunate or unfortunate; Saturn in the twelfth gives melancholic[108] illnesses; and so of the rest.

Moreover, the practice has prevailed that the Horoscope and a Planet in or ruling it are said to signify life; the Midheaven and a Planet in or ruling it, actions and honors, and so they are to be called the significators of such accidents; yet from what has been said above they are properly to be said to signify only with respect to life and actions, for although they properly may be said to signify, they are properly said to signify life or honors only insofar as they signify with respect to those things. So the Sun in the tenth, signifying honors by reason of his determination, also signifies the future of these, intrinsically and from his celestial state. And so he properly will be said to signify honors that are to be, or honors, not in any way, but insofar as they are to be, because they also can be signified as not to be, so that in fact these causes may effect and signify a future of removal and negations of these things.

In addition, when it is said that the Horoscope signifies life, it is to be understood as the beginning of that part of the *Caelum* that occupies the first space, but not as the beginning of the space itself. For the Horoscope is directed for life by the proper ascensions, which are different for each point of the Ecliptic that is in the same first space of the same horizon;[109] but the beginning of that space has no ascensions, because space itself is motionless. Accordingly, Saturn, for example, is not said to transit through the Horoscope whenever, Rising by the primary motion,[110] he passes through the beginning of that space, but only whenever by his own secondary motion[111] he transits the beginning of that part of the *Caelum* that occupied the first space at the hour of birth. Finally, a signification is what is signified by an efficient cause; but the space of the first house, or its beginning, is not effective, but only determinative. But the sign, or the part of the *Caelum*, that occupies that space is effective in accord with its determination and proper nature. And so Aries in the Horoscope causes one thing, Taurus another, &c, whether in the radix or through directions; for, of course, the direction of the Horoscope in Libra to Mars is worse than [that of] the Horoscope in Aries. From which it is still more evidently apparent that the first space does not properly signify life, nor [does] the Horoscope, its beginning; and the reasoning is the same in the rest.

Second, it is to be said: The celestial bodies, as they are determined by individuals, as by human beings, act on these in four ways; of course, by granting the accidents with respect to which they are determined, or by denying them, or by removing what has been granted (which is the middle between granting and denying), or by affecting fortunately or unfortunately in various ways the fortunate or unfortunate fate of the native that has been granted, as by granting children or denying them, or by removing those granted, or by making them fortunate or unfortunate during the life of the Father; so also with respect to a spouse, honors, wealth, &c. From which it is apparent that removing pertains to the success of the thing granted, as when it is asked of honors granted or to be granted whether they will have stability and last. And the denial of anything, such as riches, not only signifies no riches procured by his own effort are to be for the native, but even if they are received by succession from the Parents it portends their dissipation, and future poverty. Similarly, if there are causes that deny siblings the native not only will have no siblings younger than himself, but even those who are older will die; as is apparent in the Geniture of the Illustrious Mr. Tronson,[112] who had Mars and Saturn in the third house and was the survivor of twelve, both brothers and sisters, of whom he was the youngest. For this reason, the causes of granting, denying and removing are to be carefully noted. But above all [it is to be noted] whether they are powerful in their effect, and they are to be distinguished from each other; and that [is to be done] in each of the houses.

Accordingly, these two things are generally common to all Planets. First, what they signify about the native or about the occurrence of such things as pertain to him to which those Planets are determined by their bodily location, rulership, aspects and antiscion, but with the difference that a Planet is more efficacious through its bodily location than through its rulership alone, for the presence of a Planet can do more than an absent ruler. Then what they signify about granting, denying, removing, or affecting in diverse ways what is granted; from which a Planet in any house also is said to signify about things belonging to that house, as Saturn or Mars in the third of the nativity portends the removal of siblings, and thus the siblings' untimely death.

Chapter II

Of a single Planet in any house of a figure

If only one Planet should be in any house of a Celestial Figure, it acts principally on the accidents of the native that belong to that house and will principally govern them, more than ruling or aspecting Planets, whether it is in its own domicile or in a different one, owing to the reason stated above that the presence of a Planet can do more than the rulership of an absent one; because, of course, determination by bodily location is immediate, and so the most effective of all, against the opinion of Bellantius, refuted by us in the third chapter of the first Section.[113] In this matter, Garcaeus, *Book of the Judgment of Genitures*[114] and Junctinus in *Comment*[115] on Chapter 14, Book 3 of *Quadripartite*, as Origanus relates in Part 3, Chapter 8, page 581, favor us where they say that a Planet in the Horoscope—that is, located in the first house—whether it is in the ascending sign or in an intercepted one, is the principal significator of character, though its ruler [is its] partner.[116] Origanus subscribes to this opinion; and if this is true of character, why should not the like be said of wealth, spouses, honors, &c, seeing that the stars act uniformly? But if the Planet is in its own sign, those accidents are to be judged entirely in accordance with its nature and state, both Celestial and Terrestrial. Moreover, so that a judgment may be composed[117] from that Planet—whether it will confer the accidents that are attributed to that house, or whether it indeed will deny them, hinder them, remove them, or affect them either fortunately or unfortunately—the nature of the Planet first comes to be noted, then next its celestial state, and finally its determinations other than by bodily location; and from these judgment is composed,[118] which, if any of these is omitted, can only be defective, and often false.

With respect to the nature of the Planet, its sympathetic analogy with the accidents proper to the house is observed, for in the tenth the Sun *per se* confers outstanding honors because he has an analogy and agreement with them. On the other hand, Saturn *per se* will deny honors for the contrary reason. But I said *per se*, for by accident the Sun in the tenth will deny honors if he is badly conditioned in his celestial state, as exiled, peregrine,[119] fallen,[120] and square or opposed to malefics, and then (which is worse) if his ruler also is badly conditioned. Or, if he brings them because of his bodily location in the tenth and his analogy, they will be accompanied by difficulties, impediments, and misfortunes, which will be the greater the worse the condition of the Sun. On the other hand, Saturn in the tenth will accidentally cause honors if he is in his own domicile, or in exaltation, Oriental of the Sun, swift, direct, and trine the Sun, the Moon, Jupiter, or Venus; and Mars unmixed in the seventh *per se* will stir up disputes, wars, or battles, which Venus *per se* will prevent or dispel. Jupiter in the second will confer wealth, which Saturn, at least *per se*, will deny, but Mars will dissipate. Saturn in the twelfth will cause malignant illnesses, enemies, and prisons, from which Jupiter *per se* will free; and so of the rest, as set out individually in its proper place. For every Planet analogous to the signification of the house it occupies or over which it rules confers that, whether beneficial or unfortunate,[121] that is especially congruent with its celestial state, unless it is strongly hindered by another cause. But, when the contrary is signified, it denies it, hinders it, removes it, or makes it unfortunate.

About the celestial state of a Planet, it is to be known that in general every Planet well conditioned[122] by celestial state—that is, in its own domicile, exaltation, or Triangle, Oriental of the Sun, Occidental of the Moon, free from unfortunate connection by body or aspect with malefics, direct, swift, &c—is assessed as universally benefic for the whole World, for which reason it will be benefic also for any particular native in whatever house of the figure it falls, especially if it is illumined by the favorable rays of benefics. For the beneficence or malignity of the nature or state of the Planets is neither removed nor altered by the houses, but is only determined (Theorem 18, *The Elements of Astrology*); nevertheless, because the Planets are more efficacious in acting the more congruent their celestial state is with their own nature, the greater efficacy of malefics always will be suspect; indeed it will be dangerous for houses 7, 8 and 12[123]—that is, enemies, death, illnesses and prisons—because by nature the malefic Planets always have an efficacious analogy with those unfortunate accidents and are inclined to them by their nature. And so Mars exalted in the seventh house of Prince Gaston[124] roused powerful enemies against him. And likewise Mars in Aries in the eighth house of Henri d'Effiat[125] cast him down into a violent death, as may perhaps be more fully explained elsewhere. Accordingly, Saturn and Mars well conditioned are beneficial in the fortunate houses,[126] but unfortunate in the unfortunate ones.[127] And if [the malefics] are in the Horoscope or in the Midheaven, either peregrine or badly conditioned and without the power of dignity in the first or tenth, they will cause great misfortunes, and those [will be] far greater if they also strike the rulers of the first or tenth with malefic rays.

But every Planet badly conditioned by celestial state—such as exiled, fallen, retrograde, badly configured with malefics, without rays of benefics—is considered universally malefic for the whole World and for each individual native in whatever house of the figure it falls by bodily location or by rulership, because certainly in such a state the proper influx of the Planet is corrupted. But this will be worse for Planets of a malefic nature because their bad[128] state usually causes either disgrace or infamy, or mutilation, or deformity, or casting down from dignity, or exile, imprisonment, grave illnesses, or violent death, or similar misfortune, in accord with the determination of the Planet by bodily location or rulership.

Accordingly, Saturn in Leo in the eighth house of Duke Montmorency[129] signified his shameful violent death.

Finally, a Planet moderately conditioned[130]—as when it is simply peregrine, configured malefically with benefics or benefically with malefics, &c—has a moderate way of causing fortune or misfortune.

But it is to be noted that a Planet that is well conditioned in several ways by celestial state stands out as more inclined to benefit; and where badly conditioned in several ways, from that it is more prone to causing misfortune. And that both universally and particularly, for the universal mode of action springs from the particular and the universal is determined by particulars.

With these premises I now say that, in general, a benefic Planet well conditioned by celestial state in any of houses 1, 2, 3, 4, 5, 6, 7, 9, 10 and 11 of the celestial figure, which are called fortunate because they are of desired things, confers the benefits of that house in which it is bodily located, and those are real, abundant, free of difficulties, and lasting. And on that account, in the second it confers riches, especially if, like Jupiter, it signifies them from its own nature; and so the Sun in the tenth will give honors, or dignities and praise; in the eleventh, friends among Kings, Princes, or Magnates; Venus in the seventh, a beautiful wife and a happy marriage; Mercury in the first, excellent inborn talent; Sun, Saturn and Jupiter in the fourth, parents blessed with honors and wealth because, owing to their satellites,[131] these Planets are analogous to the parents; and so of other houses, in which it is always to be observed in what way the nature and state of the Planets may be congruent with the significations of the houses.

But a benefic in the fortunate houses badly conditioned by sign or connection [with other Planets] either gives nothing, or with difficulty, or by improper means, and only in small amounts, false, corrupted, unstable, or useless.

Finally, a natural benefic [in the fortunate houses] moderately conditioned certainly gives more than when badly conditioned, but gives in a moderate way by reason of quality, quantity, and stability or duration.

On the other hand, a Planet malefic by nature and badly conditioned by celestial state in a fortunate house, such as the tenth, will not confer the benefits of that house—that is, honors or dignities—but rather will prevent them from happening; or, if they should come from elsewhere, it will cause misfortunes in them, especially Saturn, whose nature is contrary to honors.

But a malefic well conditioned in a fortunate house, such as the tenth, will give honors and dignities, especially if it is in its exaltation, for exaltation above the other dignities of the Planets is analogous to honors. And [it should be] not square or opposite the Sun or Moon, both especially analogous to honors, and those [should not be] badly conditioned.

In the second, it will confer wealth, especially if well connected to Jupiter, which is analogous to wealth. And the reasoning is the same for the rest of the houses. But a well conditioned natural malefic always confers imperfect benefits, either by improper means or in difficult ways, or with some misfortune in the end, owing to the malignity of that Planet, which is inclined by nature to misfortune rather than to benefit. From which it can be said[132] that malefics well conditioned in the fortunate houses are like dissonances in Music resolved to produce a consonance.

Finally, a malefic moderately conditioned [in the fortunate houses] gives nothing and destroys nothing, but only prevents benefits from happening, especially if by nature it is contrary to the benefit, as Saturn in the tenth for honors. And so Saturn only moderately conditioned in the second neither confers nor takes away riches, but conserves with parsimony and avarice what has been conferred by succession; but Mars threatens their dissipation by wastefulness, or by foolish and useless expenditures.

Now certainly a Planet benefic by nature and celestial state in the unfortunate houses,[133] 8 and 12, removes or mitigates the misfortunes of these houses, and also those of the seventh, which, on account of disputes and open enemies attributed to it, participates to some degree in misfortune; not indeed intrinsically, but from its opposition—which is the root of disputes and enemies—to the first. And therefore Jupiter [well conditioned] in the twelfth (which is *per se* of illnesses) will make the native subject to only a few, mild, and easily cured illnesses, and will free him from prisons and also from hidden enemies, and for that reason will make the native able to overcome them. In the eighth, he will prevent a violent and shameful death, and will make it easier. From his nature and analogy Jupiter certainly does not incline to hideous illnesses, foul prisons, and violent death, and less so the better conditioned he is by celestial state, because, of course, his nature is not varied with respect to the whole Earth by his diverse placement among the houses of a figure, nor, while he is fortunately constituted, is his beneficent influx, but it is simply determined, as is set out in Theorem 18 of *The Elements of Astrology*; this follows by necessity from Physics, as he certainly promotes benefit and tempers and diminishes misfortune. And the reasoning is the same about other Planets benefic by nature and celestial state.

Yet a Planet benefic by nature but badly conditioned by celestial state in the twelfth or eighth, or the ruler of one in the other, will not ward off diseases but will cause some difficult ones; nor will it prevent a violent death, especially one otherwise signified, as is evident from Cardinal Richelieu,[134] who had Jupiter in the eighth in Gemini with the Eye of the Bull, and he perished by a malignant illness, having been several times mangled by Surgeons, for, with the sum total of exertion and tyranny, they deprive of life with a more violent death.[135] Then from Henri d'Effiat, for whom Jupiter was in the eighth with Mars and the Sun, and he was decapitated; then from Lord Des Hayes,[136] who had Jupiter in Gemini in the eighth house, with the Eye of the Bull and Mars, ruler of the Horoscope, and also the Moon in the seventh with the Head of Medusa[137] and the Pleiades square the Sun, ruler of the Midheaven, and he was decapitated by order of the King. And then from me, who had Jupiter, ruler of the eighth, and Saturn in the twelfth, and I suffered malignant and difficult illnesses, from which, however, I recovered, because illnesses, but not Death, admit of remedies; but I have several times fallen in danger of a violent death, even being seriously wounded.[138]

Finally, a natural benefic moderately conditioned [in the unfortunate houses] neither confers nor removes misfortune but only mitigates it.

On the other hand, a Planet malefic by nature but well conditioned by celestial state in the unfortunate houses of the figure does not remove misfortunes; that is, it does not prevent them from happening, on account of the malignancy of nature prone to misfortune; but, on account of the benefic state, it rescues from them or tempers them. As is apparent in Prince Gaston, who had Mars in his exaltation and Saturn in Aquarius in the seventh, and had powerful open enemies, but he always eluded their power. In like manner, the King of Sweden[139] had Mars in the twelfth in Scorpio and was neither diseased nor imprisoned nor oppressed by hidden enemies. How much more, then, will benefics in the unfortunate houses remove their misfortunes or remit them?

Note, however, that Henri d'Effiat had the Sun, Jupiter and Mars in Aries in the eighth house, and died a violent death owing to Mars, a judicial one owing to Jupiter, and a public one owing to the Sun, because this combination squares with[140] the misfortune of Mercury, ruler of the Horoscope and of the Midheaven, from Saturn, unfriendly to the eighth house in the tenth house, and also infecting with his aspect the Sun, Jupiter and Mars. From this it is apparent that there is much to attend to in Astrological judgments, all of which would be much too long to recount here.

But a natural malefic badly conditioned in an unfortunate house greatly promotes its misfortunes, and makes them worse, even with baseness, infamy, and violence. And so Saturn badly conditioned in the twelfth will cause great and long-lasting illnesses, malignant and difficult

For from a Planet that is intrinsically benefic or well conditioned, benefit and misfortune do not equally result, otherwise it would without cause be called benefic by nature or state. Nor, in the same way, from a Planet malefic intrinsically or by celestial state do benefit and misfortune equally result, for otherwise it would be wrongly said to be malefic by nature or celestial state. But benefics by nature or celestial state act benefically[143] by conferring benefit in the fortunate houses and by removing misfortune in the unfortunate ones; but malefics by nature or state do harm by bringing misfortune in the unfortunate houses and by removing benefit from fortunate ones. Otherwise, if a Planet from its own nature, or in a concordant celestial state, should confer benefits in the fortunate houses and misfortunes in the unfortunate ones, on no account could it be said to be benefic rather than malefic from its nature, or well conditioned rather than badly conditioned. And benefit is caused not only by the delivery of actual benefit, but also by the removal of misfortune, and misfortune is caused also by the removal of benefit, not otherwise than benefit is removed by the causation of misfortune, and misfortune by the causation of benefit.

With these things understood of a Planet located in any house, or determined by its bodily location, now its other determinations in the figure are examined. And first, each Planet, besides being determined by bodily location, can be determined at the same time also by rulership; and if both determinations are with respect to the same house, that Planet will be most efficaciously determined to the significations of that house, indeed notably and easily causing them if it is a fortunate place, but tempering or averting them if it is an unfortunate one. But if the two determinations are with respect to different houses, as, of course, when a Planet is in one house and rules another, then the significations of the two houses are combined; but the inclination is more to the signification of the house that Planet occupies, because doubtless the presence of a Planet has more power than the rulership of an absent one. For that reason, if a Planet is well conditioned in the second and rules the seventh, riches will befall the native from marriage, disputes, or wars; if it is the ruler of the tenth, they will happen from his profession, dignities, and actions. But if, on the other hand, a Planet is badly conditioned in the second and rules the seventh or tenth, the contrary happens—that is, [financial] hardships from marriage or disputes and wars, or from actions and the profession. Yet a Planet should not have a determination by rulership contrary to that which it has by reason of its bodily location; so if Mars in the first is ruler of the eighth, he will be the worst for life or for death, for either a violent death or the danger of it will be portended; and the reasoning is the same about the rest.

Second, a Planet determined by its location can be determined again by another Planet seen according to its own nature and analogy, and that by conjunction or aspect. And so a benefic Planet in the tenth with the Sun, or in trine to the Sun, powerfully signifies honors owing to the Sun's analogy with honors. In the second and trine Jupiter, notable wealth. But a malefic in the eighth with Mars, or in his square or opposition, violent and cruel death. In the twelfth and square Saturn, prisons and malignant illnesses; and so of the rest. And this is very much to be noted for the more certain and greater effect determined by any Planet.

Third, [a Planet] can be determined by another Planet, just as the former is determined by its bodily location or rulership; by that means, if a Planet in the first is conjoined with the ruler of the tenth, or is in its strong aspect or in that of a Planet located in the tenth, that will confer on the native propensities to notable deeds and prefigures fortunate actions, and from those, honors and dignities. If it is conjoined with the ruler of the eighth, or in its square or opposition, it portends the danger to life of a violent death. And the reasoning is the same in the rest, especially when the significations of the houses can be combined. The principal concealed treasures of judgments are hidden in these [combinations]; and therefore it is apparent, owing to the determinations of the Planets in the primary houses by bodily location and rulership, how important it is to establish the true method of constructing the celestial figure.[144] But about a single Planet in any house of a figure, these generally suffice here, for what each one does particularly in each of the houses of the figure may be sufficiently explained in its own place; and, of course, what is said about a single Planet located in any house of a figure is to be understood to be said also of the ruler of that house, but with the difference that the presence of a Planet in a house of any figure is more efficacious than the rulership of an absent one.

Chapter III

Of several Planets in any house of a figure

If several Planets should be in the same house, its essential significations are jointly governed by all those Planets, and each is considered according to its proper nature and celestial state, and by its determinations other than by bodily location, just as is done concerning a single Planet in Chapter 2. And from that scrutiny, in any case it will be discovered which of those Planets is most powerful for granting, denying, removing, or making fortunate or unfortunate[145] the significations [of the house], as said above; then whether, how much, and in what way it is helped or hindered by others, and what each will cause in a similar way with respect to the same significations. And finally, judgment will be rendered from the combination of the mixed influences, as much as foresight will be able to do; but not without difficulty, which will be the greater the more Planets there are in the same house, especially benefics and malefics mingled with each other. For where all are malefics or all benefics, judgment is easier. And about these the following are to be noted.

First. When several Planets, such as three, four, or five, are located in the same house, this house is the first, ahead of the others, that presents itself to be noted. For it prefigures something remarkable about its essential significations, and the more Planets there are in it, the more notably they prefigure benefit or misfortune. It is apparent in me, as I had Venus, the Sun, Jupiter, Saturn and the Moon in the twelfth house,[146] and I have been seized many times with even malignant and difficult illnesses; many times I have fallen in with causes for imprisonment that foolish youths think honorable; more than ten times I have fallen into danger of violent death; sixteen times I have been subject to servitude, which is not a little akin to imprisonment or captivity, and I had many hidden enemies out of envy, then also Magnates treating me unjustly, among whom was Cardinal Richelieu. And all this was caused by Saturn in the twelfth, analogous to those misfortunes, but I always escaped because of Jupiter and Venus well conditioned; though I frankly confess that I have been rescued from the dangers of violent death more than five times by Divine goodness and mercy alone, and once truly miraculously when, spun around on horseback, I was in the greatest danger of a fatal fall and drowning;[147] for which may all his Saints praise the Lord, and I with them forever, Amen.

It is also apparent in the Geniture of the very Illustrious Mr. Louis Tronson, who had the Moon, Jupiter, Venus and Mercury in the tenth under the rule of the Sun in the eleventh. And he was honored with numerous dignities by King Louis XIII for his distinguished deeds and faithful professional excellence.[148] It is apparent again in the Geniture of Henri d'Effiat, who had the Sun, Jupiter and Mars in 8, and his last day was marked by a death that was violent owing to Mars, judicial owing to Jupiter, and public owing to the Sun; and it is everywhere apparent in many other genitures.

Second. Among several Planets conjoined in the same house of a figure, each one acts in accord with its own nature and its determinations, both separately and together with the others.

Third. Out of several Planets in the same house, if any one is analogous to the significations of that house, or one is the ruler, or one is analogous but another the ruler, they are to be attended to before the others as more efficacious than the others in conferring the benefit or misfortune of that house or in removing it. So in my Geniture, Jupiter and Saturn were attended to before the others; and Mars in the Geniture of Henri d'Effiat, inasmuch as he is analogous to violent death and the ruler of the others.

Fourth. One closer to the house cusp is also considered, for it is very powerful in that house because of the strength of the cusps, from Chapters

14 and 15, Book 18.[149] And the principal signification is to be sought either from the ruler of the house or from one exalted in it, or from an analogy, or from the one nearer to the cusp. And if all these agree with the same Planet, it will be absolutely the most powerful over the significations of its own house.

Fifth. Among several Planets located in the same house, some of which are analogous to the significations of the house, others certainly contrary (as if the Sun and Saturn should be together in the tenth, to the honors of which the Sun is analogous but Saturn is *per se* contrary), it should be seen which one of them is strongest for conferring, or for removing or hindering, the benefit or misfortune of the house according to the doctrine of the second chapter, for the stronger will always prevail in effect over the weaker; yet their benefit or misfortune are combined in due proportion, so that if Saturn is in Cancer and the Sun in Leo [in the tenth], honors will appear because of the analogy and strength of the Sun, but misfortunes will not be lacking in them owing to Saturn's contrariety to honors and his bad condition. If they both are peregrine, as in Scorpio, no honors will be signified, for as much as the Sun signifies them, so much is Saturn adverse to them. Even if they will have happened from a different source, as from a trine of Jupiter to the Sun, there still will be misfortunes in honors to be expected from Saturn. But if both are in Libra, where the Sun is fallen and Saturn is exalted, honors will happen owing to the exaltation of Saturn, which the Sun favors more by analogy than he opposes them by his fall. And judgment and foresight are reasoned in the same way in the rest.

Sixth. It often happens that two benefics are found in the same house, or two malefics, or a benefic with a malefic. Two benefics always signify benefit, either by conferring benefits or by freeing from misfortunes, and that all the more efficaciously when they are better conditioned by celestial state. But two malefics always signify misfortune, either by conferring misfortunes or by denying, hindering or corrupting benefits, unless both malefics are strong in the fortunate houses, as Saturn and Mars in Capricorn in the second house for the wealth of Mr. De Chavigny,[150] or Mars in Capricorn and Saturn in Aquarius in the seventh for the marriage of Prince Gaston. But the benefit caused by malefics is ever[151] mixed with misfortune. And so in wealth, [they cause] plunder or avarice; in marriages, the death of the spouse; or they will stir up notable obstacles, however much they also can confer the things signified in the house. About a benefic Planet with a malefic in the same house, see what follows.

Seventh. If a benefic Planet follows another benefic in a fortunate house, it is very beneficial, and the benefits will be stable. But if a malefic [follows a benefic, expect] misfortune, for the benefits will end in some misfortune or they will be hindered. But in an unfortunate house, if a benefic follows a benefic, misfortunes will not happen, or they will be very mild. If a malefic follows a benefic, misfortunes certainly will come to pass by reason of the house. If a benefic [follows] a malefic, misfortunes also will happen, but after that the native will be released. If, finally, a malefic follows a malefic [in an unfortunate house], the misfortunes will be very grave, and he will not be released. But note that here by benefic or malefic we understand such either by nature, or by celestial state or determination. And therefore a benefic in the tenth applying by body to an exalted Saturn more certainly signifies honors; and a Planet in the twelfth applying to the ruler of the eighth more certainly portends illness with danger to life.

Eighth. With several Planets appearing in the same house and their ruler outside it, it is to be considered in what house [their ruler] is. For from the signification of this house will come the origin of the benefit or misfortune. So in the Geniture of Mr. Tronson, the Sun is the ruler of the Moon, Jupiter and Venus[152] in the tenth; as he is in the eleventh, he prefigured dignities from mediating friends, and those Courtiers or Magnates.

Ninth. Two Planets in the same house can be combined with each other in nine principal ways. For each is to be seen in a threefold way—

namely, by reason of nature, celestial state, and determination in the figure. But any reckoning about one Planet may be combined with the triple reckoning about another Planet, and three times three are nine. And from that comes the difficulty of predictive Astrology.

Chapter IV

Of the ruler of one house of a figure in another house. And first, does it always combine the significations of the two houses?

Now it comes to us here for taking hold of, taking apart, and elucidating the subject that occurs most frequently in all of judicial [Astrology], and is above all others unknown until now.

    For the understanding of which it is to be noted first: A Planet does not act without the sign it occupies, and depends on it inasmuch as it is a sign, as we already have said in Book 20, Section 3, Chapter 5. For it acts in dependence on it as it is a part of the *Primum Caelum*, or the first Physical cause; but this part also was determined to the nature of some Planet at the beginning of the World, from Book 15, Chapter 2.[153] So the Planet acts in dependence on that part as it is such a sign, and that is a dependence of partnership, as is already explained many times elsewhere. And this is confirmed in the geniture of a person, for any Planet certainly determines to its nature its place in the *Caelum* as it occupies this or that sign, for which reason the Planet is said to be well or badly conditioned; and its place so determined retains such a condition with respect to that native during the whole life of the native, just as the place of the Sun in Aquarius retains the badly conditioned nature of the Sun. And directions of significators to those places, and transits of the Planets through them, demonstrate that, for transiting Planets act in accord with the natures of, and their own conditions in, the places where they occur, as daily experience proves.

Second. A sign always depends in its action on the nature and formal virtue of its ruler. For it depends on it essentially inasmuch as it is such sign; and if the ruler of any sign were removed from the World, such sign would no longer act as a sign, but only as part of the *Primum Caelum* with the simple and universal virtue of the *Caelum* itself. For that reason, a Planet is rightly said to rule its sign, or to preside over it, and over the house of the figure in which that sign falls; that is, over the essential significations of that house, which depend on that ruler in becoming and being as on an efficient cause. But it is less properly said that one Planet rules another Planet appearing in its sign;[154] because, certainly, if Mars were lifted from the World, nevertheless Jupiter placed in that part of the *Caelum* that is called Aries would not cease to act with his Jovial nature, for, although Aries and Jupiter mix together their forces, yet each one acts separately in accord with his own nature, Martially and Jovially; whence, removed from the World, the Martial virtue would cease only in Aries, but the Jovial would not cease in Jupiter.

Now, of course, because a Planet acts not only by reason of its own nature, but also by reason of its celestial state, which is constantly varied by sign and connection with other Planets, therefore in acting a sign depends on its ruler, both by reason of its nature and as it is in a particular state. And experience also proves this, because, as is known, the ruler of the Horoscope in exile and in conjunction, square or opposition with malefic Planets is most unfavorable for the essential significations of the Horoscope.

From this certainly it follows that, because a Planet does not act except in dependence on the sign it occupies, and a sign, of course, in dependence on the nature and state of its ruler, for that reason a Planet in a sign not its own also will act in dependence on the nature and state of its ruler; and this is very much to be noted. For it is from this that, in judging of the significations of the Horoscope—which are life, character, inborn talent, &c—not only the ruler of the Horoscope is taken into account, but, if this is in another's sign, the ruler of this sign, which I call the secondary ruler of the Horoscope, also is to be taken into account, for on it the principal virtue for the effect and the chief part of judgment frequently depend, as I have found in many genitures; and so also for the ruler of the Midheaven, the Sun, &c. Yet I have never found that efficacious virtue extended sensibly to the ruler of that secondary ruler, lest the strength of some circle should impose on us here, for the more the light is bent, the more it weakens; and so these rulerships are to be assessed.

Furthermore, a Planet is considered as acting in two ways: namely, indeterminately and universally with respect to the whole World, and also particularly as it is determined in a celestial Theme[155] with respect to the person being born. And so a sign in its universal action is seen as dependent only on the celestial state of its ruler,[156] and in its particular action with respect to a person born, [a sign] is seen also as dependent on the terrestrial state of that ruler, or its determination in the figure mentioned above. And therefore the Sun, ruler of the Horoscope, in the tenth[157] house elevates the native to honors, and in the eighth exposes the same to the dangers of a public death, especially if he is struck in that place by Saturn or Mars.

Third. A Planet acts or signifies more efficaciously about those things to which it is determined by body in the figure than about those things to which it is determined only by rulership. For as it is customarily everywhere said, the presence of a Planet is stronger than the rulership of an absent one. Consider Capricorn in the twelfth house, signifying Saturnine illnesses, and Saturn in the tenth. Capricorn, of course, has its nature from Saturn, to which it is determined from the beginning of the World, and it causes something Saturnine. But as for illness, this is not had from Saturn but from [Capricorn's] location in the twelfth, which is the place of illnesses, which for that reason particularly determines that Saturnine sign to illnesses; and so, Capricorn in the twelfth causes Saturnine illnesses. Yet the force causing them does not belong formally to Capricorn, but to the ruler, Saturn, on which Capricorn depends for its action, as is said elsewhere; therefore, [that force] is more present in the ruler, Saturn himself, than in Capricorn, because if Saturn in the tenth has a greater force with respect to the significations of the twelfth than does Capricorn in the twelfth, then [located] in the tenth itself [Saturn] will have a much greater force with respect to the significations of the tenth than of the twelfth; for in the tenth he acts in himself, and in the twelfth through another—namely, through Capricorn. So, in short, the presence of a Planet has more influence than the rulership of an absent one, whether this is understood of the same house—as of Saturn in the twelfth or only the ruler of the twelfth outside it—or of different ones—as of Saturn in the tenth and ruler of the twelfth. And for the same reason the ruler of the first in the ninth with the ruler of the seventh inclines more to religion than to marriage, wars, &c; on the other hand, the ruler of the first in the seventh with the ruler of the ninth urges more to marriage, disputes, and wars than to Religion.

An exception is made, however, for the first house, the essential significations of which—of course, life, temperament, &c—are the first of all the accidents and the foundations of the rest, which necessarily are to be set out first so the rest may be. And so they are caused and signified more efficaciously and certainly by rulership alone than are the rest by bodily location, even added to rulership. But nevertheless, the ruler of the first in another house determines life, character, and inborn talent in accord with the significations of the house in which it is, and that more strongly if it also presides over this house.[158] Though, of course, with respect to others, the ruler of the twelfth in the eleventh signifies friends more efficaciously than hidden enemies, and that hidden enemies become friends rather than the contrary; and the reasoning is the same in the rest.

Someone will object. The Midheaven is more efficacious for actions and dignities, or profession, than the ruler of the Midheaven, even located in the tenth house, as is evident from the direction of each of them. On account of which, for the significations of the tenth, directions only of the Midheaven were attended to by Ptolemy and his followers; therefore the sign is more efficacious than its ruler, whether absent or present.

I reply: The Midheaven does not have its greater efficacy for the reason that it is such a sign or such a degree, but only for the reason that such a degree occupies the cusp of the tenth house, which is the most efficacious point of the house by whatever degree or sign it is occupied, as is said in Book 18, Chapter 15. And if a Planet occupies it, it will act still more efficaciously than that simple degree, especially if the Planet is in its own sign; for in a foreign one, on account of the mixture of diverse virtues, it perhaps will act with its own nature more weakly than through its sign by itself.

With these premises, it is now to be said that the rulers of the houses in those houses notably confer their significations if they are fortunate, and especially if those rulers are Analogous to those significations. For a Planet in its own sign is undivided in its power of action, united with itself, and independent of another in promoting its effects, and therefore very strong and always in itself benefic. And if it is in the unfortunate houses, such as 8 and 12, it very much liberates from the signified misfortunes, or tempers them. And this usually also is done by Saturn and Mars, unless they are made unfortunate in some other way, such as through connection with malefics by nature or determination, or by conjunction, square or opposition to a luminary, or if they wound the rulers of the Horoscope or of the Midheaven.[159]

But when a Planet that is ruler of one house is located in another, beyond what it does with respect to the essential significations of the house over which it rules—which is not otherwise than if it were in that house, although weaker—it prefigures, in addition, a combination of the essential significations of the two houses, to be caused by [the Planet] in accord with the possible combinations of those two houses and that ruler, and in accord with the [signification] seen as more congruent with [the Planet's] nature and Analogy, and its celestial state. And the reason is because the sign in the house that the Planet rules acts upon the significations of that house in dependence on its ruler and in accordance with [the ruler's] nature and its celestial and terrestrial state, as is already said many times. By terrestrial state, of course, is to be understood its determinations in the celestial figure, as we have said before.

Yet it is to be determined first whether a Planet located in any house of a figure but the ruler of another always combines the essential significations of the two houses, so that it can do nothing by reason of its bodily location independently of its rulership, or to the contrary; this is certainly of the greatest importance in judgments.

But this is not to be asserted until it is first proved. Every Planet is active intrinsically and from its own formal virtue independently of the sign over which it rules, from which, of course, it does not receive the formal power of action, but, on the contrary, that sign [receives its power of action] from its Planetary ruler. A Planet, therefore, can act through its determination by body without acting through its determination by rulership. And this is confirmed from the fact that Saturn in the twelfth always causes illnesses, prisons or enemies. But he does not have this from himself formally, although he is Analogous to those, for intrinsically he is indifferent to life, illness, health, wealth, &c; nor does he have this from his signs, Aquarius and Capricorn, or from the houses of the figure that those signs occupy, because in whatever house they may be, still Saturn in the twelfth will cause illnesses. It remains, therefore, that he has this through his own determination by body in the twelfth, which is [a house] of illnesses. And so a Planet causes something by its bodily location in the figure independently of its rulership in other houses of the figure.

Second. A Planet outside its own sign causes one thing by reason of the house of the figure in which it is located, and another thing by reason of its rulership in another house. Theorem 28, *The Elements of Astrology*. But these two effects do not have a necessary reciprocal subordination, such that one necessarily involves the other, for these are accidents diverse in kind and in reality distinct; therefore, &c.[160]

Third. If a Planet could not act by body without at the same time acting by rulership, then, because Saturn, Jupiter, Mars, Venus, and Mercury each rule two signs, and the reference to the two is equal, it would follow that, in every particular action of these Planets placed outside their own signs, combinations of the essential significations of three, four or five houses of the figure, in which the ruling Planet or either of its two signs are found, would always be concurring. But that is incongruous and contrary to experience; as in my geniture, Saturn is the significator of illnesses for me. And when he met by direction with the Sun in about my eighth year, he caused me a quartan fever,[161] and from the direction of the Horoscope to the square of Saturn in the year 1616, I fell into a long and malignant illness. But it is totally false that the significations of houses 9, 10, and 11—of course, religion, travels, and profession—which are ruled by Saturn, concurred with such illnesses or made a combination with them.

Similarly, in the geniture of the most illustrious Mr. Tronson,[162] Jupiter was in the tenth, prefiguring honors, and was the ruler of the second, third, and fifth, but it is false that those honors happened through combinations of wealth, siblings or kindred, and children; for by his own merit alone, from his counsels and skills,[163] he won dignities from Louis XIII,[164] and with the Lord of Luynes,[165] afterwards the Constable, they freed Gaul from the tyrannical power of Concini, the Marquis d'Ancre;[166] then he was without siblings and children, and had nothing conferred by or known from his kindred. Again, at the age of 18, a remarkable and very rare occurrence happened to the same Mr. Tronson. The Parisians who conspired against Henri Bourbon, King of France and Navarre,[167] elected as Vice-Chancellor the father of Mr. Tronson (who was the Keeper of the books of supplicants[168]). But he, a faithful but secret servant of the King, refused to accept the sacred Seal. The Parisians and petitioners, however, urged that at least his son Louis should accept the Seal and bring it to the Council on the days appointed for sealing, and that the seal should be affixed to the documents in need of it. The Father nodded his assent, fearing danger from the conspirators if he should betray his feelings towards the King, and so Mr. Tronson himself, at the age of 18 years, served for a period of six months as Vice-Chancellor. And these honors came to him by the direction of the Midheaven to the Moon, the ruler of the MC itself and the first of all the Planets in the tenth with which [the Midheaven] met [by direction]. This had nothing to do with the religion or journeys of the native, even though the Moon was also the ruler of the ninth. And the Moon herself had been directed to Venus, the ruler of the Horoscope, and was being directed to Mercury, the ruler of the Sun. And the same can be seen everywhere occurring in other genitures.

And so it is to be concluded that a Planet in any house of a figure and the ruler of another does not always combine the significations of the two houses, but sometimes it acts by reason of its bodily location, sometimes by reason of one rulership, and, if it presides over several signs and houses, sometimes by reason of another, as is apparent from the direction of the Horoscope to Mars in the first, as the ruler of the twelfth for illnesses or as the ruler of the Midheaven for actions or honors. At times, however, it combines its effects by reason of its own nature and bodily location with the significations of one or another determination by rulership, in accord with the possible combinations of those significations and the state of that Planet, but not always with all at the same time. Yet it is certain that a combination of the significations by bodily location with the significations by rulership will be made at some time if a combination is at least possible. Moreover, it sometimes happens that a Planet that is the ruler of one house in another first acts by reason of bodily location and, in consequence, combines the signification by bodily location with the significations by rulership, as in the geniture of Mr. Tronson Mars was the ruler of the second in the third, and therefore the principal significator of siblings; but by nature he signified their death, especially with Saturn, ruler of the fourth, in the third; the death of the native's siblings was threatened from both malefics in the third, of which one was the ruler of the second and the other of the fourth, and so successions and wealth were strongly signified from the death of the brothers and sisters, and therefore the native, the last of thirteen, survived the others as successor.

Conversely, a sign in any house of a figure where its ruler is absent acts always by reason of the nature and celestial state of its ruler, but not always by reason of its terrestrial state or determination in the figure. Otherwise, with the ruler of the Midheaven in the eighth, each of the actions and undertakings of the native would be combined with death or the danger of death; in 12, 7 or 4, with the significations of the twelfth, the seventh, or the fourth, which is contrary to experience; then also for the reason that the significations of the houses differ in kind and in reality, as is said above. Therefore, it can be predicted only that a combination will occur at some time, but not always in all things.

Chapter V

In what way a Planet ruling one house & in another combines the significations of the two houses

As said in the previous chapter, a Planet ruling one house and in another prefigures at least at some time a combination of the significations of the two houses. Now here it is to be said in what way such a combination is made, a matter that takes a principal place in judicial foresight and about which many things present themselves for consideration, at least the principal ones of which we will touch upon here.

First. Every house has many meanings, as the first: life, health, temperament, character, inborn talent; the twelfth: illnesses, prisons, hidden enemies who display false proof of friendship, thus deceiving and covertly harming; the seventh: marriage, disputes, contracts; the tenth: actions, undertakings, dignities; and so on of the rest, as we have set out elsewhere; and each house is of the same signification as that opposed to itself, by reason of that opposition and so only by accident. So, from experience it is evident that Mars in the second[169] threatens death and Jupiter in the eighth prefigures wealth; Saturn in the sixth portends illnesses or prisons; and Venus in the twelfth, fortune with servants and animals; and so of the rest. But it is not to be thought so about the rulers of houses. For the ruler of the fourth does not influence the significations of the tenth unless it is in the fourth, or presides over the tenth, or is strongly connected with the tenth house or its ruler. And the reasoning is the same about the rest of the opposite houses. And a Planet strong by celestial state strongly signifies the house opposite itself; weak, weakly.

But by its opposition it always signifies contrarieties or oppositions for the benefits pertaining to the opposite house, and increases its misfortunes.

As regards houses of the same triplicity, they are also to be noted here, for a Planet in the first house influences the significations of the ninth and fifth, and much more so if it rules over the ninth or fifth; and so of the rest.

Second. The essential significations that belong to the different houses are brought together with foresight in combinations that are possible. For from the ruler of the fourth in the fifth it will not be said that the Father of the native will be his son, for this is impossible; but if we say that the Father of the native will benefit his children, or that the paternal succession will go to the native's children, and things similar or contrary to these, these combinations are possible, and they can be predicted from the nature and state of the Planet that is the ruler of the fourth house. Similarly, from the ruler of the sixth in the seventh, the servant or handmaid can become the spouse, or can put together disputes against the native; or from the ruler of the seventh in the eighth, the native's spouse or enemy can bring death to the native; and so of the others.

Third. It is to be determined with notable keenness of perception which of the possible combinations of significations are more congruent with the nature and state of the Planet, then also with the condition of the native himself. For some agree with a Prince or a nobleman, others with a merchant or a peasant; some with a secular person, others an ecclesiastic; some a man, others a woman; some a child, some a youth, some an old person; and so of the rest; and only congruent things are accustomed to happen.

Fourth. All the houses are significators of the accidents of the native, and the Planets are determined by those houses to act in accord with their bodily location, rulership, and both together. And consequently, when the ruler of one house is in another—that is, when a Planet that is the significator of one accident by rulership is the significator of another by body—from that, these two accidents, both separately and combined with each other, are signified as what will be; and so sometimes one, sometimes the other, but at other times both combined, may happen. So, if the Planet that is ruler of the Horoscope is in the sixth and benefic by nature and celestial state, as it is in the sixth, it prefigures beneficial things about servants and animals of the native; if it is malefic by nature and celestial state, it portends the contrary. But as it is the ruler of the Horoscope, it signifies the temperament, character, and inborn talent of the native congruent with the nature and state of that Planet. And as it is the ruler of the Horoscope in the sixth of the native (whom the Horoscope signifies), [it signifies] the weighing down of the mind with laborious things, then love, exertion and occupation with respect to servants, animals, and household affairs. And if the Planet is malefic and badly conditioned, owing to the opposition of the sixth to the twelfth it portends prisons, exile, or illnesses being thrown against the native, and [owing to its location in the sixth], damages and dangers from servants.

Fifth. A Planet that is ruler of one house in another acts not only by reason of the house it occupies and that it rules, but also [by reason] of Planets appearing in [the house it rules].[170] And so, if the ruler of Mercury is found in the first house, it prefigures the inborn talent of the native, even if Mercury is outside the first house. And the ruler of the Sun in the tenth, honors; and so of the others. Because doubtless any Planet acts on the native by reason of both states of its ruler, of course, Celestial and Terrestrial. And therefore, if [Mercury] has his ruler in the first house well conditioned, he will act on the native by reason of the significations of the first house, and especially inborn talent, owing to the analogy; and this fortunately, owing to the well conditioned state of the ruler. But terrestrial state here is to be understood only by reason of bodily location and not by rulership in another house, except perhaps very weakly. For otherwise the efficacy of the circular would be admitted, which we rejected in Chapter 4. And consequently, with Venus located in the third house and her ruler

Jupiter in the first and ruler of the twelfth, Venus certainly will act on the native by reason of the significations of the first, but not of the twelfth. Or if Jupiter is in the twelfth as ruler of the Horoscope and of the Sun in the fourth, he certainly will act on the native by reason of his rulership in the first and fourth, then through the Sun in the fourth. But the Sun in the fourth, acting by reason of his ruler and its state, will not act through the significations of the first, in which the ruler of that Sun is not bodily found; likewise of others.

This premised, because the first house signifies substantively the native himself, then also the accidents of his body and mind contingent on the genethliacal arrangement of the *Caelum*, but the significations of the other houses are the intrinsic accidents of the same native, from this, if the ruler of the first is located in other houses of the figure or the rulers of these in the first, the combination will be reciprocal. So, if the ruler of the first is in the tenth, or the ruler of the tenth in the first, actions, Profession, and Dignities are signified for the native in both cases, with the difference, however, that in the first case the native will be aroused by his own impulse and ambition, and will work with his own purposeful diligence to acquire a position of authority or honors. But in the second, he will not strive in this way, but sometimes even unexpected dignities will happen to him. Similarly, if the ruler of the first is in the eighth or the ruler of the eighth[171] in the first, the premature death of the native is signified in both instances, of which he himself is most likely the cause, either voluntarily or unwittingly exposing himself to dangers, especially in the first case; or even by endeavoring to prevent his own death, as happens to those who, merely as a precaution, have blood drawn from themselves or arrange for their humors[172] to be purged unseasonably.

And for the same reason, from the ruler of the first in other houses, the combination of life, health, character, inclination, or inborn talent arises with the significations of those houses in accord with combinations possible and more congruent with the nature and state of the Planet, which two are especially observed to determine whether the essential significations of the houses are to be for the native, then how fortunately or unfortunately.

But of the ruler of other houses in a house other than the first, such as the ruler of the second in the seventh, it is to be judged according to a threefold consideration. In the first place, the Planet itself, because it is in the seventh, prefigures benefit or misfortune with respect to marriage, open enemies, disputes and contracts in accord with the nature and state of the Planet. Next, inasmuch as it is the ruler of the second, [it prefigures] benefit or misfortune with respect to wealth owing to the same reasons. Finally, inasmuch as the ruler of the second is in the seventh, if it is benefic and fortunate it prefigures wealth through marriage, disputes, and contracts; but if it is unfortunate, it portends the loss of wealth through marriage, disputes, and contracts. And thus arises a fortunate or unfortunate combination in accord with the nature and state of the Planet. But if, conversely, the ruler of the seventh is in the second, the same things are signified as before by reason of bodily location and rulership; yet by reason of the combination,[173] if the Planet is benefic and well conditioned it signifies an increase of wealth from the frugality or work of the spouse, or by acting in the disputes and causes of others; but if the Planet is malefic and badly conditioned, robbers, open enemies, or the spouse will plunder the native's wealth. Similarly, if the ruler of the tenth is in the twelfth, either the signification of the tenth will transition into[174] the signification of the twelfth,[175] or vice versa; but determination by bodily location is stronger than by rulership, and so the presence of a Planet is more efficacious than the rulership of an absent one; therefore, from a Planet [in the twelfth] that is ruler of the tenth, dignities, undertakings and actions of the native themselves will be the cause of illnesses, prisons, enemies, exile, &c. But if, conversely, the ruler of the twelfth is in the tenth, enemies, prisons, exiles, &c will be the cause of honors and eminent dignities, received especially if that ruler is benefic and well conditioned.

The first was apparent in me in that I have Saturn, ruler of the Midheaven, in the twelfth. The second was apparent in Cardinal Richelieu, who had Venus, ruler of the twelfth,[176] near the heart of the *Caelum*;[177] and so of the others, always paying attention to how the Planets and their states are congruent with the significations of the houses.

But it is necessary to carefully observe in which house a Planet that is ruler of another house is located. For in the pivots,[178] it is strong to benefit or to harm, especially if placed in its domicile or exaltation. Though if it is located in a house congruent with the significations of its rulership, as the ruler of the second in the fourth, seventh, or tenth, wealth is certainly signified by that, for from the significations of these houses—that is, successions, marriages, and dignities—wealth is accustomed to occur; but if it is located in a contrary one, as the ruler of the second in the twelfth, squandering of riches is portended as a cause of illnesses, exile or prison;[179] for in most of these combinations the signification of the house lacking its ruler is converted to[180] or transitions to the signification of the house in which that ruler is located. So, if the ruler of the tenth is in the twelfth, the dignity of the native will be a misfortune for him, or he will fall from it, or he will leave it, as happened to me in the Profession of Medicine from Saturn, the ruler of the tenth in the twelfth; or he will be imprisoned owing to actions and undertakings. But if the ruler of the twelfth is located in the tenth, the native's enemies, exiles, prisons, or misfortunes will be a cause of honor and dignity, as for Cardinal Richelieu, from Venus, ruler of the twelfth, on the Midheaven by orb of virtue and in the ninth by body. And so, the ruler of the eleventh in the twelfth turns friends into enemies, as often with me; but the ruler of the twelfth in the eleventh causes the reverse. Similarly, the ruler of the tenth appearing in the eleventh [signifies that] the native's actions and honors will be for him the cause of friends; but the ruler of the eleventh in the tenth prefigures the reverse; and the reasoning is the same for the rest.

From these certainly it follows that if the same Planet is the ruler of two houses and is outside them, the significations of these will transition into the signification of the house where that ruler is, or they will be affected by that signification; and so the badly conditioned ruler of the first and the eighth in the seventh portends the native will be killed or wounded by enemies; and the reasoning is the same about the rest. But always, to render judgment the nature of the Planet and its analogy with the significations of those houses, and its state, both Celestial and Terrestrial, are to be carefully attended to. For a Planet badly conditioned, and especially a natural malefic, is of no value for the fortunate houses it influences by body or rulership, but denies, hinders, or causes misfortune to their benefit. But if it is in the unfortunate houses, it certainly will promote the misfortunes of these, but not the benefits of the houses over which it rules; and so a transition will not happen, except, perhaps, of unfortunate significations by rulership into the significations by body.

You will object from Section 8, Book 18.[181] A house of the celestial figure is seen materially in two ways: The primary, of course, which is a fixed space, and the secondary, which is the part of the *Caelum* that occupies that space. Because the primary house is a fixed space, therefore the tenth house, for example, will not be the house of the dignities only of the native, but will be the house common to the honors of all those born on that horizon, or it will be the house proper to honors in such horizon or place on Earth. And the same is to be said of the eighth house for death, of the seventh for the spouse or disputes, &c; and so if the ruler of the third is in the eighth, from that the death of the siblings will be signified; if it is in the tenth, honors will be signified for them, &c.

But I reply: The reckoning is not the same for the native and the siblings, parents, children, &c, for the eighth house is only the eighth house on that horizon with respect to the first, and so the meaning of the eighth—death, of course—is such meaning only with respect to the meaning of the first—the native, of course—and not with respect to the third, or siblings. And therefore, the ruler of the third[182] in the eighth takes on the signification of death with respect to the native, and that from the siblings or for their sake, but not with respect to the siblings. But the tenth house is the eighth with respect to the third, and, therefore, the ruler of the third in the tenth signifies the death of the siblings, as I have often observed, and it signifies dignities for the native from the siblings; therefore it can be gathered that, through the death of his sibling, the native will succeed to his [sibling's] dignities, or from his [sibling's] inheritance he will acquire dignities for himself. And the reasoning is the same about the rest.

But again attention is due to the Planet with which the ruler of any house is engaged.[183] For the ruler of the first with the Sun inclines the native to, or makes him suited to, association with Kings and Magnates, then also to praise, fame and dignities; the ruler of the second with Jupiter promises certain wealth; the ruler of the eighth with Mars threatens violent death, or its dangers are threatened; and so of the rest, considering the analogy between the house and the Planet that is with that ruler. Moreover, in the meeting of two Planets it is to be seen over which houses they preside. For if the ruler of the first is with the ruler of the twelfth or eighth, it will be unfortunate on account of illnesses or death; if it is with the ruler of the tenth or eleventh, it will be beneficial for actions and honors, or friends. Similarly, if the ruler of the second is with the ruler of the tenth, wealth is signified from actions, endeavors, and dignities; or if the ruler of the twelfth is with the ruler of the eighth, illnesses and prisons almost always will be dangerous to life. But of these things more will be said in the following Book.[184]

Furthermore, it is to be known here about the eighth house that its signification—death, of course—is nothing substantial, nor is it undertaken for or causative of anything, but only causable by the significations of some house. And for that reason the ruler of any house in the eighth causes death through the signification of the house over which it presides, which is thus converted into the signification of the eighth. And so the ruler of the twelfth in the eighth prefigures that illness will be the cause of death, or that the native will die in prison; the ruler of the seventh in the eighth, the wife or war; of the tenth house, dignity or action undertaken; the ruler of the first in the eighth, the native himself will be the cause of his death; the ruler of the second, avarice or theft, &c. On the other hand, the ruler of the eighth appearing in any house passively causes death by reason of the signification of that house; so the ruler of the eighth in the seventh prefigures that the native will suffer death, not from his wife, but for the sake of his wife; in the eleventh, on account of a friend, &c. But when a Planet in the eighth presides over two other houses, it is to be seen with which the eighth more easily or more efficaciously combines by reason of its significations, and with which the Planet in the eighth more congruently brings death; and judge from these.

Chapter VI

Of several Planets ruling the same house, or one Planet ruling several houses

When a house is ruled by a single Planet, the state of the essential significations of that house will be simple, but simpler if that Planet is in its own domicile, and truly simplest if it is [also] in that house, because then there is no division in the governance of those significations.

But when several Planets rule the same house, then, because the governance of the significations of that house is subject to rulers of diverse kind and virtue, their condition suffers a mixture, a division, and sometimes a contrariety. And that will be greater when one of the rulers is a benefic Planet but the other malefic; and certainly greatest if, in addition, it happens that one is strong by celestial state, the other weak, and the two are squared or opposed.

Moreover, the Planet that presides over the cusp is to be preferred in the governance of the significations of that house, yet another [ruler] is not to be neglected. And the reason is that the cusp of each house is the most efficacious point of the whole house, as is said elsewhere; but because the degree of the sign that occupies the cusp acts only by virtue of its ruler, it follows also that this [ruler] takes precedence over another, especially if it is analogous to the significations of the house, is stronger by celestial state, and, above all, if either it or a Planet it aspects with its own strong ray is in that house. In fact, all the following are to be noted: Whether they are both benefic or malefic, or indeed one benefic and the other malefic; whether they are both analogous, or one of them; whether they are both strong by celestial state, or both weak, or whether indeed one is strong and the other weak; whether they are both inside that house or both outside, or one inside and the other outside. Then which presides over the cusp, or is closer to it, or is connected by a stronger ray to it or to a Planet in that house. According to these, the winner is to be pronounced.

Finally, when the same Planet presides over several houses, even if it occupies none of them, it nevertheless prefigures the combination of the significations of those houses. As, if the same Planet is the ruler of the Horoscope and the Midheaven, the native is promised actions, undertakings, profession, or dignities. The same ruler of the seventh and eighth [promises] dangers to life or death from enemies, especially if it is malefic and badly conditioned. It is to be seen also with which house the Planet has a greater analogy, for the significations of such a house will prevail. But if the ruler is in another house, that is to be judged according to Chapter 4.

Chapter VII

Of the accidental determination of the Planets by reason of exaltation & Triplicity

It is well known among Astrologers taught by experience that Planets placed in their exaltations are very efficacious for benefit or misfortune in relation to the significations of the houses of the figure where they are located and [where they] rule; then also that through its connection by body or aspect an exalted Planet strengthens other Planets by pushing forward their effects. But here it is to be determined whether a Planet placed outside its exaltation has some power with respect to the significations of the house in which the sign of its exaltation is placed, or in the significations of another Planet that occupies that sign, as if the Sun should be in the tenth in the sign of Cancer and Jupiter outside the tenth; in this circumstance, by reason of Cancer, in which he is exalted, something [of Jupiter] may be in the significations of the tenth, and also in the Sun as the Sun is bodily in the tenth, much in the same way as he is ruler of the eleventh where Leo is found.

What is brought out here is evident from Ptolemy and all Astrologers. Ptolemy, in *Quadripartite*, Book 2, Chapter 6 on the election of the ruler of an Eclipse, then in Chapter 13 on the election of the Apheta,[185] takes the Planet that is most powerful by domicile, exaltation, and Triangle[186] in the principal places of the figure; from which it follows that, if that Planet has power in the general significations of the Moon suffering an Eclipse by reason of domicile in the place of the Moon, it also will have power by reason of exaltation in the same place. And the same is considered every time in the election of the ruler of the Geniture, about which it is asked which, based on those grounds, is more powerful in the principal places of the figure, and indeed also when it is desired to be known of any Planet which other Planet is stronger and more efficacious in its place.

But although I have discovered by experience in almost all figures that the causes of effects are rendered sufficiently evident by the bodily location, rulership, and aspects of the Planets, so that there is scarcely any effect from the stars that is not sufficiently reduced to these causes, yet it is certain that the dignity of exaltation in another house very often not only concurs with the causes already mentioned, but sometimes also acts with the strength of its proper and solitary allotted efficient power. So in the geniture of Prince Gaston, Saturn in the seventh with his exaltation in the fourth signified his wife by whose cause he was made lord of very extensive landed estates and also of two Provinces. So also for me an almost perpetual eagerness for the exaltation of praise attached to my geniture, not only from Mars, ruler of the Horoscope, in the exaltation of Jupiter and all the other Planets except Mercury in the exaltation of Venus, ruler of the first,[187] but especially because the Sun and Moon have their exaltations in the first house, which is the house of character and inborn talent, from which I too much incline to esteem myself above the rest owing to the gifts of my inborn talent and the more sublime sciences known to me; and it is very difficult for me to resist such a propensity unless I turn to my faults and from that am confounded, and sincerely judge no man so base and deserving of contempt. And also from those causes my achievements and name became famous in the World; and many similar examples occur everywhere, so that, accordingly, it does not seem useless to draw an opinion about the significations of any house not only from the Planet that is the ruler of that house, but also from the Planet that would be strong by exaltation in that house; so, if Libra is in the Horoscope, character is judged from Venus and Saturn and their state; and so of the others. And similarly if Saturn is in Libra, Saturn's effects are to be judged not only from the fact that he is exalted, but also from his ruler,

Venus, and from the mutual relationship between the two; for if Venus is well conditioned and applies to Saturn by conjunction or trine, for this reason Saturn will act more efficaciously. Again, if the Sun is in Pisces, he will act in Pisces as in the domicile of Jupiter, and for that reason with Jupiter himself; but also he will act with Pisces as the exaltation of Venus, and for that reason with Venus herself, and that is proved by authority, reason, and experience. The authority is that of all the Ancients, who say the Planet that is more powerful in some place of the *Caelum* is that which has more dignities by domicile, exaltation and Triangle. The reason is that for no other cause is it said to be powerful in that place through those dignities than because on account of those dignities it works powerfully with respect to the significations of that place; for if it did not act with respect to those significations by means of those dignities it would wrongly be said to be powerful in that place. Finally, the experience is apparent in the examples given above. But yet, other things being equal, the ruler of the house prevails over the ruler by exaltation, but both are always to be observed.

As regards the Triplicities, the Arabs[188] predicted almost everything from the rulers of the Triplicities, as is evident from their Books; but because until now there has been no certainty among Astrologers about those rulers,[189] as we have explained in Book 15, Chapter 6, no wonder such judgments abound with errors. And so far truths have been predicted from them only to the extent that the erroneous assignment of the Triangle rulers of the Ancients happened to be congruent with truths and natural things, as handed down by us in [Book 15,] Chapter 7.[190] This can be proved from the comparison of the Triangles established by us with the figures of Albohali,[191] in which he judges the fortune or misfortune of the native from the rulers of the Triplicity of the Sun if the geniture is diurnal, but from the rulers of the Triplicity of the Moon if it is a nocturnal geniture. But that judgment is too universal, and is common to half of the whole Earth, and on that account incongruous; and nothing is predicted by him through Triplicities that could not be more strongly and evidently predicted through the locations, rulerships, and aspects of the Planets.

So in the first nocturnal figure of Albohali, the Moon is the ruler of the second in the sixth with Saturn, and in Scorpio, where she is fallen; and Mars, the ruler of the Moon, is in Aquarius square to the Moon and Saturn. What more truly miserable state of the second ruler can be conceived for poverty? Therefore, without Triplicities the cause of poverty was very evident and very strong. Through the Triangle rulers truly set down by us, poverty is also signified. Indeed, it is well known that the Moon is the principal ruler of her Triplicity, with Mars a participant. Now it is true that the Moon and Mars are in cadent houses, as the Moon is in the sixth and Mars in the ninth, which suffices for the rule of Albohali; but I add that the Moon, the ruler of the second, is fallen and wounded by conjunction with Saturn and by a square from Mars, which is much more efficacious.

In the second figure of Albohali, which was diurnal, the Sun is in the eleventh in Aquarius with Mercury; and so, according to Albohali and me, Saturn and Mercury were the rulers of the Triplicity of the Sun. And Saturn was with Mars in Scorpio in the eighth, and so Saturn and Mercury were in succedent houses, from which Albohali infers the greatest offices, the highest honors, and the greatest good fortune; this certainly could not happen from Saturn and Mercury, because they were squared, but from other stronger and more evident causes—namely, from Venus, ruler of the second in the tenth and trine the second, and so in her Triplicity; then from Jupiter in the fourth and in his exaltation, from which he mutually receives the Moon in domicile. Therefore, from Jupiter and Venus, well conditioned and analogous to wealth, and in places congruent with honors, great wealth, honors and prosperity flowed, which the malefics—trine Jupiter and sextile Venus, and also in the eighth, from which by opposition they signify wealth—were not against, but also favored; and all these square with the doctrines posited by us above.

I could offer many similar examples from Albohali and others, both Ancient and Modern Astrologers, but these are all alike. Yet we may say that virtues certainly are in the rulers of the Triplicities and that judgment can be had from them, because doubtless when in any sign any change occurs this in a certain way belongs to the whole Triplicity of that sign on account of an identity of nature, as we said in Book 15, Chapter 7, and the signs act in accord with the nature and state of their rulers, as is often said. But yet judgment from the ruler of the sign is much more certain than it is by means of the ruler of the Triangle, because, of course, the ruler of the sign is the more proximate cause and that on which the sign itself essentially depends for its action; but the ruler of the Triangle is plainly a cause more remote, and one on which the sign does not *per se* depend. In fact, I rate the power of the aspects to be far more efficacious than the power of the Triangle rulers alone, to which in Astrology I judge minimal powers are to be attributed on account, of course, of the general agreement of the elemental nature of signs of the same Triplicity, which, however, differ completely from each other in any formal virtue of the signs. Accordingly, Cancer is a sign in kind, or in formal virtue, Lunar; Scorpio, Martial; Pisces, Jovial, even though they are generally of the same watery nature; and, accordingly, consideration of the Triangle rulers is judged more valuable with respect to temperaments and constitutions of the air than with respect to the rest of the accidents of a person.

And so the determination of one Planet by [domicile] rulership over the significations of any house, other things being equal, overcomes the determination of another Planet by exaltation with respect to the same significations, and [overcomes] a determination simply by rulership of the Triangle. But it must be taken for certain that each Planet acts on the significations of the houses of the celestial figure by reason of its dignities in the houses of its exaltation and Triangle, in whatever place that Planet may be and whether or not it aspects those houses. As brought out above, domicile and exaltation belong to a single Planet. But by Triangle three

Planets preside over the same sign; and so it is to be seen whether the celestial figure is diurnal or nocturnal, so that only two Planets are to be looked at, one of which is the primary ruler of the triplicity but the other only the secondary.

And it is a common opinion that by the dignity of domicile a Planet signifies about the stability of things, or about stable things; by the dignity of exaltation about sudden and significant changes; and by the dignity of Triangle about joining two-by-two and in fellowship.[192] But Ptolemy in Aphorism 72 of the *Centiloquy*[193] judges about the rearing of the Native from the Triangle ruler of the Horoscope, and about way of life[194] from the Triangle ruler of the Moon. Cardanus in Aphorism 166, Section 3, however, is of the opinion that Planets appearing in diverse Triplicities make people more adapted in all things, but in a single Triangle, more adapted to fewer things but in some excellent; and this is true.

Chapter VIII

Whether the Planets are efficaciously determined in the figure for the native by their essential debilities (as they call them), namely, exile & fall

A Planet in its exile, or placed in fall,[195] is said to be badly conditioned by celestial state—that is, universally and with respect to the whole Earth—because it is in signs contrary to its nature and virtue. And in exile its power is corrupted; but in fall it wilts and as it were grows numb. But simply peregrine is not an essential debility, for it is contrary neither by nature nor by virtue, at least influential (which is essential); for a peregrine Planet is neither in its own signs—namely, domicile or exaltation—nor in contrary ones, but simply in foreign ones. For we do not call the Sun in Aquarius and Libra simply peregrine; in Aquarius and Libra he has no dignity, but in Aquarius he is exiled and in Libra fallen, which is much more than a simple wandering in a foreign place. But he is simply peregrine in all of the watery and earthy Triplicities, then also in Gemini; and the reasoning is the same about the rest. And therefore a Planet simply peregrine has itself in a middle way between an essentially well conditioned and badly conditioned state; this is always to be understood *per se*, for by accident a Planet that is simply peregrine can be, because of an accidental and congruent connection with other Planets, in a better and more effective state than another essentially well conditioned.[196]

Here, however, it is not inquired whether a Planet in exile or placed in its fall is determined with respect to the significations of the house of the figure in which it is located, so long as, of course, it is in its exile or fall. For experience very evidently proves that this is true, because certainly

Saturn in exile in the twelfth will cause more malignant illnesses, and in the eighth a more shameful death, and fallen in the tenth he may cause unskilled idleness and unreliability, or give a base occupation, or completely prevent a worthy occupation, or cause a fall from it or dishonor in it, which Saturn himself would not have caused if he were not exiled or fallen in those places. And so the ruler of the Horoscope or of the Midheaven exiled or fallen is unfortunate for the significations of these houses. But it is inquired here whether by reason of its fall or exile a Planet is determined with respect to the signification of the house occupied by the sign of its exile or fall in the absence of that Planet.

And as to this, although we may see the Astrological causes of the effects sufficiently rendered without taking into account this determination, yet, if experience and reason are consulted, we may discover either that it concurs with other causes, or even that it causes something peculiar [to itself]. As far as regards reason, it is certain that any Planet in its domicile or exalted in a house of any figure is exiled or fallen in the opposite, and signifies the latter, for the significations of opposite houses are in a certain way reciprocal, as is said before. And this deceived the Ancients, and Ptolemy himself, who believed that the sixth house is essential for illnesses and the eleventh for children, although they have such significations only by accident and by reason of opposition to the twelfth house, which is for illnesses, and the fifth, which is essentially and *per se* for children. Owing to this cause, therefore, a Planet in its own domicile located in the sixth will prefigure with respect to the significations of the twelfth house, but that unfortunately, from a double cause. First, on account of the opposition, which is an intrinsically unfortunate ray. Second, on account of the exile; for what good can a Planet do or signify in a place where its nature or virtue is corrupted?

As regards experiences, these occur very often, but here I will speak only of myself. I have Jupiter and Venus in the twelfth house and in Pisces, the domicile of Jupiter and exaltation of Venus, from which I certainly escaped many bad illnesses and causes for prison, and I prevailed over hidden enemies, even the Magnates signified by the Sun, in such a way that by their own will and power they will not have altogether harmed me. But in service I was always unhappy, except with two young students of excellent nature, aside from whom I was compelled to change to others almost monthly; if not so often changed, tedium and patience, my own vices or deficiencies, truly all day long would have prevailed.[197]

From which I deem it sufficiently apparent that even this determination is not to be neglected or to be rejected, though sufficient causes of its effects are at hand elsewhere. And consequently, Mars can be seen as in exile in the domicile of Venus, the exaltation of Saturn, and the triplicity of Saturn, Venus, and Mercury;[198] so of others.

You will object. If this were a determination of any virtue and efficacy, it is certain that this always would have to be taken into account in predictions or judgments, so that surely contradiction or confusion in judgments always would be seen. Therefore it is not efficacious.

I reply. The conclusion is false. For in the examples given above, no confusion or contradiction is found in the significations, and the significations of opposite houses are connected; therefore such a determination is not in the least to be neglected any more than is determination through multiple dexter and sinister aspects, which is to be seen for each Planet; from which it is apparent that many things are to be attended to about every Planet; for it is to be discerned what it does by reason of its bodily location and opposition, then by domicile, exaltation, Triangle, exile, fall, aspects, and its subjection to other Planets by domicile, exaltation and Triangle. All these render judgment difficult, at least for human capacities, but not impossible because the effect always follows the nature and state of the most powerful Planet.

Moreover, although Aries placed in the Horoscope acts with respect to the significations of the Horoscope in accord with the nature of its ruler, Mars, and against the nature of Venus, or Leo so placed acts in accord with the nature of the Sun and against the nature of Saturn, yet Venus or Saturn is not on that account said to act on the significations of the Horoscope, for they cannot act except by their own nature which is not in the Horoscope where, of course, contrary powers are. But it is not otherwise than if Jupiter should be the ruler of the Horoscope and it in his trine, where the benefic effect of the trine would be increased by Jupiter's dignity in the Horoscope. But if Saturn's exile is in the Horoscope, and it in his square or opposition, the malignity of the square or opposition will be increased by the contrariety of Saturn to the sign in the Horoscope. It by all means follows, and from experience is most true, that in that position such contrariety is in that sign, which is intrinsically effective in accord with the nature of its ruler, but Saturn does not act with it without an aspect. And so, without this aspect by square or opposition, Saturn is not to be attended to as a significator of the misfortunes of the Horoscope; so of others.

Chapter IX

Of the accidental determination of the Planets by aspect, & in what way this is to be understood

How great is the power of the aspects or rays[199] of the Planets is not only well known by the experience of all Astrologers, especially in directions, but is also highly worthy of admiration.

So it is to be known that by the ray of its body, which they call a conjunction, a Planet acts formally on these inferior things as much according to its elemental as its influential forces. But its other rays—the opposition, quincunx, trine, square, sextile and dodectile[200]—act only through the eleven parts of the *Primum Caelum*, which are determined from the body of that Planet by those aspects, as is said by us in Book 14, Section 1, Chapter 4. Therefore, those parts, or places, determined to diverse kinds of aspects, act on these inferior things by virtue of those determinations, in accord with the nature of the aspect they form; but yet they depend on the nature and formal virtue and on the state of the aspecting Planet, just as is said above that a sign acts with the formal virtue of its ruler and in accord with [its ruler's] state; and so a Planet through its aspects communicates its power universally, that is, to the whole World, but in diverse ways according to the nature or kind of each aspect, and therefore it also acts universally in diverse ways. But by means of the same aspects it acts on the native particularly in accord with the significations of the houses in which those aspects fall, or in accord with the significations to which the Planets are determined, and that, in the common way of speaking, are affected by those aspects. For the Planets properly [speaking] do not affect or color each other by their aspects; as, when the Sun is said to be in the square of Mars, it happens that the square of Mars falls in the same place with the Sun, and the square of the latter with the former, so they act on these sublunary things as partners—not unlike what is said in Book 2, Section 2, Chapter 5 of Planets acting with the signs as partners in the same action. And certainly the partnership of benefic aspects from benefic Planets is beneficial; malefic aspects from malefics, unfortunate; but the partnership of benefic ones from malefic[201] Planets, or of malefic ones from benefics, is middling, which also comes to be understood of aspects to the cusps of the houses. Therefore, in those two ways in which a Planet acts in a particular way through its aspects,[202] those aspects are said to be determined with respect to particular things.

From these things it surely is apparent that a force of action is in the aspects, as in the signs, by virtue, of course, of a determination that depends on the formal virtue of the Planets; and so, those aspects act, or, if you prefer, a Planet acts through its aspects. In fact, [a Planet] is seen, at least in some cases, to act more strongly by aspect than by rulership, because experience certainly proves that it is worse for the Horoscope to be afflicted by a square or opposition of Mars or Saturn than to be under their rulership. On the other hand, it is better for the Horoscope to be in the trine of Jupiter than for Jupiter to be the ruler of the Horoscope, which yet is understood with other things being equal; for if Jupiter, the ruler of the Horoscope, is in the Midheaven well conditioned by celestial state, it is far better than his being in the eighth badly conditioned and trine the Horoscope; and the reasoning is the same about the rest. And from this it can be deduced[203] that a Planet may signify more efficaciously the house to which it is opposed than does the ruler of that house located outside the house, especially if [the ruler] is weak and does not aspect [into the house].

From this it is to be noted that the aspect of a Planet acts more efficaciously by reason of the house in which that Planet appears than by reason of the house it rules. And so, Mars, ruler of the third in the fourth and trine the Horoscope of some native makes him favored by his parents but hated by his siblings.[204]

Chapter X

That by their aspects the Planets cause benefit & misfortune, & in what way

Although some Planets by their nature are benefic, as Jupiter and Venus are commonly considered, others surely are malefic, as Saturn and Mars; yet not all aspects of the benefics are beneficial on account of the diverse nature or quality of the aspects, some of which are intrinsically beneficent, or suitable for benefiting, while others are in fact maleficent; therefore, each Planet by its aspects benefits and does harm at the same time, or causes benefit and misfortune at the same time, because it pours out from the *Caelum* at the same time benefic and malefic rays. Yet the distinction is preserved that benefic Planets are more prone to benefit by their benefic rays and by their malefic ones less prone to misfortune than malefic Planets. Therefore, the benefit of any Planet flows through the aspects of the trine, sextile and dodectile, which are benefic by nature, and of these the trine is the most efficacious, the dodectile the weakest, and the sextile in the middle. But misfortune flows from the opposition, square and quincunx, which are by nature malefic; and the strongest is the opposition, the weakest the quincunx, and the square in the middle.[205] On the other hand, the conjunction—that is, the body of the Planet or its place in the *Caelum*—is not an aspect properly speaking, although it is counted among the aspects, but it is only the beginning of the aspects and is intrinsically indifferent to the quality of its effect; for the conjunction of benefic Planets is beneficial, of malefics, unfortunate; and these things are said in general.

Further, a Planet benefic by nature benefits easily and abundantly through its *per se* benefic rays, causing benefit in the fortunate houses it aspects and preventing or mitigating misfortune in the unfortunate ones; but its malefic ones only put in the way difficulties, obstacles and misfortunes to be overcome.[206] Yet by accident, by reason of the malefic state of that Planet, both Celestial and Terrestrial, its benefic rays will produce little, but it will do much harm by its malefic ones, as, in the geniture of Cardinal Richelieu, benefic Jupiter, exiled in the eighth, the [place] most hostile to life, and with the violent fixed star, the Eye of the Bull;[207] his opposition meeting by direction with the Horoscope, the primary significator of life, at last killed him, notwithstanding his many attendants; and he was, in fact, many times little distant from having died a violent death, and as many times he evaded it, either by supreme care or by remarkable fortune. For which reason what is often said by common Astrologers in such a case is false—namely, that the square and opposition of the benefic Planets are of no harm.

On the other hand, a Planet malefic by nature very much harms through its *per se* malefic rays, causing misfortune in the unfortunate places of the figure and preventing or corrupting benefit in the fortunate ones, unless the malefic rules the place of the malefic aspect; for then in the fortunate houses that aspect will benefit, but violently and with corruption or misfortune. In the unfortunate ones, it is certainly worse, so that Mars, as ruler of the eighth in the second, almost always kills. But by means of its benefic rays, it prefigures the acquisition of beneficial things by difficult means, as, in the geniture of the King of Sweden, Saturn, ruler of the second, by his trine to the Sun in the first signified great riches for him, which he acquired in war owing to Mercury, the ruler of the seventh cusp in the second; and he was most fortunate in acquiring them owing to Jupiter, Mercury, Venus and the Part of Fortune in the second under the rulership of that Saturn. But yet if the state of a malefic Planet, both Celestial and Terrestrial, is unfortunate, these do great damage also through their benefic rays, as in the same King's geniture, Saturn, exiled in the eighth, struck by the square of Mars from the twelfth and trine the Sun in the first, brought an unfortunate and violent death, especially because Jupiter, the ruler of the Horoscope and the Sun, applied to the opposition of Saturn and squared Mars. For it is always to be noted whether the house of the aspecting Planet is congruent with the benefit or misfortune of the house it aspects. And so it is apparent that the same aspect can be at the same time beneficial for one thing and unfortunate for another, which is worthy of note.

Accordingly, a malefic by nature and sign in the malefic aspect of a malefic by nature or determination is unfavorable; in the benefic aspect of a benefic, it is milder; but if a benefic by nature badly conditioned by sign is in addition in the unfortunate ray of a malefic, it certainly will harm.

Moreover, it is to be carefully noted here that a Planet influences threefold by its aspects. First, by reason of its own nature, for the Sun influences in a solar manner, the Moon in a lunar manner, Saturn in a Saturnine manner, &c. Second, by reason of its celestial state through the sign it occupies and its connection with other stars, for a Planet depends on this state as on its partners in an action, as is said many times; and so, well conditioned it will be of use, at least through its benefic rays; badly [conditioned], it will harm, at least through its malefic ones. Third, by reason of its Terrestrial state, and this is twofold—namely, by bodily location in a house of any figure, and by rulership. A Planet, however, always influences through its aspects by reason of its nature and celestial state, yet not always also by reason of its bodily location and rulership at the same time, but sometimes by reason of the latter, sometimes of the former, and sometimes both at the same time, as, with Jupiter in the first and trine the Midheaven, the native will be fortunate in actions undertaken and honors,[208] in accord with the nature and celestial state of that Jupiter; if also Jupiter is the ruler of the Midheaven, it prefigures much more certain and greater fortune in these things. But if, in addition, he aspects by a trine the Sun in the tenth, it then prefigures the greatest good fortune. And the reasoning is the same for the rest of the aspects, whether for benefit or for misfortune. Indeed, in general, any Planet in each of its aspects to Planets or to cusps, or by meeting those significators in directions, makes the significations of these fortunate or unfortunate according to its own significations by reason of the nature of the bodily location, of the rulership, and of the nature of its own aspects. And so Mars, ruler of the fourth and eleventh in the seventh aspecting by trine the Sun in the Midheaven, will promote honors for the native through disputes, combat, the spouse, parents and friends. Then if he has met that Sun by direction.[209] And the reasoning is the same in the rest. But in addition to the three things already mentioned, it is necessary to pay attention also to whether the Planet is aspecting by application or by separation, because application is more efficacious than separation, other things being equal; and when one Planet applies to another, the latter also is looked at with respect to its nature and both states, Celestial and Terrestrial, and from that it is to be judged. So, therefore, in the geniture of the King of Sweden, Jupiter, the ruler of the Horoscope, in the second applying to the opposition of Saturn, a natural malefic exiled in the eighth and struck by the square of Mars, portended a violent death for that King.

From what has been said above, therefore, it is evident that as Planets, according to their bodily location and rulership in the celestial figure, either confer benefit or misfortune or remove it, so they do the same also by their aspects, according to how these are determined. In fact, two Planets constituting an aspect mutually determine each other to the significations of the houses where they are located. So, if Jupiter is in the first and trine the Sun in the tenth, the Sun will determine Jupiter to the significations of the tenth—of course, to honors and dignities—and Jupiter [will determine] the Sun to the significations of the first—of course, to character and fame or praise. Similar is Saturn in the eighth and Jupiter, ruler of the Horoscope, in the second, aspecting each other by opposition.

Section II | Chapter X

The opposition of Saturn to Jupiter will color the Jovial character and a Saturnine influx will stain it. On the other hand, this opposition of Jupiter and Saturn can prefigure death by judicial decree. And so the same aspect of two Planets to each other always signifies diverse things, which indeed was not heeded by the Ancients when they handed down to us the effects of the aspects. And the Planets have in addition that by their aspects they may increase, diminish, or corrupt the power of other significators, sometimes remarkably and sometimes moderately, as, if Jupiter is in the tenth, he will be the significator of honors. If then the Sun blesses him with a trine, his force for conferring especially great honors will be magnified. But if Saturn unfortunately squares him, that force will be not only diminished but also corrupted, and it will portend something unfortunate in dignities and actions. Moreover, from the essential significations of the Planets and their positions in the celestial Figure, the nature or kind of effect of their connection by body or aspect can be discovered. So, because Jupiter signifies foresight and Mars audacity, if the two are conjoined in the tenth house and celestially well conditioned, they prefigure dominion and great power, because this foresight and audacity are realized in undertaking and acting; if they are in the second, they will signify vast wealth to be procured by skilled taking,[210] and notable expenses. And what has been said here about the conjunction is also to be understood about the aspects between Planets, at least the stronger ones, considering the nature of the aspects and of the Planets, and their Celestial and Terrestrial state.

Someone will object. If a Planet is determined by all its aspects to the significations of the houses in which they fall, it will act as a result on all the accidents of the native. And so it will be the significator of them all, and also will be considered in each kind—life, wealth, siblings, parents, &c; and each one will be judged from all the aspects of each Planet, taking into account the bodily location and rulership of that Planet. And in the judgments of the effects of the stars this could not fail to meet with inextricable difficulties and confusion; the greatest, with no means of discernment. Therefore the Planets do not act through their aspects, or all judgment is completely uncertain and delusive.

I reply. The action of the agents of causes is double—one perceptible, the other imperceptible. The action of the Sun is perceptible to all, but the action of a fixed star of the sixth magnitude is perceptible to no person, yet it is not to be denied that it acts. So, therefore, in Astrology, although any accident signified by the stars depends in some way on all the Planets and on each of the aspects of each one, it does not depend on them equally, but on some more, on some less, and on others least. Now certainly an Astrologer judges effects only from particular and stronger causes; namely, from the Planet occupying the house to which such an accident belongs, or from its ruler, and their celestial state; then from the stronger aspects into that house, which are the opposition, trine, square and sextile, and which all the Ancients observed. The two remaining, dodectiles and quincunxes, rarely act unless they are partile; and if the force of action is sometimes extended to the secondary ruler of a house, yet it does not advance further into the circle, at least sensibly, as is said above. And similarly, even if the Planets influence each house with some of their rays, yet among several rays affecting the same house, the stronger ones frustrate and suppress the force of the weaker ones. And so, having brought together the concurring strengths of the Planets and of all other causes of some accident, Astrologers pronounce on the question of the proposed accident according to the assent of the winning party. It is very far removed [from reality] that it cannot be done without confusion and that the science is groundless, for even at first sight of a figure a true judgment is composed, with attention directed only to the evident beneficence or malignity, then the strength or weakness, of the proper and more principal causes of an accident, which always overcome the unsuitable and less principal ones; although I have never urged on anyone a precipitous judgment, but circumspection, lest he dishonor himself and the art.

Chapter XI

Of the connections, or aspects, of the Planets compared to each other in diverse ways

The aspects of the Planets are compared in multiple ways. First, with respect to the cusps of the houses. The Planets are moved to the cusps by the primary motion, that is, on the *primum mobile* from Rising to Setting,[211] and so their dexter, or preceding, aspects are commonly supposed to be more efficacious than their sinister, or following,[212] ones of the same kind; but this is not absolutely true and, as such, requires a distinction. If a Planet applies by dexter square to one cusp, such as the Midheaven, but departs from a sinister one to another, such as the Horoscope (which is to be understood only in a comparison between different figures),[213] the dexter will be more efficacious; but if by the primary motion it departs from the dexter to the Midheaven and applies to the sinister to the Horoscope, the sinister will be more efficacious; and the reasoning is the same in the rest. But note that the Horoscope here is to be understood as the cusp itself, or the circle of position[214] that begins the first house, and not the part of the *Caelum* that occupies that cusp. For when a direct Planet applies to the cusp itself by the primary motion, it departs at the same time by the secondary, or proper, motion from the part of the *Caelum* occupying it. And this doctrine is founded on the fact that application is more efficacious than departure, at least other things being equal, because in application the force is directed toward the aspect as it becomes closer to partile, but in departure it is slackened; from this it is also to be deduced that a preceding Planet does not have power superior to one following unless the former also applies to the latter.[215] And this is to be carefully noted when the strengths of the Planets are counted up to discover which one is preeminent.[216]

Second. Aspects between Planets, which move towards each other by the secondary, or proper, motion from Setting to Rising,[217] are to be compared. And so sinister [interplanetary] aspects are stronger than dexter according to the common opinion,[218] which, however, also requires a distinction. If Venus, either direct or retrograde, applies by sinister trine to Mars, such an aspect is stronger than the dexter trine of Mars to Venus; that is, Venus[219] more efficaciously affects the significations of Mars, both essential and accidental, than Mars affects the significations of Venus. But if, on the contrary, Venus applies by dexter trine, the dexter trine here will be stronger than the sinister trine by which Mars departs from Venus; and the reasoning is the same in the rest.

Third. The same kind of aspect from the same Planet is compared to itself as the placement of the Planets differs; so the square of Mars and the Moon does not always produce the same kind of effect, as the Astrologers who put together Tables about the powers or effects of the aspects of the Planets have supposed. For that aspect can vary twelvefold, through the twelve signs of the Zodiac in which Mars and the Moon can be found. For Mars does one thing in Aries and another in Taurus, and the same is to be said of the Moon; therefore, although, in general, their square portends contrariety and misfortune, yet the misfortune will be one kind if Mars is placed in Libra and the Moon in Capricorn, and another if Mars is placed in Capricorn and the Moon in Libra; but in particular, there will be one kind of misfortune if Mars is placed in the first house of a figure and the Moon in the tenth, and another if Mars is placed in the tenth and the Moon in the first, which is apparent from *The Elements of Astrology*; and the reasoning is the same in the rest; and so for the most part the Tables will be found to be misleading.

Fourth. The same kind of aspect, or the same kind of connection, between two Planets is considered according to the reason for the victory of one Planet over the other; so that if two Planets are conjoined, squared, or opposed, it is asked: Which of the two will prevail? To which the answer must be fourfold. First, on account of the dignity of the Planets. For, other things being equal, the Sun and Moon, because they are the Planets of the first rank arranged as primary around the Earth,[220] surpass the rest of the Planets in virtue, and the Sun himself [surpasses] the Moon. Of the rest, Saturn, Jupiter, and Mars are superior, and predominate over Venus and Mercury, the inferior ones.[221] And so the significations of Venus placed in the square of Saturn will be more strongly affected by the square of that Saturn than the significations of Saturn by the square of Venus. Second, by reason of celestial state; for the stronger celestial state—of course, domicile, exaltation, Triangle, position in relation to the Sun, &c—will prevail over the weaker. And so Mars from Capricorn square the Sun in Libra will wound [the Sun], or his significations, more powerfully because Mars is in his exaltation and the Sun in his fall. Third, by reason of Terrestrial state, for the Planet that is determined in several or more efficacious ways to the significations of the houses in which its aspects fall, or to the contrary of these, will prevail, as, if Jupiter is in Sagittarius in the Horoscope, he is determined to life by nature, bodily location and rulership. If, therefore, he is conjunct or square the Moon, the not [otherwise] unfortunate ruler of the eighth, that Jupiter will prevail for life, notwithstanding the square of the Moon to the Horoscope. But if Jupiter is exiled in the Horoscope and conjoined with Mars, ruler of the eighth, Mars will prevail in bringing death because, strongly determined to death by nature and rulership, he very much wounds the significator of life. Fourth, by reason of application and departure; for a Planet that applies to connection with another by body or aspect is counted as the stronger in the connection, as is said in Chapter 10. Nevertheless, it is certain that from this the application is said to be stronger than the departure also because the Planet to which the other applies is more strongly affected by the application than [the other] by the departure, either for benefit or for misfortune, according to the nature of the aspect and of the [applying] Planet and its Celestial and Terrestrial state. Further, after the prevailing Planet is recognized, it is also to be seen whether it predominates by a little or by much; and the other always is taken into account because, of course, both concur in the same effect as partners in the same action, for neither the square of Saturn to the Sun nor the departure of the latter from the former can be ineffective; and to the degree the [prevailing] Planet is in a Celestial and Terrestrial state stronger for benefit or for misfortune, it is to be noted to that extent more diligently in which houses its aspects fall, for it will strongly influence their significations for benefit or misfortune according to the nature of the aspect.

Fifth. Two aspects of different kinds are compared to each other in two ways. First, as they are from a single Planet. And so the opposition of the same Planet is *per se* stronger than its square, and the trine stronger than the sextile. I say *per se*, and universally, because the square is half the opposition, and the sextile half the trine. For by accident, and by reason of the determination both of the Planets and the aspects, it can be contrary; for Jupiter, the ruler of the Horoscope in the eleventh, will have more power with respect to the temperament, character, and inborn talent of the native by his sextile to the Horoscope than with respect to his siblings by his trine to the third. And Mars, ruler of the eighth in the tenth, will have more power against his life by his square to the Horoscope than with respect to parents or inheritance by his opposition. Second, as they are from two Planets to the same significator; so, if Jupiter trines and Mars squares the Horoscope, one of the two will prevail in the concourse, or mixture, with respect to the life and character of the native; because the rays are mixed and they act as partners, or as hot and cold coming together, something intermediate comes from them. And this can be considered in five ways.

First, simply and absolutely; and so, because the trine is the aspect first in virtue for benefiting, and the square only the second for doing harm, which certainly is only half the opposition, therefore the virtue of the trine of Jupiter will surpass the square of Mars, and so the latter will harm life less than the former can help. Second, with respect to the celestial state of Jupiter and Mars; for if Mars is strong, as in Scorpio or Capricorn, but Jupiter is weak, as in Gemini, the square of Mars will do more harm than the trine of Jupiter is able to help. Third, with respect to terrestrial state, or the determination in the figure to the accident in question. And so Mars, ruler of the eighth square the Horoscope, will harm life more than the trine of Jupiter, ruler of the eighth or the twelfth, will help it, because, for Jupiter to be most beneficial for life through his trine, he should be determined to life by nature, body, rulership, and aspect, but also free from the signification of illnesses or death, which, however, will not be the case if he is in the eighth, or the ruler of it or of the twelfth. And the reasoning is the same about other aspects fighting each other for the same significator of life, dignities, marriage, &c. For when the concurrent aspects agree, whether for benefit or for misfortune, there is no difficulty in judging. Fourth, with respect to the distance to the significator; and so, from the aspects of two Planets to the same significator, such as the Horoscope or the Sun, the nearer or more partile is preferred to the more remote of the same kind, especially if it attains union first. Fifth, with respect to approach or departure; and so the one applying is preferred to the one departing, as is often said.

Sixth. The same kind of aspect from the same Planet in fortunate or unfortunate celestial state is compared; but it can be doubted whether Saturn, from his own domicile or exaltation, does more harm through his square or opposition than if he should be in his exile or fall. But the doubts are removed by comparison with Jupiter, which, if he is in a fortunate celestial state, will help more through his trine than if he were unfortunate; but in an unfortunate celestial state, he will do more harm through his square than in a fortunate one, about which matter no Astrologer doubts. Therefore, why would not Saturn in an unfortunate celestial state harm more through his square than when fortunate? Saturn, therefore, will always harm, but more so if he is unfortunate, as is evident from the direction of the Midheaven to the square of Saturn in Leo in the eighth, which killed the King of Sweden. And so the trine of Jupiter from his own domicile is the best trine; the square is harmless, or only slightly harmful; but from exile, the trine is useless, or very little useful, and the square assuredly is harmful. And similarly, the trine of Saturn from his own domicile benefits, and his square wounds; but from exile, the trine is useless, or rather, harmful, and the square is worse; which is understood *per se* and other things being equal. From this certainly a conjecture is made about the intermediate state of the Planets, when, namely, they are simply peregrine.

Seventh. Aspects of the same kind are compared with respect to their beneficence and maleficence; so, although all squares and oppositions are intrinsically unfortunate, they are worse from the malefics, Saturn and Mars, and even worse if these Planets are unfortunate and corrupted in their celestial state; but they are worse still if they are determined by bodily location or rulership to be significators of the unfortunate houses of the figure or of those opposed to them;[222] but the worst if, in addition, they have afflicted the rulers of the first or the tenth, or of the twelfth or eighth, or Planets located in those houses, but especially the Sun and Moon. But before the rest, oppositions of latitudes of different denominations, if they are partile or diametrical, are malignant,[223] especially between Mars and Saturn, for they soon kill when the other one of them is the ruler of the Horoscope. On the other hand, although all trines and sextiles are intrinsically beneficial, yet they are better with Jupiter, Venus, Sun, Moon and Mercury, but still more fortunate if those Planets are fortunate in their celestial state; but they are even more fortunate if those same Planets have been determined by body or rulership to the significations of the fortunate houses. Yet they are best if, in addition, they aspect the houses that are significators of beneficial things, or the Planets in them, especially Jupiter,

Venus, Sun, Moon, or Mercury. Therefore, the opposition of Saturn in Leo and the Sun in Aquarius is the worst; the trine of Jupiter in Pisces and the Moon in Cancer the best.

Eighth. Conjunctions and aspects are compared with respect to the following or preceding one. For if a benefic one immediately follows a benefic one, benefit is certainly and easily signified. If a malefic one [follows] a malefic one, certain and even sudden misfortune is portended; if a malefic one follows a benefic one, the apparent benefit will be turned to misfortune; if a benefic one [follows] a malefic one, the contrary will happen. But the strength of the following aspect, on account of its nature and that of the Planet, and also [the Planet's] Celestial and Terrestrial state, is always given attention; for where it is stronger, the more certain and efficacious the accident, as has been said above. But in addition, the aspect, or the Planet, immediately preceding it is noted. For departing from a benefic aspect to a benefic one is fortunate; from a malefic one to a malefic one, very unfortunate; the others, middling.

Ninth. The conjunctions or aspects are compared with respect to the rulership of the connected Planets. For the ruler of the first with the ruler of the eighth and partile, or the latter applying to the former, or both mutually [applying], all cause the same effect—namely, premature death. For the cause is entirely the same, and only the house in which they meet is to be noted. For if they meet in the twelfth, death from illness, or from prison or exile, is signified; if in the seventh, death will be from war, combat, or a dispute or robbers, according to the ruler of the connected Planets or other aspects to them (in the common way of speaking) that agree. If they mutually depart, dangers will occur that will be avoided; finally, if one applies to the other, as the ruler of the first [to the ruler of the eighth], Death, or rather his own fault, will carry away the native; and the reasoning is the same in the rest.

Moreover, from what has been said so far, it is apparent that one can pass judgment on the signification of each house from the nature of the sign that occupies that house, and from the nature and Celestial and Terrestrial state of the Planets that either are in that house by body or aspect, or that preside over it by domicile, exaltation, or Triangle. From these a wide field for prediction is established which, if human ability, to the extent it is adequate, should develop the strength, it could predict even the smallest things about the accidents of natural fate; but notwithstanding the weakness of human discernment, at least it should not err about the most notable things. And these things said of the determination of the Planets by body, rulership, exaltation, Triangle, and aspect are sufficient.

Chapter XII

Which things about any Planet & its aspects are principally to be looked at so that a truer judgment of them may be composed

These are collected here from the previous chapters. And so in judgments of the Stars, the nature of each Planet is to be considered first—that is, whether it is benefic or malefic. For from benefics more is to be hoped and less is to be feared; from malefics, the contrary, at least other things being equal.[224]

Second. Whether it is in its own domicile, or in a foreign one. For in its own, it acts purely, and independently of any other Planet, at least in this respect. But if it is connected to another Planet, it will depend on it as on a partner in action, yet of different virtue. If a Planet is in a foreign domicile, first it is to be seen to what ruler it is subject, whether benefic or malefic. Then in this domicile, or in this sign, that Planet either will be powerful with the dignity of exaltation or Triangle, or it will be unfortunate in exile or fall, or it will be simply peregrine. If it is exalted, it will act powerfully and suddenly with respect to the things to which it is determined, at which time it will burst into action. If it is exiled or fallen, it will confer nothing beneficial, or it will act in a corrupt manner and will bring destruction. If it is simply peregrine, it will work weakly.

Third. Whether it is direct, retrograde, stationary, quick, slow, or medium. For from these it acts analogically with respect to its significations, as is said more fully elsewhere;[225] and from that the Planet is strengthened or weakened.

Fourth. Its position in relation to the Sun and Moon. For Oriental of the Sun and above the Earth during the day, and similarly Occidental of the Moon, are more efficacious and bring out notable effects. In the contrary position, they are weaker, and act obscurely.[226]

Fifth. Its connection with other Planets. For if a strong Planet is connected to no other by body or aspect, it is said to be feral, and it will act purely in accord with its own nature, especially if placed in its own domicile. Every feral Planet portends something unusual, [either] beneficial or unfortunate according to the nature of the Planet. So Saturn feral in the first [signifies] a hermit or monk. If, on the other hand, it is connected with any Planet, that one is either strong, weak, or intermediate in essential dignities or debilities, or it is simply peregrine. If strong, a notable effect will follow; if weak, obscure; if intermediate, middling. And the quality of the effect in beneficence, maleficence, ease or difficulty will be according to the nature of the aspect. But with respect to a weak Planet—that is, fallen, exiled or peregrine—if it is feral, from that some worse unusual thing is portended. But if it is connected with another, that one too is either strong, weak or intermediate. If strong, in the beginning scarcely anything will be done, yet in the end it will make progress. Or there will be misfortunes and obstacles in the beginning, but none in the end; misfortune will end in benefit; rewards will follow efforts; victories, wars; health, illness, &c, in accord with the bodily determination of that debilitated Planet. But understand that this is about a connection through the application of a fortunate ray, for through an unfortunate one nothing beneficial will be signified, except with great difficulties; if it is weak, the greater the misfortune that is portended from it, or the greater the deprivation of benefit; if intermediate, no effect, at least none chosen, will soon come from it.

Sixth. Whether a Planet in a foreign domicile is connected to its ruler, and how, and the state of both. For a Planet connected to its ruler depends more on it in its action, and is more subject to it, and both work more efficaciously, especially if the connection is strong and congruent. Moreover, if a Planet is badly affected by Celestial or Terrestrial state, or both, but its ruler is well [affected], harms and misfortunes will be signified in the beginning, but benefit and good fortune will follow, especially if that Planet applies to its ruler by a fortunate ray. If, however, a Planet is well affected but its ruler badly affected, benefit will end in misfortune and hope will be fruitless. If both are well affected, this will be the best, whether the Planet is in the fortunate houses of the figure conferring their benefits, or in the unfortunate ones removing or mitigating their misfortunes. Finally, if both are badly affected, this will be the worst, whether the Planet is in the unfortunate houses of the figure conferring their misfortunes, or in the fortunate ones removing or obstructing their benefits.

Seventh. With which fixed stars a Planet is conjoined, and with which it rises, culminates, and sets, for the bright stars produce remarkable and unexpected effects, as frequent experience confirms.[227]

Eighth. To what a Planet is determined in the celestial figure by body, rulership, or aspect; then [the same] of its ruler if it is subject to another. For benefic Planets determined to benefits are beneficial, such as Jupiter for riches, Venus for marriages and children, both for inborn nature or dignities; and it is better by far if they are well conditioned by celestial state. But if benefics are determined to misfortune, the misfortune is less because they free from misfortunes, or at least mitigate them. But the malefics, Saturn and Mars, determined to benefit are unfortunate unless they are well conditioned by celestial state; and this notwithstanding, if they are square or opposed to the Sun or Moon, or to the Horoscope or Midheaven or their rulers, they certainly cause misfortune; nor will conjunction with benefics remove all malignity, as is apparent in my geniture, in which Mars trines Jupiter, and the latter conjoins Saturn; and, nevertheless, from Saturn and Mars I have suffered, suffer and will suffer many and notable misfortunes. But [malefics] determined to misfortune—

such as illnesses, prisons, disputes, and death—are very unfortunate; and it is truly worse if they are also badly conditioned. And the Sun and Moon in the fortunate places of the figure cause splendid and illustrious benefits, especially when well conditioned and with benefic aspects; but in the unfortunate ones certainly [they cause] remarkable misfortune, especially when badly conditioned and with malefic aspects. Moreover, each Planet is determined to different things at the same time; namely, to one by body, to another by rulership, and to others by aspects. And although bodily determination is intrinsically the strongest of all, it yet can happen that determination by rulership or aspect is stronger, certainly if, for example, the Planet that rules or aspects is analogous in its significations to the house of the figure in which the aspect or rulership falls, but not to that it occupies. And the same Planet can be determined at the same time in several ways to the same kind of effect, or one congruent with that; and if this happens, the effect signified is more certain and more ample than when it is determined to that [effect] in a single way. Furthermore, if a Planet is in a foreign domicile, and it and its ruler agree with each other in nature and in determination by body or rulership, an outstanding effect will follow, especially if they aspect each other in accord with the effect; as, if benefic Planets are in the second, their benefic ruler in the tenth, and they bless each other with a trine; or, if malefic Planets are in the twelfth, their malefic ruler in the sixth or the eighth, and they square or oppose each other. Any Planet, of course, acts only according to its own nature, celestial state, and determination in the figure.

As for Planets in or ruling the first or tenth house, their celestial state and determination are especially noted. For badly conditioned by celestial state, they are very bad for the significations of those houses, especially if they apply to badly conditioned Planets, and that by an unfortunate ray; for if they apply to well conditioned ones, especially by a fortunate ray, benefit will follow after misfortune. But it will be much worse if, in addition, one or the other is determined to misfortune, as, if the ruler of the first is in the twelfth or the eighth, or the contrary,[228] or [if the same Planet is] either the ruler of the first and twelfth, or of the first and eighth;[229] a Planet in or ruling the tenth is to be judged in the same way. Moreover, from such a consideration alone of the Planets in the first or tenth, [and] of the rulers [of those houses], a judgment can be made at the outset whether the geniture is fortunate or unfortunate;[230] and one may judge of any fortunate house in a similar way.

Ninth. Whether a Planet is in a house analogous to its nature. For then it works powerfully in accord with its nature; so, Jupiter lavishes great wealth in the second; the Sun in the tenth, great honors, and in the first, notable fame; Saturn in the twelfth, malignant illnesses, prisons, servitude, hidden enemies; Mars in the seventh, enemies, disputes, wars; Venus in the seventh, a spouse, and in the fifth, children, &c. But by reason of the ruler of the sign and connection [with other Planets], the contrary may happen; on the other hand, Planets in the places of the figure not analogous to their nature obstruct, suppress, or overturn the significations. So in the twelfth Venus *per se* obstructs illnesses; in the tenth Saturn [*per se* obstructs] honors; I said *per se*, for if Venus is badly conditioned in the twelfth, she will bring illnesses, and Saturn well conditioned in the tenth will confer honors.

Tenth. Whether the Planet is in the angular houses of the figure, or in succedent or cadent ones. For Planets in the angles signify constant things, especially in fixed signs, as is apparent from Cardinal Richelieu with Mars and Venus in the first and tenth in fixed signs, from which he always had a mind for wars and had firmly established power until he died. But in cadent houses and moveable signs they signify inconstancy; and intermediate in succedent.

And as regards aspects, seven [points] are considered for each aspect. (1) What the Planet is. (2) The quality of its celestial condition. (3) To what it is determined by body and rulership. (4) Which aspect it is. (5) In what sign it falls, and what is the ruler. (6) In what house of the figure.

(7) Circumstances before or after the aspect.[231] For as any one of these seven varies, the effects of the aspects also vary.

Similarly, seven states of the Planets with respect to the houses and their rulers are to be considered as proper to this arcane skill.[232]

1. A Planet in the first house, and strong by sign and connection with benefics or strong Planets, strongly influences the significations of that house in accord with its own nature and state; and the temperament, character, inborn talent, &c of the native will be what it is from this, and perseveringly.

2. Whereas debilitated in the first, but connected to its own ruler or the ruler of the Horoscope, it certainly influences more weakly, and that by reason of the debilitation of the Planet in the first, the state of the aspecting Planet, and the virtue of the aspect.

3. But debilitated in the first, connected neither with its own nor the Horoscope's ruler, it influences most weakly the significations of the first.[233]

4. But a Planet outside the first, strong in the first, and especially the ruler of the first, if it aspects a Planet in the first or the Horoscope, powerfully carries off the life, character and inborn talent of the native to the significations of the house in which it is [located].[234]

5. If, however, [a Planet as described in item 4] aspects neither a Planet in the first nor the Horoscope, the same also will be set in motion, but perhaps it will not come to pass.[235]

6. But a Planet outside the first and debilitated in it, if it is connected by rulership or aspect to the ruler of the first, or aspects the Horoscope, will very weakly influence the significations of the first.[236]

7. If, however, [a Planet as described in item 6] is connected neither to the ruler of the first nor to the Horoscope, it will influence nothing about the significations of the first, unless perhaps very obscurely by reason of its debilitation in the first, such as exiled, fallen, &c.

And what is said here of the first house is to be understood to have been said similarly of the others. And for that reason, never judge of a marriage, for example, except from the Planets in the seventh, or the ruler of the seventh, or the rulers of these rulers, or those aspecting the seventh or its ruler. And note how these Planets have rulership of or connection with the Planets analogous to the male or female spouse; and the reasoning is the same in the rest.

Chapter XIII

Of the accidental determination of the Planets of one natal figure when they are found in the places of the Planets or of the principal significators of another figure

This chapter provides a place for the doctrine of Aphorism 47 of Ptolemy's *Centiloquy*, which is: *When one will have been born with a malefic that falls into the place of a benefic in the geniture of another, he who has the benefic will suffer loss from him who has the malefic.*

In truth, this doctrine must be extended much more generally, and must be taken apart and defined from its true foundations. Because it excludes the greatest concealed treasures about the character, inborn talent, actions, fortunes, and misfortunes of any two natives between whom such combinations occur.

I say, therefore, first, that this determination is to be looked at both by reason of the signs as much as by reason of the Planets. And we will begin with the signs, as the parts of the *Primum Caelum*, which is the first Physical cause.

And so if the sign of the first house of one natal figure is in the first house of another figure, the ascendant will be the same for both, and the ruler of the ascendant will be the same, which ruler can be also of the same or of diverse Celestial and Terrestrial state. If the Celestial and Terrestrial state is the same (which happens very rarely), there will be the greatest agreement between those natives about the significations of the first house and of that in which the ruler is found. If the state is different, then, for judgment of the accidents that will be for each of the natives, the significations of the first house will be combined with the significations of the houses in which that ruler is found in both figures, taking into account the celestial state of each.

If the sign of the second, third, fourth, fifth, &c houses of one figure is in the first house of the other figure, those houses of the two natives will have the same sign and the same ruler, and the Celestial and Terrestrial state of these may be the same or different. If the same, the combination of the significations of those second, third, and fourth houses of the first figure with the significations of the first house of the other figure will be strong and effective. If the state is different, then the significations of the second, third, and fourth houses of the first figure will be combined with the significations of the first house of the second figure, taking into account the houses in which that ruler is found and its celestial state in both figures. But what I said about the sign of the second, third, fourth, &c of one figure in the first house of another figure is to be understood to be said also of the sign of the second, third, fourth, &c house of the first figure in the second, third, fourth, &c house of the second figure.

But now it is to be known that the combinations of the Planets are to be seen in two ways. First, when the Planets of one figure are found on the cusps or in the houses of another figure, and especially in the Horoscope or in the Midheaven. Second, when the Planets of one figure are found in the places of the Planets of another figure.

Therefore, if a Planet of one figure is in the Horoscope of another figure, the first thing to be noted is the determination of the Planet in the former figure by the house it occupies and by its nature and celestial state. For according to these three things it will have power with respect to the character, inborn talent, and life of the latter native;[237] and so if the Planet [in the first house of the latter figure] is in the first or is the ruler of the first in the former figure—that is, determined to the significations of the first—there will be between the natives a great agreement of character, inborn talent, and ways of life, because these things will be caused by the same sign and Planet in both figures. If it is determined to wealth, or the significations of the second house in the former figure, the former native will have a circumstance with the second native for causing wealth to him, or conferring it, or receiving it from him. If it is determined to the significations of the third house in the former figure, the former native will be connected with the other through a relative, or will be associated by reason of travel or religion. If it is determined to the significations of the seventh—of course, marriage or disputes—if they are persons of the same sex, they will have disputes or mutual contracts; if they are of different sexes, they will be coupled with each other in matrimony, or instead be subjected to disputes or mutual contracts, or business. If it is determined to the significations of the eighth in the former figure, because the former native has the significator of his death in the place which, for the other native, is the cause of life, let [the former] be careful not to incur the danger of death from this. If it is determined to the significations of the tenth in the former figure, the former native will depend on the other native in his undertaken actions and dignities,[238] or will use [the other] for such things, or he himself will be subjected to such things.

But if a Planet appearing in the second house of one figure is found in the seventh of another figure, the significations of those houses will be combined, and the natives will affect each other accordingly; and the reasoning is the same for the rest of the houses.

But when a Planet in one figure is found in the place of a Planet in another figure: In a similar way, the first thing to be noted is the determination of both Planets by reason of the house in both; then the nature and celestial state of both—of course, benefic or malefic, and also strong or weak; and then these are to be wisely judged, combining them as above. For all the discernment of these judgments revolves around making possible and congruent combinations, and defining their effects.

But to predict quickly the effects of these combinations is surely easy for Angels owing to the intuitive and most keenly penetrating, and minimally obstructed, light of their understanding; but for human beings, for contrary reasons, it is extremely difficult, and impossible without frequent error. However, I have said here in general in what such a skill[239] truly consists. Be diligent in it and practice to try to be as perfect as you can so that you are adequate to predict the agreement or disagreement of any two nativities, and the kind.

The Planets of one figure are also combined with the Planets and significators of another figure through aspects, in which the benefic or malefic nature of these comes to be especially considered.

Finally, I see that it does not matter in these combinations which one is older because that which is signified by the combination for the native whose figure is the first happens as much to him through a younger native as through an older.

From what has been said above, it is indeed apparent that not only is this doctrine by far more extensive than the 47th Aphorism of Ptolemy, but also that the Aphorism frequently can be false. For if someone has Saturn in Aquarius in the first house and another has Jupiter in the same degree in the first house, the agreement of both nativities in the significations of the first house will be great and fortunate; and each one will be helped by the other with foresight, counsel, seriousness, and authority rather than be affected by loss.

Chapter XIV

Whether by reason of their essential significations the houses of the natal figure determine the celestial bodies with respect to the native alone, or also with respect to other persons

Here the question is not whether from the genethliacal figure of the native others can be extracted for parents, spouse, children, &c, as, after Ptolemy, other Astrologers have wanted, for we will examine that in another proper place.[240] But here only what is proposed in the title of this chapter is asked.

For a more accurate understanding of which, it is to be known that in the genethliacal figure the essential signification of each house is first and *per se* the accident only of the native himself and not of another person, as the signification of the first house is only the life, character, and inborn talent of the native, not of another; the signification of the twelfth[241] house is the illnesses of the native whose figure it is, but not of another person; the signification of the eighth is the death of the native, but not of another; and so of the others. Accordingly, a Planet, or sign, or aspect, in a house of any figure is determined to its essential signification, not indeed absolutely or indifferently, but insofar as it refers to the native and pertains to him; and so a Planet in the seventh signifies with respect to marriage, disputes and enemies of the native, but not of another person; accordingly, a house of the natal figure, by reason of its essential signification, determines the celestial bodies with respect to the native only, and not other persons; and the celestial causes, insofar as they are determined by the houses with respect to the native, cause and signify only those things that pertain to the native himself, in accord with the mode of their determination; and in that [mode], or in accord with it, insofar as they are of that native, they influence him, and not another person with respect to whom they are not determined by reason of the same [mode].

From this it is apparent how much the Ancients erred, who, not attending to this, took from the eighth house of the figure of the native judgments about the death of parents, spouses, children, servants and friends or enemies of the native; and if, for example, the ruler of the fifth is in the eighth, or the two rulers are connected to each other by a square or opposition ray, they want that the death of the children should be signified. And their reasoning is the same for the ruler of the eighth with the ruler of the seventh for the spouse, or with the ruler of the fourth for the parents; or if the ruler of the fifth is in the tenth, [they want] honors to be signified for the children; if the ruler of the third, for the siblings, when, however, the eighth and tenth are the death and honors of the native only and not of another person, owing to the reason stated above.

Someone will say that in any horizon the space of the eighth house is the common or universal house of death for all those born or living in that horizon, as is evident from the universal figures of the annual revolutions of the World, Eclipses, Lunations, &c, in which, if, for example, a luminary suffering an Eclipse or its ruler is in the eighth house, mortality is signified in that region; if they are in the seventh, wars are portended; from the ruler of the third in the eighth of the natal figure, therefore, the death of siblings will be signified; and so of the rest.

But I reply: Universal figures differ from particular ones in this because the latter are erected at the moment of some particular effect, such as the birth of a person, and the whole *Caelum* is determined by the spaces, or primary houses, with respect to him and his accidents inasmuch as they are of his own birth; but the former are erected at the moment of some universal cause, such as a New Moon or an Eclipse, and so that cause acts universally, or indifferently, in the region for which that figure is erected. And, therefore, if the ruler of an Eclipse, or the disappearing luminary, is in the eighth, it certainly signifies mortality by famine, pestilence, or sword, in accord with the nature and state of the Planets, but only universally and indiscriminately, and not, at least from the power of that house, more for one person than for another. But in the particular figure of any native, the ruler of the third in the eighth acts on the native by reason of its determination; that is, inasmuch as it is in the eighth, it acts and signifies with respect to the death of the native; or, to speak more truly, it acts on the native with respect to death; and inasmuch as it is the ruler of the third, it influences the native with respect to siblings; but inasmuch as it is the ruler of the third in the eighth, it combines both matters; that is, it influences the native with respect to death, and at the same time siblings; otherwise, the native, contrary to experience, would not be affected by the rulers of the houses; therefore, the ruler of the third in the eighth does not signify the death of the siblings, but rather of the native from the siblings, or for their sakes; and so of the rest. Of course, each signification by house, sign, and Planet in the natal figure is first and *per se* with respect to the native himself. And if the eighth house were the death of the native, of parents, spouses, children, &c, it would strengthen the universal reasoning in a particular figure, which is incongruous to suppose; for by the same reasoning, the first house would be the life, character and inborn talent not only of the native himself, but also of his parents. spouse, children, &c; and so of the other houses, which would have caused the greatest confusion in Astrology, and would have utterly turned away from experience.

Because it is indeed certain that from the figure of the native many things are signified for and happen to the parents, wife, siblings, children, &c, it justly may be asked by what celestial cause these things are brought about and on what they depend. Whether, of course, only from his own birth, or from their natal constitution of the *Caelum*, or from some means common to both?

Lucio Bellantius, in Question 19, Article I against Pico della Mirandola, supposes that the figures of parents, inasmuch as they are earlier, have the force of a universal cause with respect to the figures of their children, as also of other descendants, in that those are later; and so from the latter, by some influx of their powers, the former are determined to the accidents that are to come after birth, not otherwise than the annual revolutions of the World are determined by the Lunations. And he says he knew a nobleman who had the house of children unfortunately disposed, all of whose children perished by a violent death. But such an apparently plausible comment does not by any means satisfy. First, because even if the figures of father and child were subordinated as a universal and particular cause by reason of priority and origin, yet regarding the birth of siblings, relatives, spouses, servants, friends, &c the same cannot be said, for their figures do not admit of such subordination or dependence. Moreover, the example Bellantius offers overturns his reasoning; for either the figure of the father or, on the other hand, the figures of the children or the children themselves, determined the violent death. But it cannot be said that the figures of the children determined the figure of the father to the death of the children, because the figure of the father was already determined from itself to such an effect; therefore, another reason is sought.

But neither can it be said that the siblings or the spouse of the native have only from their own figure that the native will die early, for, at least in a natural death, it depends more on his own fate as a *per se* and immediate cause than on one belonging to another and more remote. And similarly, if the native in his own figure is signified to be killed by the spouse, servants, or siblings, he does not have that only from the celestial figure of the spouses, servants, or siblings; for he has that also from his own, from the hypothesis that in it such an accident is signified. It is to be said, therefore, that such effects are produced by their own cause and are common to both persons, which, of course, is not some particular figure or constitution of the *Caelum* distinct from others, but is the reciprocal agreement of these to such an effect by which that effect is reduced from a common potential to a particular act. For that reason, it is predicted for the father that the children will perish by violent death because this was signified not only in the figure of the father, but also the figure of each of the children portended a violent death, from which the signification agreed on both sides and was confirmed. In the same way, therefore, the native will survive the wife because this is signified for the native not only in his figure, but also in the figure of the wife, or at least from the comparison of the two figures, from which it is apparent the Husband is predeceased; and the reasoning is the same of other accidents between different persons.

Therefore a truly admirable Divine Providence, which is a mystery incomprehensible to us, connects genitures agreeing in common effects, or permits them to be connected, so that a native who is to be murdered by an enemy will not lack an assailant, as we have already said elsewhere, nor will one who is to marry unfortunately lack a wife suitable for such a misfortune; and the reasoning is the same in the rest.

But yet certainly also in the figure of the native is another admirable determination of the celestial bodies with respect to the accidents of parents, spouses, children, &c of the native, which is known to me by frequent experience, and that has not been noted up to now.[242] That is, that the ruler of the third in the tenth, especially a malefic and badly conditioned, signifies the death of the siblings, because the tenth house is the eighth with respect to the third; and similarly, the ruler of the fifth in the twelfth[243] portends death to the children by the same reasoning, especially if Saturn or Mars is in the twelfth, because, of course, the twelfth is the eighth, and therefore of death, with respect to the fifth. But from this the doctrine laid down by us above is more strongly confirmed, because certainly the eighth house with respect to the first is the death only of the native, as the eighth with respect to the fifth is the death of the children. But these other subjects, as of the figures of parents, spouses, &c derived from the figure of the native, we will take up with Ptolemy and other ancient Astrologers, where we will illustrate this doctrine with histories of those experiences.

With regard to the truth of the directions of universal significators, which Cardanus calls significators according to substance, and which Cardanus and others direct—as the Sun for the life and accidents of the Father, the Moon for the life and accidents of the Mother, &c—we will examine them in their place, and refute them as contrary to reason and experience.[244]

It will be objected. Question 15, Article 2 of Lucio Bellantius against Pico della Mirandola did not appoint the Sun or Saturn as the chief significator of the Father, Jupiter of wealth, Mercury of inborn talent, &c, but the rulers of the fourth house for the father, the second for wealth, the first for inborn talent, &c. Therefore, at least not all Astrologers have erred about these things.

I reply. Indeed, Bellantius had examined this matter a little more attentively than his predecessors, but he himself had been hallucinating about it, for he looks at four significators of, for example, wealth. Namely, the sign of the second house, Planets analogous in nature to wealth—Jupiter, of course—Planets in the second house, and the Planet [that is] ruler of the second, in which he agrees with other Astrologers, and this is certainly correct. But he says a sign cannot be the primary significator because of its weakness to act (for he wants to have the signs as matter, and the Planets in the signs as the form of these). Nor a Planet appearing in such a sign, because this can be its exile or fall, and the Planet is not permanently in that sign; but the primary significator, he says, must be such by something fixed and permanent; nor a Planet analogous by nature to wealth—namely, Jupiter—for, he says, the houses of the figure cause a greater diversity of accidents from the stars than do the signs, and the force of the stars varies most through the kind of house, so that the principal expression of the virtue of the stars is according to the houses; from which he concludes that the ruler of the second house is the primary significator of wealth, then Jupiter, then the Planet in the second by body or aspect, and finally the sign of the second house; and this is their order by reason of virtue, at least other things being equal, because it is possible that the first in the order here posited is so weak that the second or third is to be preferred to it. And such is the doctrine of Bellantius.

But he deviates from the truth. First, when he supposes that the signs have their nature as signs in the manner of matter, or passively rather than actively, and that by the Planets present in them they are shaped and rendered efficacious for what is to be done, when, however, even unoccupied signs act in themselves, as we have said elsewhere; and from the sign that a Planet is in, but by no means rules, different virtues pour out and are mixed together in action. Second, when he rejects the Planet located in the second house because the sign it occupies may be the exile or fall of that Planet. For a Planet in the second house does not have from the sign it occupies that it signifies with respect to wealth, but from its location in the space of the second house, by which it is determined to wealth. Nor does it matter that the sign in the second house is the exile or fall of the Planet, for while a Planet in the second in fact signifies with respect to wealth, if it is well conditioned by celestial state it certainly will signify wealth; if badly, it portends either none or little, or its dissipation, however much Jupiter—not determined by body, rulership, or strong aspect to wealth or to such congruent associated significations—is well conditioned; from which it is apparent that a Planet in the second place should be chosen as the primary significator of wealth. And in that, Bellantius errs with many others, in that he always wants to choose as the primary significator of wealth the stronger, or the more blessed by celestial state, as if, contrary to experience, wealth is signified to be for all natives; and they commit the same error about the significators of honors, marriage, &c. Third, when he supposes that the houses of the figure cause a greater accidental diversity in the Planets than the signs, &c. For it is false that the [qualities of] the forces of action of the Planets are varied by the houses of the figure, which certainly does not happen; rather, they are varied through the signs, for a sign and a Planet act as partners with mixed forces, and [they do] that with respect to all Sublunary things; and when a Planet transits into another sign, the virtue of the latter is likewise combined with the virtue of the former so they act at the same time together. But no active force is in the houses, but only that determinative of the virtue of the Planets and signs, as we have said elsewhere. And so the virtue does not vary when a Planet crosses from the third house into the second by the primary motion, but this always remains the same, only being determined to wealth. The primary significator of wealth, therefore, will be a Planet in the second, then the ruler of the second, then the sign of the second, and finally an aspect to the second; but Jupiter outside the second, without rulership or exaltation in, or connection by body or aspect with, the second, will be of no virtue, at least *per se*, for the wealth of the native. I say *per se*, for if he is well conditioned in the seventh, he will accidentally signify wealth from marriage; if in the tenth, wealth from dignities or the profession; and the same of the rest.

Chapter XV

Of the double determination of the essential significations of each house of the figure: of course, intrinsic & extrinsic

The primary houses actively determine the celestial bodies, but those bodies passively determine the essential significations of the houses, as is already said elsewhere. Further, the essential significations of each house are determined in general in two ways—namely, intrinsically and extrinsically. And they are determined intrinsically by everything that falls into that house, whether it is a sign, a Planet, or an aspect. So Mars in the first house confers a Martial nature, as for Cardinal Richelieu; Sagittarius, Jovial, as for B.P. Charles de Condren;[245] a partile sextile of Mercury to the Horoscope, Mercurial, as for me. Now this determination is called intrinsic because it is from celestial causes intrinsic to that house. But that beyond these is another that is extrinsic is proved from this: That a native with Jupiter in the Horoscope is indeed of a Jovial nature, but if it happens that Jupiter is also the ruler of the Horoscope, then he will be of a simple or unqualified Jovial nature that is indifferent to all things; but if Jupiter, ruler of the Horoscope, or of the first house, is in the tenth, he will be of a Jovial nature inclined to honors; if in the ninth, to religion and sacred things; if in the fifth, to pleasures, &c; the essential signification of each house, therefore, is determined intrinsically by celestial causes appearing within it, but extrinsically by causes of the same signification established outside that house.

Moreover, intrinsic determination occurs in nine ways. First, a Planet in a house of the figure and in its own sign, with the aspect of another Planet. Second, a Planet in a house and in its own sign, without the aspect of another. Third, a Planet in a house, outside its own sign but with the aspect of its ruler. Fourth, a Planet in a house outside its own sign but with the aspect of another Planet, but not its ruler. Fifth, a Planet in a house outside its own sign without the aspect of another. Sixth, a sign in a house and with the aspect of its ruler. Seventh, a Planet aspecting [into a house], without rulership in that house. Eighth, a Planet only in antiscion to the house. Ninth, a sign alone in a house, with no aspect or antiscion to that house. In these nine ways the signification of the house is intrinsically determined by the nature of the Planet that occupies, rules, or aspects that house, in the order of virtue that is placed here. And any way may be simple, as specified above, or composite—namely, if several Planets, several signs, or several aspects are in the same house, all of which will be useful to notice and distinguish. But extrinsic determination also happens in nine ways. First, from the ruler of the house in another house but in its own sign, with the aspect of another Planet. Second, from the ruler of the house in another house and in its own sign, without the aspect of another; and so of the rest, as in intrinsic determination. And it is to be understood similarly of a Planet aspecting any house. But of the active determination of the celestial bodies by Sublunary things, what has so far been said is sufficient.

From which surely will be found to be restored whatever good is contained in the Books of Ancient Astrologers of the Arabs, Greeks, and Latins, who received the truth of this divine science by tradition solely from Adam and his posterity, and left it to us, but without cognizance of first principles, and vitiated by many figments, delusions, and groundless things; the truth itself, nevertheless, compellingly directed them to the locations and rulerships of the Planets in the houses of the celestial figure, the effects of which were more conspicuous than other things, but they did not look into the universal and primary cause, which is nothing other than the determination of the celestial bodies set forth by us above and handed down by no one before us; for the celestial bodies do not act except as they are determined to particular things.

Chapter XVI

That nothing among Physical causes more perfectly imitates God's way of acting than the celestial bodies

Of the powers and modes of action of the *Caelum* and the Stars, many wonderful things, verified by experience, have been said in all of this Book. But here, in the chapter of the place of the coronis,[246] we will show that God's way of acting can be no more perfectly imitated by Physical causes than by the celestial bodies through the force of their influence.

But it is to be noted that, besides the celestial bodies, only four Elements are given in Nature, or what are equivalent to these, the three chemical principles of bodies: salt, sulfur, and Mercury,[247] and then the Sublunary bodies that are mixed from them, whether they are meteors or minerals, vegetables, and animals. But in none of these Elements or mixtures is found a virtue comparable to the influential virtue of the celestial bodies. Indeed, the magnet has captivated the human mind in admiration of its virtue, especially in this age when it became widely known,[248] nor is anything known among Sublunary things more admirable than the virtue of its action; but we have said in Chapter 6, Section 3, Book 12 how great the difference is between the influence of the celestial bodies and the magnetic force. And so it remains that, because God has most excellently impressed the imprints of his Omnipotence and Wisdom on the celestial bodies, as if they are his vicars in nature through which he distributes and governs the fate of natural effects, we may compare with each other the forces and ways of action of the latter with the former.

First, therefore, as God's power of action is something very simple and ineffable,[249] which we call God's will, so the formal power of action of the *Primum Caelum* or of each Planet is something very simple and, at least to us, ineffable, which is called the influence of the *Caelum* itself or of the Planets, from Chapter 2, Section 3, Book 13.

Second, God's power of action is absolutely Omnipotent, so the virtue of the *Primum Caelum* and of each Planet is accordingly something Omnipotent, in that certainly there is no natural effect with which the *Primum Caelum* and the Planets do not concur with their own virtue.

Third, as no creature can resist the power of God, so there is no Sublunary body that has the strength to resist the influential impression of the celestial bodies, for the virtue of the celestial figure is continuously imprinted on these Sublunary things and is received by each in the manner of the receiver; and that power penetrates the whole globe of the Earth, as is said elsewhere.

Fourth, just as God by the same act of will causes at the same time whatever happens, so the *Primum Caelum* and the Sun, by the same unmixed virtue proper to their influence, cause at the same time whatever can be caused by their influential virtue. And the same is to be said of the Moon, Saturn, Jupiter, Mars, &c, to which the same is common. The Sun, however, does not accomplish that which is proper and formal to the Moon or Saturn, but as the Planets differ in their specific nature, so each one acts according to its own nature in all and in every Sublunary thing.

Fifth, as God causes whatever the *Primum Caelum*, Sun, Moon, Saturn, Jupiter, &c cause—because, certainly, as the absolute first cause he concurs with each one—so the *Primum Caelum* causes whatever the Sun, Moon, Saturn, Jupiter, &c cause, because as the first Physical cause it concurs with each one, which is treated in Chapter 1, Section 1, Book 14. Therefore, among Physical causes, the *Primum Caelum* is most like God, as befits the first Physical cause.

Sixth. God, by his power—that is, by his will—causes at the same time diverse classes, kinds, and individual things,[250] not only in different subjects, but in the same one, such as in a person; because life, action, marriage, and suffering differ in kind, from the cabala of houses;[251] but God causes all these things at the same time in different persons and in the same one, because, of course, he concurs with Physical causes, which cause the same thing at the same time; therefore, he causes at the same time diverse kinds of things in different persons and in the same one. And when in different persons and in the same one diverse kinds of things result, and also diverse individual things, and God concurs with the secondary causes effecting them, it is also apparent that God causes at the same time diverse classes, kinds and individual things in different persons and in the same one. But the Sun imitates God in all these things, for his bodily location is at the same time in each of the houses of the figure with respect to not one, but to all inhabitants of the Earth, or all those born on the Earth; and so with respect to all things taken together he causes at the same time diverse classes, kinds, and individual things. Nor does he cause these only through his bodily location, but also through his rulership and aspects. But with respect to the same thing, he can cause one thing by bodily location, another of a different class by rulership, and another of a different class and kind, or individual thing, by his aspects and connections with other Planets; and the reasoning is the same with the Moon, Saturn, Jupiter, &c. But the *Primum Caelum*, to which neither rulership nor aspect belong because it is above these, in its simplicity and eminence causes all things by its universal corporeal location, both with respect to all and with respect to individuals; but in each one it causes diverse things, according to its diverse positions. But, nevertheless, the individual effects of the *Caelum* in the same subject are not from the whole *Caelum*, but from its parts occupying the houses of diverse figures. For any part of the *Caelum* causes something in the same thing, and the whole [causes] all things, just as some part or other [causes] all things with respect to different things.

Seventh, as God, acting in nature, acts sometimes as a universal cause and sometimes as a particular one, so [also do] the *Caelum* and the Planets. For when God acts with Physical causes through his concurrence, he always acts as a universal cause, from our definition of a universal cause; but when, in the time of the Pharaoh, he causes the Sun not to shine on Egypt but on the Land of Gibeon,[252] and lets the fire mildly warm the Hebrews in the furnace of Babylon while it burns the ministers standing by,[253] this he does as a particular cause; for no natural cause subordinate to him can be assigned besides God that would cause this; in the same way, the Sun begetting a human being with a human being is the universal cause of the begotten, but the Solar influence on the character through bodily location or rulership in the first house is the particular cause of character.

Eighth, as God subjects to his rule all that he causes, so the *Caelum* and the Planets subject to their influential rule whatever they cause, with the ruling order and in the times established for accidents; the explanation of which is seen from the definition of influence handed down in Book 12, Section 3, Chapter 2. And this agreement of God and the celestial bodies is the greatest and most marvelous of all.

From these things, therefore, it is apparent that in this Book and elsewhere it has been shown that the celestial bodies by far more perfectly imitate God's way of acting than any other Physical cause is able to do. To him alone honor and praise: Amen.

END OF THE TWENTY-FIRST BOOK

Appendix of Charts

All charts, except those from Abû 'Ali al-Khayyât, are cast in Regiomontanus houses with the Mean Node. The positions of royal fixed stars are listed below only those charts for which Morin mentions them in his comments on the chart in Book 21. Although one may use the modern planets in accord with the method Morin sets out, they are omitted here to reproduce the charts as Morin saw them. And though Morin drew charts in the traditional square format, we reproduce them here in the circular format now customarily used.

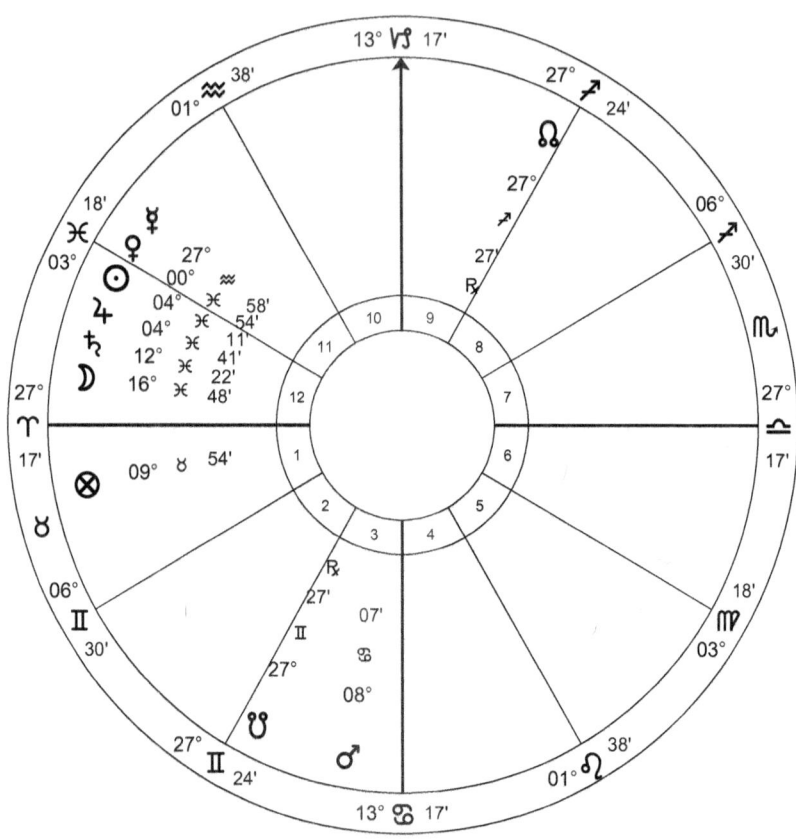

Jean-Baptiste Morin de Villefranche
23 February 1583 8:46:42 am LMT   Villefranche, France 45°N25' 04°E49'
Matching ASC from Morin *Astrologia Gallica*, Book 17, Section 2, Chapter 2

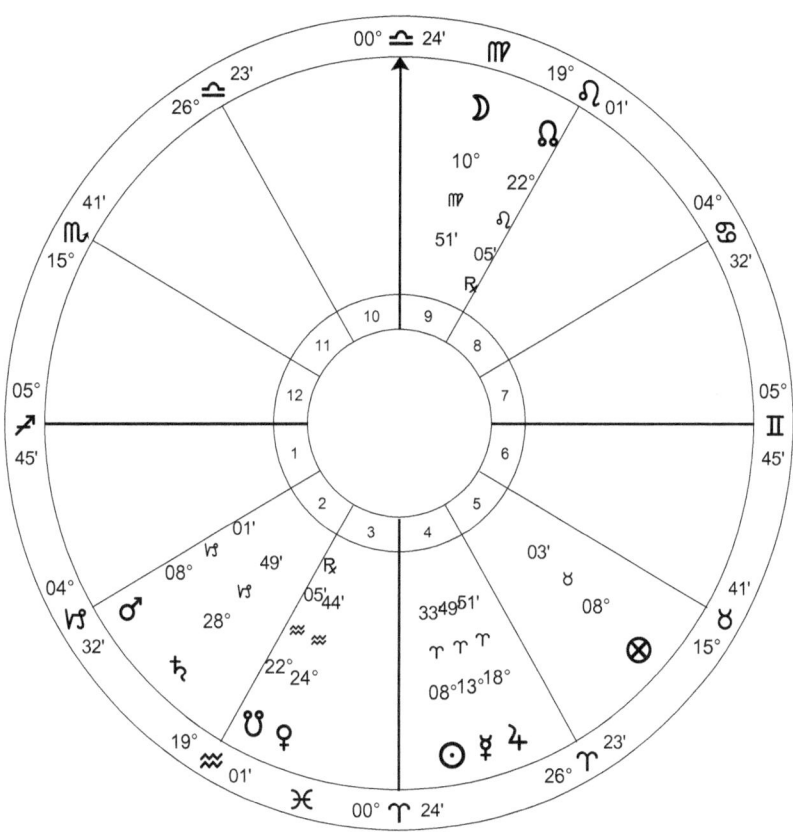

Leon Bouthillier, Count of Chavigny
28 March 1608 11:35 pm   Paris, France 48°N52' 02°E20'
Time estimated from *Astrologia Gallica*, Book 21, Section 2, Chapter 3

Morin's Book 21

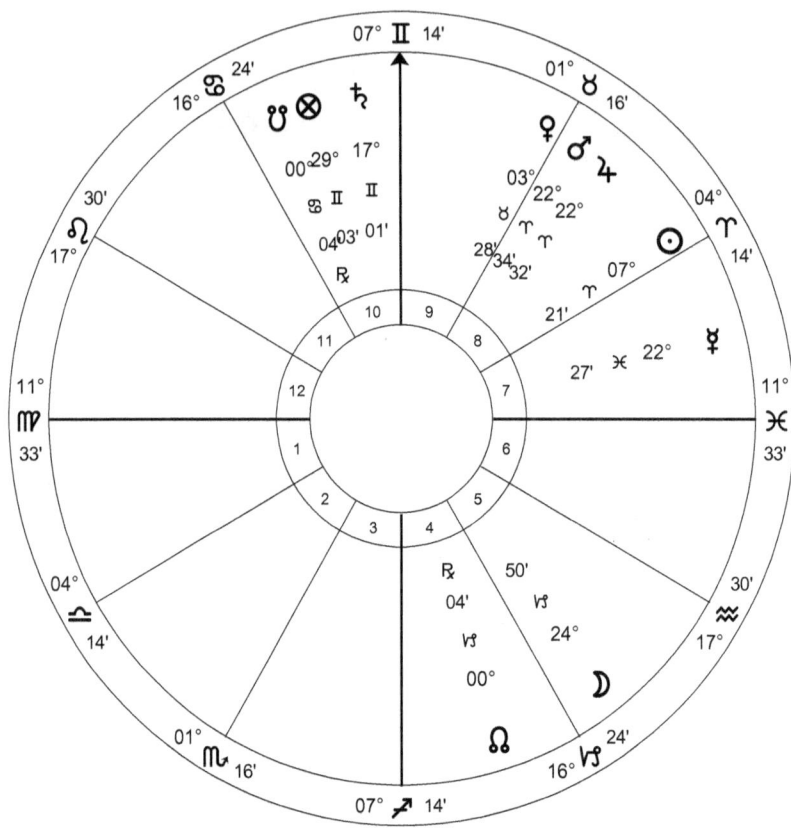

Henri Coiffier d'Effiat, Marquess de Cinq-Mars
27 March 1620   4:00 pm LMT   Effiat, France   46°N02'   03°E15'
Time estimated from *Astrologia Gallica*, Book 21, Section 2, Chapter 3

Appendix of Charts

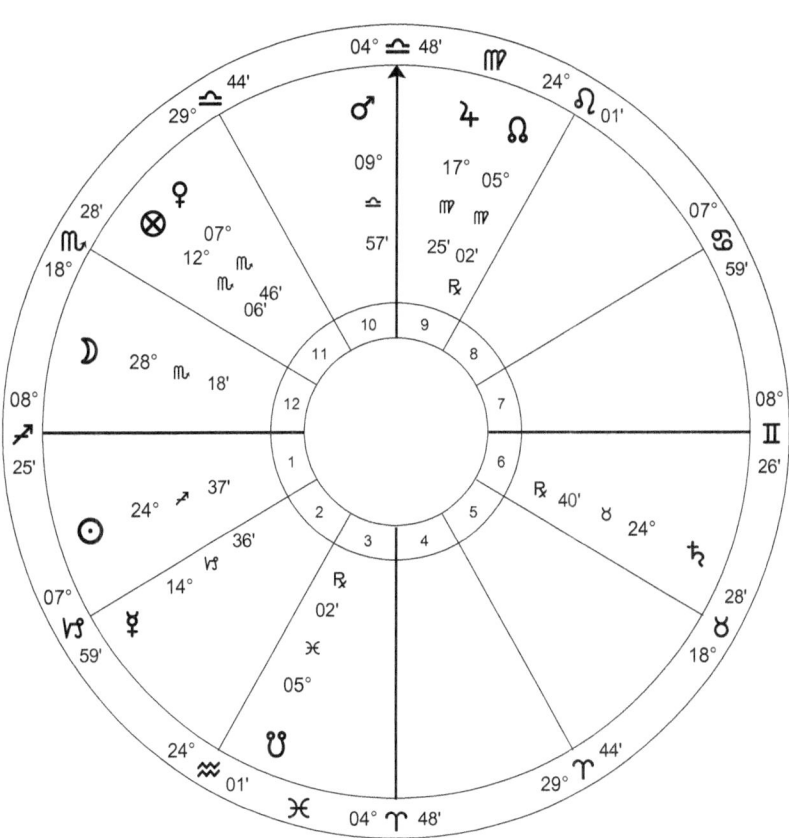

Rev. Father Charles de Condren
16 Dec 1588 6:37:40 am LMT   Vaubin, France 49°N23' 03°E19'
Matching ASC from Morin, *Astrologia Gallica*, Book 23, Chapter 7
Antares 4° Sagittarius 01'

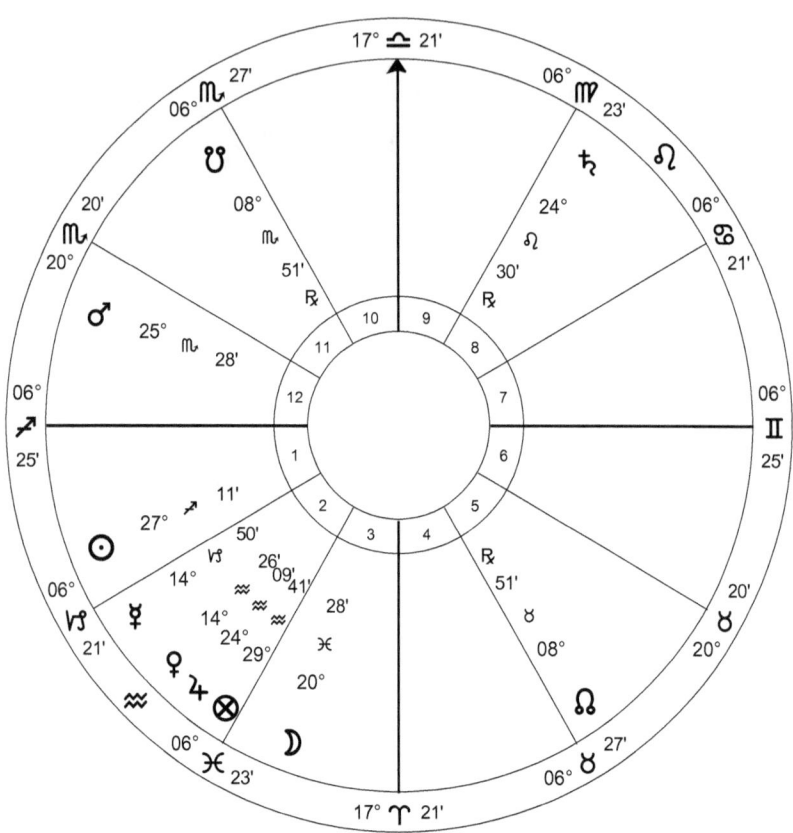

Gustavus Adolphus, King of Sweden
19 December 1594 7:14 pm LMT   Stockholm, Sweden 59°N20' 18°E03'
Matching ASC from Morin, *Astrologia Gallica*, Book 23, Chapter 7

Appendix of Charts

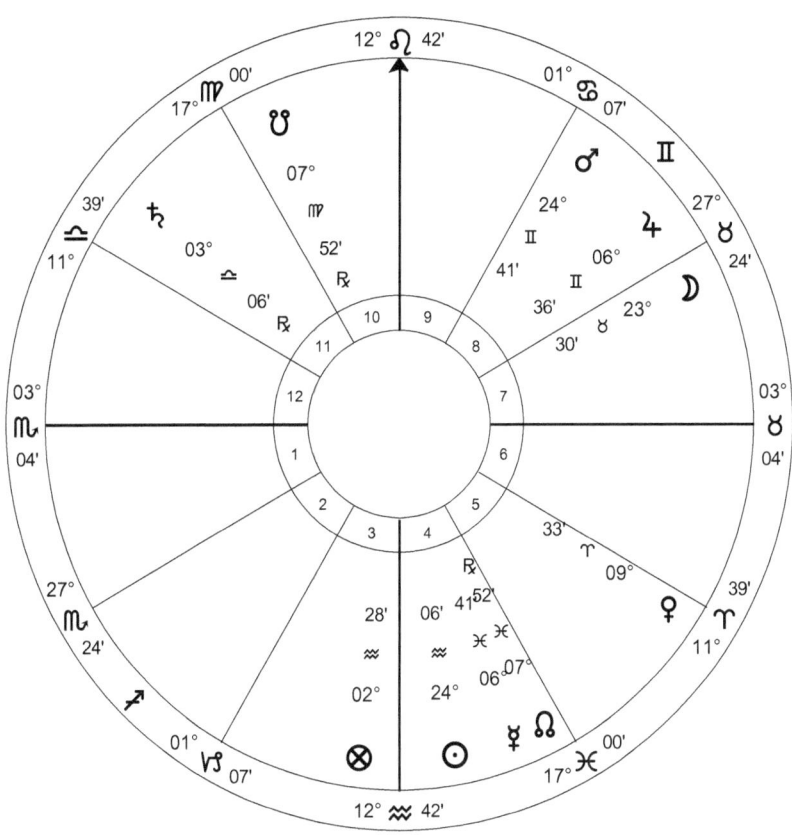

Louis Des Hayes de Courmenin
12 February 1598 11:30 pm   Montargis, France 48°N00' 02°E46'
Time estimated from *Astrologia Gallica*, Book 21, Section 2, Chapter 2
Aldebaran 10° Gemini 04'   Algol 20° Taurus 34'   Pleiades (Alcyone) 24° Taurus 23'

Morin's Book 21

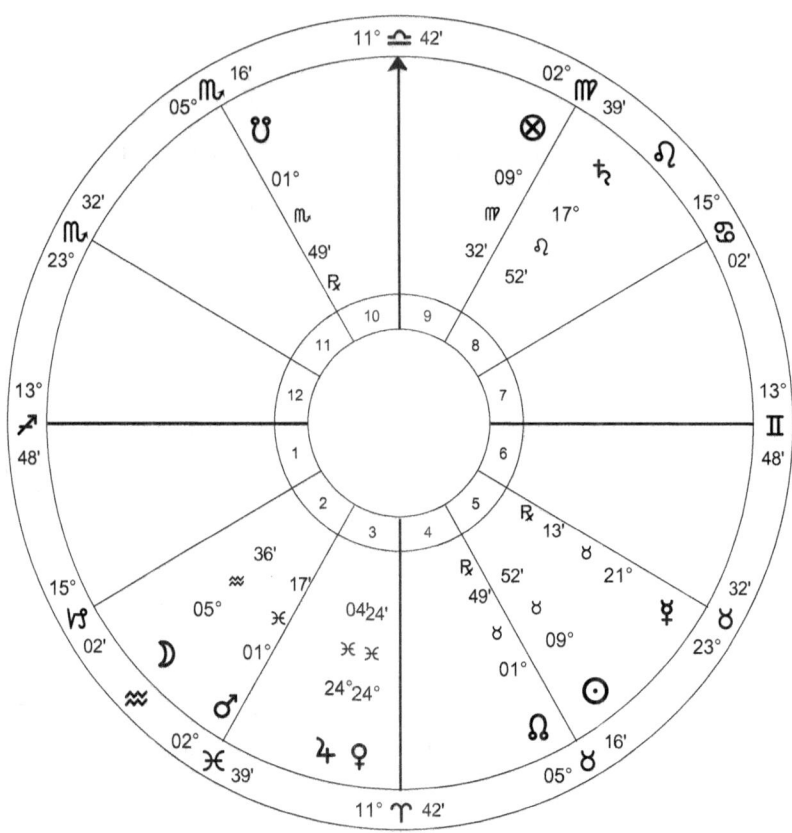

Henri II, Duke of Montmorency
30 April 1595 10:10 pm LMT   Paris, France 48°N52' 02°E20'
Matching ASC degree from Morin, *Astrologia Gallica*, Book 17, Section 2, Chapter 2

Appendix of Charts

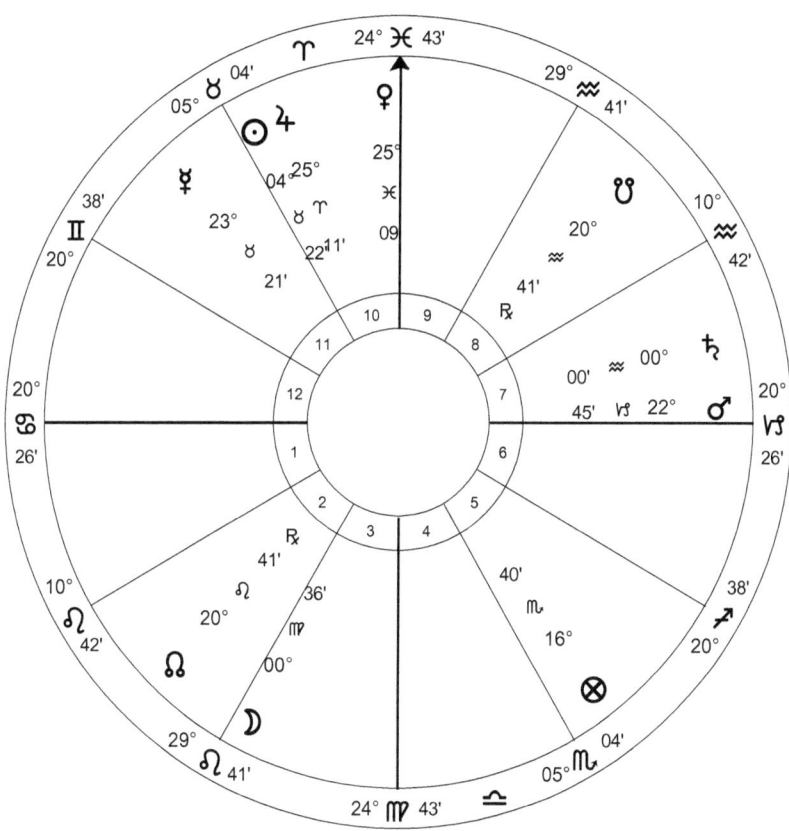

Gaston de Foix, Duke of Orleans
24 April 1608 9:30 am LMT   Fontainebleu, France 48°N24' 02°E42'
Time estimated from *Astrologia Gallica*, Book 21, Section 2, Chapter 7

Morin's Book 21

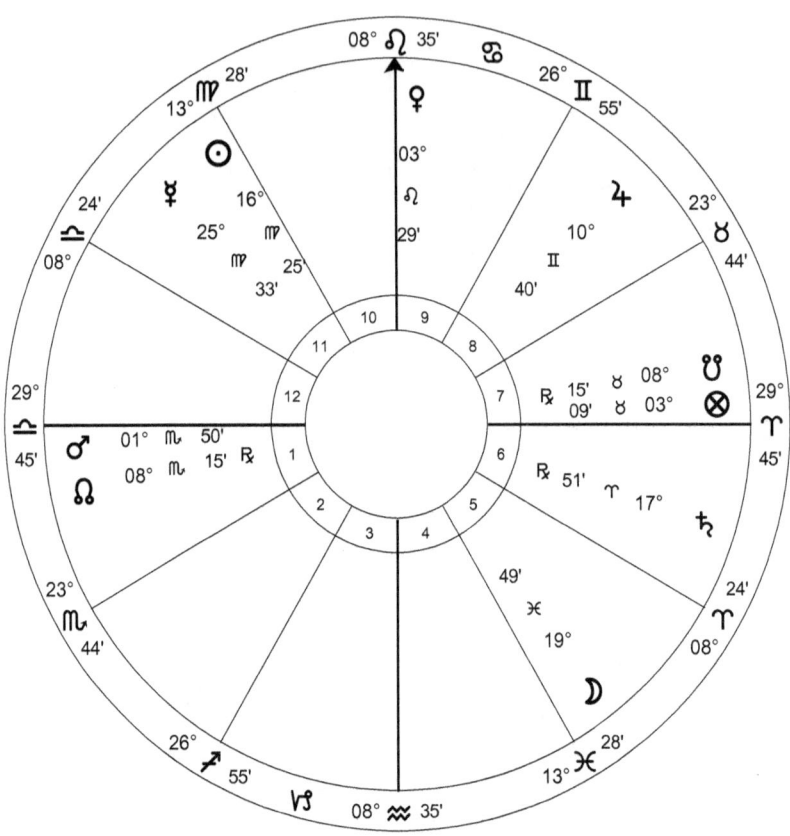

Cardinal Richelieu
9 September 1585 9:31:05 am LMT   Paris, France 48°N52' 02°E20'
Matching ASC from Morin, *Astrologia Gallica*, Book 23, Chapter 7
Aldebaran 04° Gemini 00'

Appendix of Charts

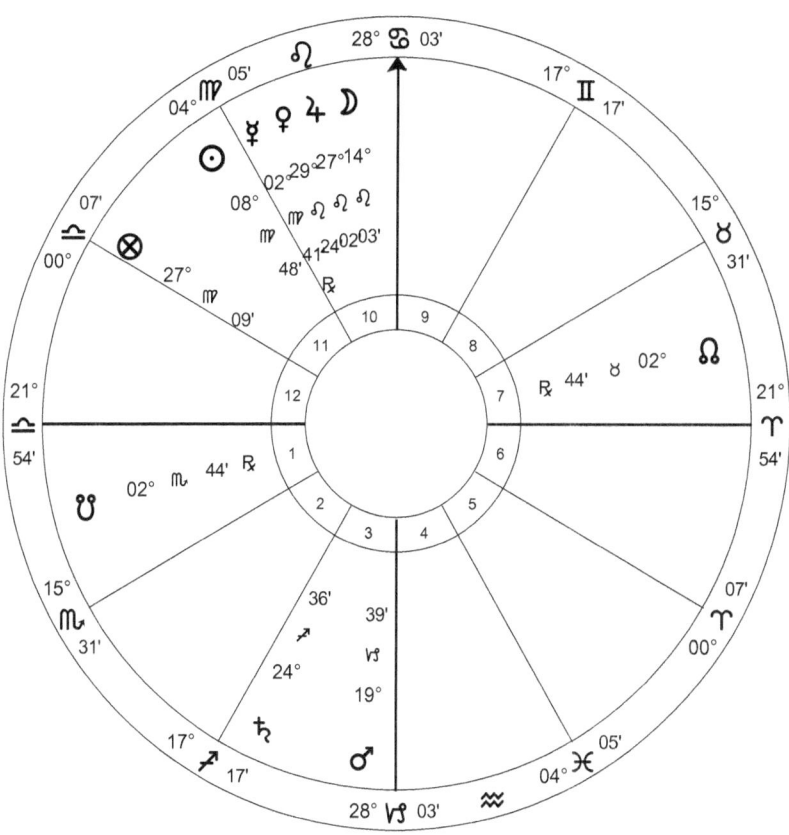

Louis Tronson
23 Aug 1576 9:18:30 LMT   Paris, France 48°N52' 02°E20'
Matching ASC from Morin, *Astrologia Gallica*, Book 23, Chapter 7

Morin's Book 21

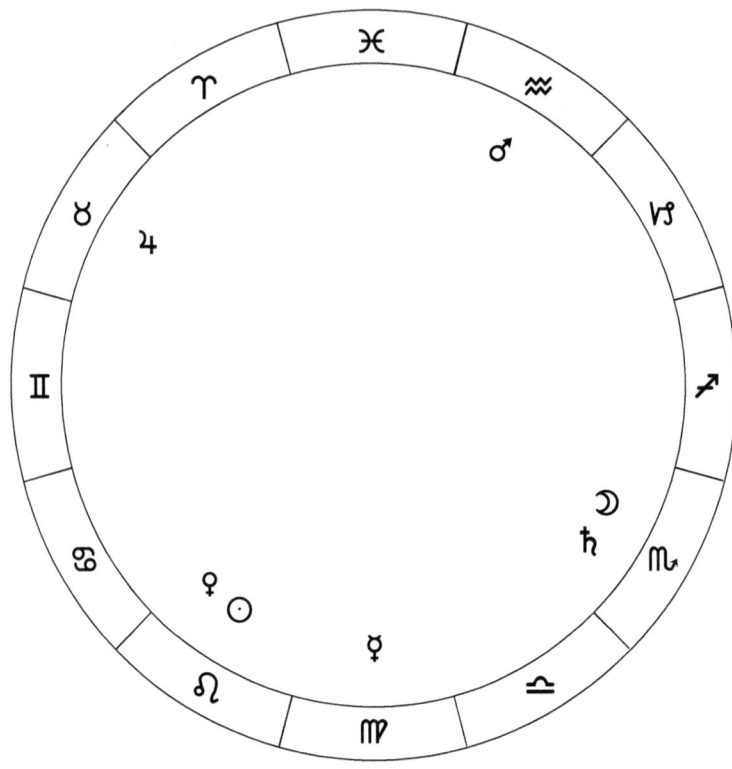

Chart #1 Nocturnal from Abû 'Ali al-Khayyât
Discussed in Book 21, Section 2, Chapter 7
From Abû 'Ali al-Khayyât, *Kitâb al-Mawâlid*, Chapter 7, Example 1

Appendix of Charts

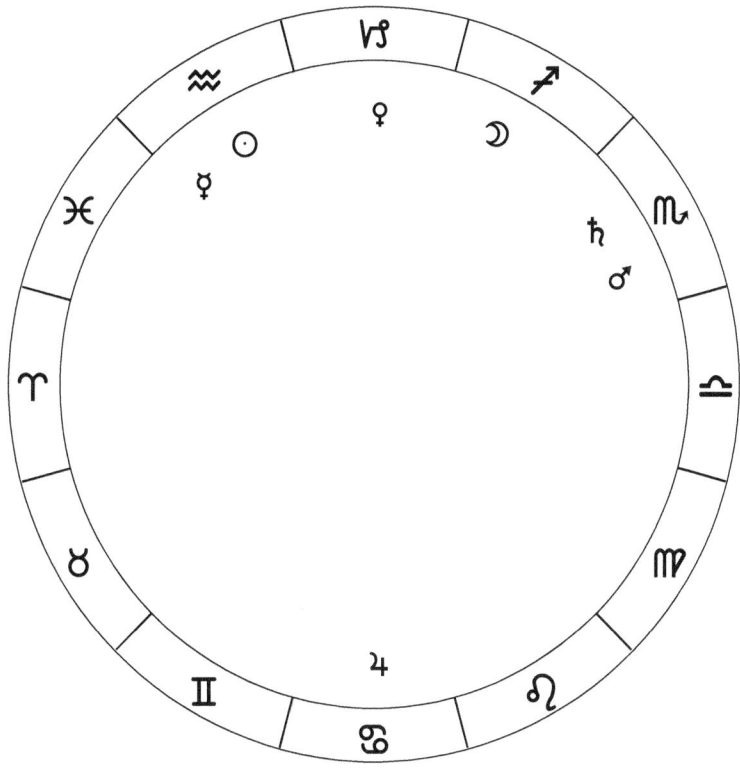

Chart #2 Diurnal from Abû 'Ali al-Khayyât
Discussed in Book 21, Section 2, Chapter 7
From Abû 'Ali al-Khayyât, *Kitâb al-Mawâlid*, Chapter 7, Example 2

Notes

Translator's Introduction

1 A bibliography of Morin's published work, *Liste Compléte des œvres de J.B. Morin* ("Complete List of the Works of J.B. Morin") is found in J. Halbronn's edition of Morin's *Remarques astrologiques de Jean-Baptiste Morin sur le Commentaire du* Centiloque *de Ptolémée*, pp. 299-303.

2 These figures are from Abû 'Ali al-Khayyât's *Kitâb al-Mawâlid*. Mâshâ'allâh used these figures. Dorotheus used the first one and used a figure similar to the second.

Preface

3 Morin refers here to what are now called "profections," or sometimes "symbolic progressions." See *Astrologia Gallica*, Book 24, trans. J.H. Holden, Section 1, for Morin's statement of his reasons for rejection of these techniques.

4 One can disagree with Morin that terms, decans (or faces), many of the Parts or Lots, profections, and other traditional definitions and techniques are figments, and still agree with his theory of astrological signification and the method of determination he sets out as proper horoscopic method. And despite disagreements, one may find great value in much of what Morin prescribes for use of horoscopic method. Those prescriptions, and their implications, include the use of houses, signs and planets in accord with their proper functions and inter-relationships, adherence to rules for assessment of a planet's significations in a chart and its effects on matters of a house, consistent use of techniques such as house combinations and derived houses, and a systematic, properly prioritized, and stable approach to every chart.

5 Morin attributed to astrologers writing in Arabic techniques they received from Hellenistic texts. His reference to Chaldeans is in line with the practice of referring to Mesopotamian astrologers or, in the Hellenistic period, to astrologers in general, as Chaldeans. For a summary of the early history of Western astrology, see C. Brennan, *Hellenistic Astrology*, Chapters 1 and 2, pp. 1-49.

6 Morin introduces here from the start the idea that universal, or general, significators do not function as particular, or accidental, significators in individual charts.

7 Jerome Cardan (1501-1576), known by the Latinized name Cardanus, was a leading Italian astrologer, an important and innovative mathematician, a physician and polymath, and author of the *Commentary on the Quadripartite* and numerous other works, including others on astrology.

8 Translating *ingenium* as "inborn talent." The word is literally "that which is inborn," from *in-*, "in," plus *gigno*, "to beget, to be born." The word *ingenium* refers to inborn qualities or abilities, and is often translated as "nature, innate quality, character, natural capacity, talent, abilities, ingenuity or genius," and, particularly by astrologers, sometimes as "intelligence."

9 Morin refers to his "Table of the Universal Rulerships of the Planets," in which he sets out at length the planets' analogical or universal significations. See *Astrologia Gallica,* Book 13, *The Proper Natures and Strengths of the Individual Planets and the Fixed Stars,* trans. J.H. Holden, Section 3, Chapter 3.

10 Referring to the technique of directions, often now referred to as "primary directions," a principal traditional forecasting technique.

11 Claudius Ptolemy (c. 100 CE-c. 170 CE) was a leading Alexandrian astronomer, mathematician and geographer who wrote works on geography, optics, harmonics, and other topics, including astronomy and astrology, and made important contributions to the development of multiple fields of study. He is the author of the *Tetrabiblos* ("The Four Books"), known in Latin translation as the *Quadripartite*, a work that became a leading text on astrology for centuries. His publications on astronomy also became for centuries leading works on the topic. In those works, he set out the geocentric model of cosmos, which became known as the "Ptolemaic system," and was for centuries the accepted model.

12 For this history as now known, again see C. Brennan, *Hellenistic Astrology*, Chapters 1 and 2, pp. 1-49.

13 Morin's reference to Adam and Noah is his way of stating his intention to reach back to astrology in what he conceives as its original and uncorrupted state.

14 Morin apparently refers here, and in his immediately preceding comment on Ptolemy and the ancient method, to the following:

> [W]e shall decline to present the ancient method of prediction which brings into combination all or most of the stars, because it is manifold and well-nigh infinite, if one wishes to recount it with accuracy. Besides, it depends much more upon the particular attempts of those who make their inquiries directly from nature than of those who can theorize on the basis of the traditions; and furthermore we shall omit it on account of the difficulty in using it and following it.

Ptolemy, *Tetrabiblos,* ed. & trans. Robbins, iii.1, p. 227. As James Holden explains, when Morin cites Ptolemy he apparently cites the Latin translation of the *Tetrabiblos*, known as the *Quadripartite*, as published in Cardan's *Commentary on the Quadripartite*. The numbering of some of the chapters, though not the one cited here, in that version of Ptolemy's work differs from those in the Robbins translation. See *Astrologia Gallica*, Book 17, *The Astrological Houses,* trans. J.H. Holden, *Translator's Preface*, p. xii.

15 The word *caelum* can be translated as "sky" or "heaven." The Latin word is retained here and throughout this translation.

16 In his general reference here to Ptolemy's use of the ancient method, Morin may refer to the following:

> In the first place, we should examine that place of the zodiac which is pertinent to the specific heading of the geniture which is subject to query; for example, the mid-heaven, for the query about action...; then we must observe those planets which have the relation of rulership to the place in question....After this, to determine the quality of the prediction, we must consider the natures of the ruling planets themselves and of the signs in which are the planets themselves, and the places familiar to them. For the magnitude of the event we must examine their power and observe whether they are actively situated both in the cosmos itself and in the nativity, or the reverse.

Tetrabiblos, ed. & trans. Robbins, iii.3, pp. 237-239 (omitting Ptolemy's statement of considerations not part of the ancient method to which Morin refers, and omitting footnotes). Ptolemy's reference to places "familiar" to a planet apparently refers to other places the ruling planet rules, and likely also to those it aspects. His reference to planets actively situated "in the cosmos" and "in the nativity" may be what in Morin's terms would be a reference, respectively, to planets' "celestial state" and their "terrestrial state."

17 Translating *Horoscopi*, an inflection of *Horoscopus*, from Greek *hōroskopos*, literally "hour-marker." In the way the term "Ascendant" is now generally used, Morin uses the term *Horoscopo* to refer specifically to the cusp of the 1ˢᵗ house and also, at times, to the 1ˢᵗ house as a whole. Similarly, Morin uses the term *medius Caelum*, "Midheaven," to refer either to the cusp of the 10ᵗʰ house or to the 10ᵗʰ house as a whole.

18 Translating *nutu Dei*, which, as a reference to divine will, finds a history in Homer's *Odyssey*, in which Zeus gives assent to the realization of fate with his nod.

19 Translating *scientiam*, an inflection of *scientia*. *Scientia* did not mean to Morin what the word "science" means in modern usage. *Scientia* is "a knowing or being skilled in anything, knowledge, science, skill, expertness." C.T. Lewis and C. Short, *A Latin Dictionary*, entry under *scientia*. https://www.perseus.tufts.edu/hopper/text?doc=Perseus:text:1999.04.0059. Accessed 4 October 2023.

Section I, Chapter I

20 The word "physical," from Latin *physicus*, "natural, physical," is related to the Greek *phusis*, "nature, growth," and *phuein*, "to bring forth, produce, to make grow," and to the Proto-Indo-European (PIE) root **bheu-*, "to be, to grow." In its original meaning, and in the meaning that Morin uses, "physical" means "natural, of nature." It refers to that which grows, and, therefore, to that which is born or naturally generated. Morin does not use the word "physical" in its modern meaning that refers only to the stuff of the body or *corpus* of things, or that polarizes with "mental."

21 An agent is one who acts, and by acting becomes a cause. More broadly, an agent is anything that is a cause of effects. An inferior agent is a cause that is the effect of a prior or superior cause. An inferior agent, caused by a superior agent or cause, goes on to have its own effects in a chain, or network, of causation.

22 An accident is simply an occurrence. It is something that happens. An accidental effect of something is an effect that may or may not result from the thing, depending on circumstances. As Morin uses the term here, the accidental effect of a celestial body is an effect that does not follow of necessity from the body's nature or essence.

It is an effect that depends on the object on which the celestial body acts, or on other circumstances in which it acts.

23 A thing's formal effect is an effect that results of necessity from the thing's essential nature. It is an effect a thing has by virtue of being the thing it is.

24 Morin often uses the term "influence" or "influential" as a term of art to distinguish the celestial—as opposed to elemental or ethereal—nature and effects of the celestial bodies. See *Astrologia Gallica*, Book 13, trans. J.H. Holden, Preface and Section 1. And see *Astrologia Gallica*, Book 14, *The* Primum Caelum *and its Division into Twelve Parts*, trans. J.H. Holden, Section 1, Chapter 2 on the distinction between the influential and elemental nature of the zodiacal signs.

25 A thing's essence—from *esse*, "to be,"—is what the thing is in itself; that is, intrinsically, or *per se*. It is the thing's nature, or its essential or formal nature, which defines the thing as the thing it is.

26 The term "subject of inherence" is a translation of *inhaesionis subjecto*. In Aristotelian and scholastic philosophy—which inform in fundamental ways Morin's natural philosophy—a substance is a thing that subsists on its own: *ens per se subsistens*. In contrast, an accident, or a quality, is *ens en alio*, a thing that exists in another. An accident, or quality, requires a substance in which it inheres—a "subject of inherence." That is, a quality or other occurrence cannot exist except as it is a quality of something, or an occurrence that happens to something.

27 "Virtue" is used as a term of art in astrology. It refers to the force, or power, that flows from the nature or essence of each of the celestial bodies. The virtue of a celestial body is the body's force or active power imbued with the body's essential nature. It is the force or power by which the body acts with the qualities and effects of its essential nature.

28 Morin uses "determination" as a term of art, and he distinguishes the *formal determination* of the *Primum Caelum*, the Planets and the fixed stars from their *accidental determination*. In Morin's theory, by a formal determination at the beginning of the World, the Author of nature created the celestial bodies and gave to each its formal or essential nature. An accidental determination of a celestial body gives qualities, states or conditions to the body.

29 The *Primum Caelum* is the "First Heaven." In the geocentric model of cosmos, which is also called the Aristotelian or Ptolomaic system, the *Primum Caelum* is the highest, or outermost, and starless sphere of cosmos. Morin refers often to the *Primum Caelum* as the first physical cause, and characterizes it as the thing most like God in the physical World. He describes the *Primum Caelum* as a perfectly homogenous and undifferentiated sphere that contains in potential, virtual or eminent form all that can be in the physical World. See Morin's comments on the *Primum Caelum* especially in Book 14, trans. J.H. Holden, Section 1, Chapter 1, throughout Section 1 of Book 21, and in Section 2, Chapter 16.

30 The term "proper" is from the Latin *proprius* "one's own, particular to itself." A virtue of a thing that is proper to the thing is a virtue that is intrinsic to the thing. It is part of the thing's essential nature.

Notes to page 8

31 In Book 3 of *Astrologia Gallica*, Morin set out his theory that the World is divided into three regions—not simply into the sublunary and celestial regions. In Morin's model, which shares basic characteristics with other traditional geocentric models of cosmos, the celestial region comprises the *Primum Caelum* and the sphere of the fixed stars. The region below the sphere of the Moon, which is the sublunary region of Earth, is the elemental region. In between is the ethereal region where the planets move. In Morin's theory, the planets are composed of celestial, ethereal and elemental substance, not of a purely ethereal substance. Accordingly, the planets have a celestial, an ethereal and an elemental nature, and they pour out their celestial, ethereal and elemental virtues by which they act on sublunary things. See *Astrologia Gallica*, Book 13, trans. J.H. Holden, Section 1.

32 Translating *eminente*, an inflection of *emineo*, "to stand out, to project," and figuratively, "to rise above, exceed other things in quality or degree." In Aristotelian and Scholastic theories of causation, and according to Descartes and others up to the present, a cause, it is said, cannot give what it does not have to give. That is, a cause must contain its effect. This principle of causation finds application in arguments for the existence of God. It plays a part also in Morin's explanation of the nature and action of the *Primum Caelum* and of the planets and fixed stars. God is understood to be the formless Source, or cause, of all that takes form in the physical World. Yet God is absolutely perfect and entirely without the formal qualities, limitations and imperfections of all things that exist or can exist in the physical World. God, therefore, contains eminently, but not formally, all that is and all that can be in the World. As God is the first absolute cause of all things, the *Primum Caelum*—the thing most like God in the physical World—is the first cause in the physical World. As such, the *Primum Caelum* is entirely simple and completely homogenous, undifferentiated, unchanging and incorruptible. Though as a thing in the physical World, the *Primum Caelum* has a formal nature, it is without the formal qualities and imperfections of differentiated sublunary things. It is of a formal nature that rises above, or is more perfect than, the elements and even the planets and fixed stars. The *Primum Caelum*, the first physical cause, therefore, contains eminently—or virtually or potentially—but not formally, all else that is and can be in the physical World. The word "virtual"—which fits well with the nature of the *Primum Caelum*—refers to "being something in essence or effect, though not actually or in fact," a meaning likely from the sense of "capable of producing a certain effect."

33 *Astrologia Gallica*, Book 14, trans. J.H. Holden.

34 Translating *situm domualem* as "house placement," and taking it to refer here to all factors that define a planet's situation within the houses of a horoscopic figure, including house location, house rulership, and aspects into houses or to or from house rulers.

35 Morin adopted the geocentric model of cosmos proposed by Tycho Brahe (1546-1601), the Danish astronomer, astrologer and alchemist known for his accurate astronomical observations and measurements. In Tycho's model of the geocentric cosmos, the Sun and Moon, the primary planets, orbit the central and stationary Earth, and the five minor planets, also called the secondary or lesser planets, orbit the Sun. Morin refers here to that model.

36 Morin refers here to the construction of the houses in the Regiomontanus system of house division, which divides the celestial equator to mark the boundaries of the 12 houses. Like all quadrant house systems, the Regiomontanus system first quadrates the celestial sphere with the great circles of the horizon and meridian. Then, in the Regiomontanus system, the intermediate house cusps are marked with great circles, called "circles of position." The circles of position that mark the intermediate house boundaries are drawn parallel to the horizon and trisect each of the quadrants with equal divisions of the equator. They intersect at the north and south points of the horizon, where the horizon and meridian also intersect with each other and with these circles. This system, often called the "Rational System," uses the equator as the circle on which to equally divide the houses because the equator is the circle of the primary motion. That is, the equator is the circle on which a planet, or the degree of a sign, moves in the primary motion to accomplish its daily spin through the houses from rising to culmination, through setting and anti-culmination and back to rising. Accordingly, in the Regiomontanus system, each planet and each point in a sign is placed in a house that is marked out by equal divisions of the very circle on which it moves from house-to-house through its daily circuit around Earth. See *Astrologia Gallica*, Book 17, trans. J.H. Holden, Section 2, Chapter 5, to which Morin refers here in the text, for his explanation of the division of the sphere in the Regiomontanus system. R.W. Holden, *The Elements of House Division*, gives clear explanations, with diagrams, of most, if not all, proposed systems of house division—though this book may now be difficult to find.

37 Correcting reference to Book 18 to Book 17, here and once again below in this chapter.

38 Morin distinguishes the "primary houses" from the "secondary houses." The primary houses are the divisions of space surrounding Earth that are generally referred to as simply the "houses." The secondary houses are arcs of the *primum mobile* intercepted between the cusps of the primary houses. For Morin's distinction between the primary and secondary houses, see *Astrologia Gallica*, Book 17, *The Astrological Houses*, trans. J.H. Holden, Section 3, Chapter 3.

39 The term Dodecatemoria, literally "Twelfth-Parts," refers to the zodiacal signs with a term that draws attention to the theory that the signs are created by a determination that divides the *Caelum* into 12 parts. It also draws attention to the highly important and consequential significance that Morin attributes to the fact that the division that forms the signs is a 12-part division. See *Astrologia Gallica*, Book 14, trans. J.H. Holden, Section 1.

40 The *primum mobile*, the "first mover" or "first moving thing," refers to the highest or outermost sphere in the geocentric model of cosmos. Although Morin usually uses the term *Primum Caelum* to refer to the outermost sphere in the geocentric model of cosmos, he often uses the term *primum mobile* in contexts that invoke the motion of this sphere.

Section I, Chapter II

41 The word "nature" is from *natura*, which is the inborn constitution, property, or quality of a thing; its character. A thing's nature is what the thing is in itself; it is its essence, or what it is to be the thing it is.

42 Correcting Section 3 to Section 2.

43 Morin refers here to *Astrologia Gallica*, Book 19, *The Elements of Astrology, or the Principles of Judgment*, trans. J.H. Holden. This short volume of *Astrologia Gallica* is a collection of formally stated definitions, axioms, and theorems from which Morin proposes to deduce astrological theory, method and doctrine by way of proofs of a mathematical nature.

44 Translating *genere vel specie*.

45 The elemental qualities of planets are especially effective in universal or mundane figures for the quality of the air or weather, and in nativities for delineation of temperament. Morin makes a similar statement at Section 2, Chapter 7, p. 97.

46 Morin comments further on the independence of a planet's elemental nature from the elemental nature of the sign it occupies in *Astrologia Gallica*, Book 13, trans. J.H. Holden, Section 1, Chapter 1.

47 David Tost (1558-1628/29), known by the Latinized name David Origanus, was a German astrologer and professor of mathematics and Greek who, among other things, published for more than three decades the first regularly published ephemeris, *Ephemerides Novae Brandenburgicae*. Morin likely refers here to Origanus' *Natural Astrology*.

48 Morin distinguishes the extrinsic, manifest or formal elemental natures of the minor planets from their intrinsic, latent or eminent elemental natures. See *Astrologia Gallica*, Book 13, trans. J.H. Holden, Preface; Section 1, Chapter 2; and Section 2, Chapters 1 and 2.

49 For Morin's theory that the eminent elemental nature of the minor planets is part of their celestial nature, not part of their formal elemental nature, see *Astrologia Gallica*, Book 13, trans. J.H. Holden, Preface, and especially Section 2, Chapter 2. In Section 2, Chapters 1 and 2, Morin also relates the planets' formal and eminent elemental natures to their sect and sex.

50 As Morin explains, heat and moisture are the generative elemental qualities; cold and dryness are the corruptive qualities. Earth, as in Capricorn, is dry and cold; air, as in Aquarius, is moist and warm. When the earthy, very dry and very cold Saturn combines with his very dry and cold earthy domicile, the qualities that work against life, especially when excessive, accumulate and intensify. See *Astrologia Gallica*, Book 14, trans. J.H. Holden, Section 1, Chapter 5 for Morin's comments on the generative and corruptive elemental qualities, for his assignments of elemental natures and strengths to the signs, and for his rationale for those assignments. See *Astrologia Gallica*, Book 13, trans. J.H. Holden, Section 1, Chapter 2 for his assignments of elemental strengths to the planets, and his rationale for those assignments.

Section I, Chapter III

51 The translation of this passage from the Loeb Classical Library edition is: "Now the sun and Saturn are by nature associated with the person of the father and the moon and Venus with that of the mother, and as these may be disposed with respect to each other and the other stars such must we suppose to be the affairs of the parents." Ptolemy, *Tetrabiblos*, ed. & trans. Robbins, iii.4, p. 241.

52 Translating *animae*, an inflection of *anima*.

53 The translation of this passage from the Loeb Classical Library edition is: "Of the qualities of the soul, those which concern the reason and the mind are apprehended by means of the condition of Mercury observed on the particular occasion; and the qualities of the sensory and irrational part are discovered from the one of the luminaries which is the more corporeal, that is, the moon, and from the planets which are configurated with her in her separations and applications." Ptolemy, *Tetrabiblos*, ed. & trans. Robbins, iii.13, p. 333.

54 Translating *moribus*, an inflection of *mos*, which can be translated as "habit, conduct, behavior, custom, a measuring or guiding precept or rule of life," and in plural form, "morals."

55 Translating *generibus & speciebus* as "classes and kinds."

56 Translating *animi mores* as "habits of mind."

57 Morin again cites this famous passage from Cardan in Book 23, where he again refers to Cardan's *Liber de Revolutionibus* ("Book of Revolutions"). See *Astrologia Gallica*, Book 23, *Revolutions*, trans. J.H. Holden, Chapter 7. The work to which Morin refers likely is Cardan's *De Revolutione Annorum, Mensium, et Dierum, ad dies Criticos, et ad electiones Liber* ("Book of Annual, Monthly and Daily Revolutions, and of Critical days, and of elections").

58 Translating *prave affectus*, here and for the most part throughout, as "badly conditioned."

59 Correcting the glyph for the square aspect to "trine."

60 Morin refers, at least in part, to his mother not giving him what would have been a customary testamentary gift. For more on Morin's inheritance from his mother, see *Astrologia Gallica*, Book 17, trans. J.H. Holden, Section 2, Chapter 2.

61 Morin defines "partile" with a very narrow orb. In practice, as here, he does not confine his use of the term to those narrowly defined limits. For Morin's calculation of partile orbs, see Book 16, trans. J.H. Holden, Section 1, Chapter 14.

62 Morin had antipathy for Richelieu, and considered him to be his hidden enemy. See, e.g., *Astrologia Gallica*, Book 16, trans. J.H. Holden, Section 2, Chapter 3. And see especially Morin's delineations of relevant solar and lunar revolutions, and accompanying directions of the radix and the revolutions, in *Astrologia Gallica*, Book 23, trans. J.H. Holden, Chapters 7, 10, 13 and 16. In consulting those charts, note that inaccuracies in the Moon's position stated in the *Rudolphine Tables* resulted in inaccuracies in lunar revolution charts. See *Astrologia Gallica*, Book 23, Translator's Preface, p. x, and the translator's notes to the individual lunar revolution charts.

63 Inserting *situm*, "location," so the Latin text would read *praesertim [situm] & dominium*.

64 Translating *arcanum*, generally translated as "secret, hidden, concealed, private." The word derives from *arcere*, "to close up, enclose, contain," and *arca*, "chest, box, place for safe-keeping." It originates in the PIE root **ark-*, "to hold, contain, guard," from which also derive the Greek *arkos*, "defense," and *arkein*, "to ward off," and the English "ark," whose meanings include "box, coffer." The word suggests something more than simply

Notes to pages 21–24

a secret or a mystery. It suggests something valuable and hidden for safe-keeping—a concealed treasure.

65 Translating *animae*, an inflection of *anima*, which could be translated as "soul, vital force, vital principle, life, breath, seat of feeling, or consciousness." Though I have used the translation "mind" here, note that "consciousness" and "mind," taken as referring to the seat of thought or rationality, are given more often to *animus*.

Section I, Chapter IV

66 To Scholastic philosophers, Aristotle was "the Philosopher," and he had a strong influence on Morin. He posited chains of causation that originate with the Unmoved Mover, or First Cause, and yet he allowed for indeterminacy. Despite the power of prior and superior causes that act in accord with natural law, indeterminacy leaves room for a break or redirection in causal chains. According to the view of what has been referred to as "agent causality," human agents can intervene in chains of causation. By our actions, we can initiate new causal chains that are not fully determined by prior and superior causes, or we can redirect or otherwise affect existing ones. Morin's statement here refers to the capacity for human self-determination, made possible by our capacity to learn and understand, and realized in our actions.

67 *Astrologia Gallica*, Book 16, *The Rays and Aspects of the Planets*, trans. J.H. Holden.

68 Morin's reference here to directions "of or to" places where the rays of the planets fall seems to imply by its terms that aspects can function as significators or as promissors in directions. In fact, however, as Morin explains, the aspects of the planets function in directions as promissors, but not as significators. Morin enumerates and discusses significators and promissors in directions in *Astrologia Gallica*, Book 22, trans. J.H. Holden, Section 1, Chapters 3 and 4.

69 Lucio Bellanti (d. 1499), known by the Latinized name Bellantius, was an astrologer who was born in Siena and was in exile in Florence when he published there his *Responsiones in disputationes Johannis Pici adversus astrologicam veritatem* ("Reply to the Disputations of Giovanni Pico Against the Truth of Astrology").

70 Giovanni Pico della Mirandola (1463-1494), born a nobleman near Modena in northern Italy, was a leading scholar and philosopher of the Italian Renaissance, and author of the famous *De hominis dignitate* (written in 1486 and published posthumously in 1496). This work, which came to be known as the *Oration on the Dignity of Man*, became a leading philosophical work of Renaissance humanism. His also famous *Disputationes adversus astrologiam divinicatrium* ("Disputations against divinatory astrology") was published posthumously in 1496. Pico died at the age of 31 under mysterious and questionable circumstances.

71 Johannes Kepler (1571-1630) was a German astronomer, astrologer, mathematician and natural philosopher. He is especially celebrated for his three laws of planetary motion according to which the planets revolve in elliptical orbits around the Sun. Morin refers to Kepler's *Judicium de trigono igneo* ("Judgment of the fiery triangle"). published in 1603. In that work, Kepler wrote on the coming series of Great Conjunctions of Jupiter and Saturn in fiery signs that began in December 1603 and continued without interruption into the late 18th century.

72 Kepler's *De stella nova in pede Serpentarii* ("Of the new star in the foot of the Serpent Handler") (1606), is on the supernova that stirred great interest, speculation and controversy following its appearance in 1604 in the constellation Ophiucus.

73 Translating *characteris*, an inflection of *character*, which could be translated as "impressed mark or sign, stamp, brand, character."

74 Morin refers here to Kepler's novel, *Somnium* ("The Dream"), published posthumously in 1634 by Kepler's son, Ludwig Kepler, under the full title *Somnium, seu opus posthumum De astronomia lunari* ("The Dream, or a posthumous work On lunar astronomy"). The novel is a magical and science fiction story, and in some of its details a scientific work. It includes a detailed description of how Kepler imagines the Earth would appear from the Moon, and what life would be like there. In part, the novel is an argument for the Copernican system, with which Kepler agreed and Morin did not.

75 Translating *figuris*, "shapes, forms, figures," which refers to aspects, or rather to the angles of aspects.

76 Translating *anima*.

77 Translating *indoles*, "inborn quality, nature, disposition."

78 A reference to the sharp or choleric nature of yellow bile, one of the four humors, which are yellow bile, blood, phlegm, and black bile. These belong, respectively, to the four temperaments, which are choleric, sanguine, phlegmatic and melancholic, and, again respectively, to the four elements of fire, air, water and earth.

79 Morin refers here to the four kinds of accidental determinations of the *Primum Caelum* that he sets out in this chapter: (1) The determination that divided the *Primum Caelum* into the 12 signs at Creation and gave to each sign its essential nature—a determination formal with respect to the signs but accidental with respect to the *Caelum*; (2) the accidental determination by the movement of the planets and fixed stars under the *primum mobile*, by which they determine to their nature the places under which they are seen and the places of their aspects and antiscia; (3) the accidental determination of the *Caelum* by the subject—that is, the receiver—of celestial influence; and (4) the accidental determination of the *Caelum* by terrestrial state—that is, by its local determination through its placement among the houses of a figure. The former two are universal determinations; the latter two are particular determinations.

80 Correcting the Latin text from *cratoris*, and translating *crateris*, which is an inflection of *cratera*, "bowl, bucket, aperture of a volcano, crater." Translated here as "fallen," *crateris* could be translated as "cratered, caved in."

Section I, Chapter V

81 Morin more than once in *Astrologia Gallica* uses the image of two men steering or pulling the same ship as an image of the way a planet and a sign, or two planets, work together as partners in an action. In the image of two men steering the same ship, imagine that one steers the wheel and the other works the rudder or sails. In a place where Morin applies essentially the same image to two connected planets, he explains the image as follows:

> [W]hen two Planets, either conjoined or connected by some aspect, concur in the same effect, these are not to be said properly and *per se* to confer their

forces on each other, but only by accident. Indeed, they act *per se* by their own rays sent out to us, not unlike two men applied to pulling the same ship, neither of whom confers his own force on the other, but each acts separately. But the motion or the pulling of the ship is common to both agents from the concurrence of the actions of both. And the reasoning is the same with all other non-subordinate agents. For when heat and cold come together, neither heat gives up its power to cold nor cold to heat, but from the concurrence of both a mixture is produced.

Astrologia Gallica, Book 16, Section 1, Chapter 17 (my translation).

82 The references are, in turn, to Julius Firmicus Maternus, a 4th century Roman astrologer, lawyer and writer of the senatorial class, and author of *Matheseos libri VIII* ("Mathesis"); Johannes Stoffler, a late 15th and early 16th century German astrologer, astronomer, mathematician and priest; and Heinrich Rantzau, a 16th century German astrologer.

83 The Eye of the Bull (*Oculus Tauri*) is the malefic royal fixed star Aldebaran. The Heart of the Scorpion (*Cor Scorpionis*) is the malefic royal fixed star Antares.

84 Translating *depravantur*, an inflection of *depravo*, "to corrupt, pervert, distort, disfigure, deprave."

85 Translating *Sol & homo generant hominem*. Aristotle, *Physics*, Book 2, Part 2.

86 Translating *Trigonum* as "Triangle" rather than "Trigon." Morin sometimes uses the term "triplicity" and sometimes uses "Triangle" when he refers to the triplicities of signs or their rulers. He no doubt uses "Triangle" as a way to remind that a triplicity of signs forms a triangle, and that the four triangles of signs participate to structure the circle of signs. His use of "Triangle rulers" also draws attention to the rationale for his assignments of these rulers. In Morin's system, planets rule by triplicity in signs of the same elemental nature as a sign they rule by domicile. Morin no doubt capitalizes "Triangle" because of the role triangles play in his cosmology and astrological theory as the expression and vehicle of divine love. See, e.g., *Astrologia Gallica*, Book 14, Section 1, Chapter 4 on the triangle and trine. There Morin refers to Pythagoras, Plato, Proclus and Kepler as masters of the "speculative numerical science," which today might be referred to as "sacred geometry." He applies to the 12-part division of the *Caelum* into the houses, and to the definitions of the aspects, principles of geometrically based meanings that are analogically related to those he applies to the division of the *Caelum* into signs. See *Astrologia Gallica*, Book 17, Section 1, Chapter 4 (on houses); and *Astrologia Gallica*, Book 16, Section I, Chapter 10 (on aspects).

87 The inferior World, or inferior region, is the sublunary, earthly, or elemental realm. That is, it is the region below the sphere of the Moon in the geocentric model of cosmos. The superior regions are those that begin with the sphere of the Moon.

Section I, Chapter VI

88 Note the distinction Morin makes between a sign acting universally and a sign acting as a universal cause. He makes the same distinction immediately below in his discussion of the planets as universal and particular causes.

89 Section 2 of Book 20 has no Chapter 4 or 5. Morin perhaps intends to refer to Section 3 of Book 20, here and three more times in this chapter.

90 "Antecedent" is a term of logic that refers to a statement that, it is argued, implies a statement that follows from the first, called the "consequent." Morin here is doing what is called "denying the antecedent." If the antecedent is false, it cannot support the implication that the consequent is true. Here the antecedent is: Every particular cause is subject to some universal cause.

91 That is, the same is true about the Sun's influential, or celestial, force, as about the elemental force by which he illuminates and heats.

Section I, Chapter VII

92 *Causa causae*—"the cause of the cause"—is a Latin legal phrase, and fits with the Aristotelian idea of a First Cause or Prime Mover. This idea, given Christian form, is important in Morin's cosmology, natural philosophy and astrological theory. For Morin, the Christian God is the cause of all causes who acts in the World through the *Primum Caelum*, the first physical cause, and through the planets, the Governors of the World who are God's regents in the World.

93 Cardan, J., *De Interrogationibus Libellus* ("The Little Book of Interrogations").

94 Correcting *confirmationes* to *conformationis*, here and twice in the following paragraph.

95 See *Astrologia Gallica*, Book 22 (on directions); Book 23 (on revolutions) and Book 24 (on transits).

96 Translating *sciens*, which could be translated as "knowing."

97 By the term "universal" figure, Morin refers to what is now commonly called a "mundane" chart or figure.

98 Translating *lites*, which can be translated as "lawsuit" or "litigation." A lawsuit is one kind of dispute, and is included in the essential significations of the 7th house.

99 Translating *malis*, a form of *malum*, which for the most part is translated throughout as "misfortune." It might be translated as "evil" or "bad thing."

Section I, Chapter VIII

100 Correcting *Hermininga* to *Hemminga*. Sixtus ab Hemminga (1533-1586) was a Frisian physician known for his *Astrologiae, ratione et experientia refutatae liber* ("Astrology refuted by reason and experience"). He was a one-time student of astrology who later opposed it. Morin refers numerous times to ab Hemminga in *Astrologia Gallica*. He devotes a chapter of Book 22 to refuting him (Section 5, Chapter 3), and another to a discussion of directions calculated for his nativity (Section 5, Chapter 4).

101 Alessandro de Angelis (1562-1620) was a Jesuit and, Morin says, the Prefect of Studies in the Roman College of the Society of Jesus. He was known for his five-volume work, *In Astrologos coniectores* ("Conjectures against the Astrologers"). Morin writes numerous times in *Astrologia Gallica* against de Angelis' opposition to astrology. See, e.g., Book 16, Section 1, Chapter 19; Book 22, Section 5, Chapter 2; and Book 14, Section 1, Chapter 8.

102 Correcting *intrinseca* to *extrinseca*.

103 Translating *adjunctis*, and taking it to refer broadly to planets joined to the part of the *Caelum* in question by rulership, conjunction or aspect, or by antiscion or opposite house location.

Section II, Chapter I

104 Translating *Sol & homo generant hominem*. Aristotle, *Physics*, Book 2, Part 2.

105 Translating *bona*, an inflection of *bonum*, as "good fortune." It can be translated as "good" and refers to "what is valuable, beneficial, estimable, fortunate, favorable, or pleasant, physically or mentally," or to what is "profitable, advantageous, serviceable, useful, or correct."

106 Morin defines a secondary house as the arc of the *primum mobile* that is intercepted between two circles of position that mark the boundaries of a primary house. See *Astrologia Gallica*, Book 17, trans. J.H. Holden, Section 3, Chapter 3.

107 Correcting *duodecima* to *undecima*.

108 Based on the four bodily humors, a melancholic illness is one to which a melancholic constitution or temperament is susceptible. Saturn rules melancholy, and has an analogy with melancholic illnesses.

109 To calculate arcs of direction, ascensions are measured along the equator. They differ for different zodiacal degrees because the ecliptic is oblique to the equator.

110 In the geocentric model of cosmos, the primary motion, also called the "diurnal motion," is the motion of the celestial sphere from east to west by which, in the model, the sphere spins daily around the central and stationary Earth. In the model, every planet, sign and fixed star is carried daily in the primary motion of the celestial sphere through all the houses drawn for any horizon.

111 In the geocentric model, the secondary motion, also called the "proper motion," is a planet's own motion as it moves on its planetary sphere around the central and stationary Earth. A planet moves in its proper motion from west to east when it is in direct motion.

112 See Section 2, Chapter 3, and especially Chapter 4, for more on Louis Tronson.

Section II, Chapter II

113 Morin does not mention Bellantius in Section 1, Chapter 3. He apparently here intends to refer to his comments in Section 2, Chapter 14, on Bellantius and the identification of the principal significator of any matter.

114 Johann Gartz (1539-1575), known by the Latinized name Garcaeus, was a German astrologer, Lutheran theologian and pastor. Morin likely refers here to Garceus' *Astrologiae methodus, in qua secundum Ptolemaei, exactissima facillimaque Genituras qualescunque iudicandi ratio traditur* ("A method of astrology, in which, according to Ptolemy, the most exact and easiest method of judging Genitures of any kind is handed down").

115 Franciscus Giuntini (1522-1590), known by the Latinized name Junctinus, was an Italian astrologer, mathematician and theologian. Morin likely refers here to Junctinus'

were against the Huguenots and against Habsburg Spain. Though he held important governmental positions, he was one of the noblemen who objected to the king's suppression, through Cardinal Richelieu, of the power of the nobility in favor of an absolute monarchy. In 1632, Montmorency joined with other nobles and Prince Gaston in an attempt to remove Richelieu from power. In the fighting, which his side lost, he was wounded and captured. Abandoned by Gaston, he was condemned to be beheaded. On his way to the scaffold, he revealed Gaston's forbidden secret marriage.

130 Translating *mediocritate affectus* as "moderately conditioned."

131 Galileo Galilei's (1564-1652) observation of the satellites of Jupiter was among the discoveries of the early 17th century that resulted from his development of the telescope. His *Siderius nuncius* ("The Starry Messenger"), published in 1610, contains drawings, diagrams, descriptions and theories based on his telescopic observations of the Moon, selected constellations, and the satellites of Jupiter. The four satellites of Jupiter that he saw came to be known for a time as the "Medicean Stars," because Galileo, seeking patronage, dedicated the work to Cosimo II de' Medici and named those satellites after the four Medici brothers. When Galileo saw the rings of Saturn through his telescope, he initially speculated that he might be looking at two satellites. In the late 1650s, shortly after Morin's death, Christiaan Huygens (1629-1695) recognized that what Galileo saw near Saturn were Saturn's rings.

132 Omitting *non* from *Unde non abs re dici potest*.

133 Translating *pravis domibus*.

134 Armand-Jean du Plessis (1585-1642), Duke and Cardinal de Richelieu, generally known as Cardinal Richelieu, was a French clergyman and statesman and, from the early 1620s until his death, the chief minister of King Louis XIII. Among Richelieu's principal aims during his ascendancy were centralization of power and establishment of royal absolutism in France, and strengthening France's power in international politics. He centralized power by reigning in the formerly very powerful feudal lords of the French nobility, and worked to overcome the Huguenots, French Protestants of the 16th and 17th centuries. Richelieu became, particularly in the later years of the war, a key figure in the devastating Thirty Years' War (1618-1648) that ravaged Europe. In that war, Richelieu allied Catholic France with Protestant nations in northern Europe, including Sweden under King Gustavus Adolphus. He made these alliances with Protestants as a means to oppose the power of the Austro-Spanish Catholic Habsburg dynasty that had held dominant power in Europe for centuries, including for part of that time as rulers of the Holy Roman Empire.

Richelieu came to the French court and advanced there as an ally of Concino Concini. Through a circuitous route, he fairly soon came into the good graces of Louis XIII. After the death in 1621 of the Duke of Luynes, a chief advisor of the king, Richelieu became the king's advisor and ally, and quickly rose to great power in the court. Power struggles, court intrigues, beheadings, and war, and his notable political savvy, consolidated Richelieu's power and, along with repeated plots to assassinate or otherwise unseat him, became characteristic during his time as an outstandingly powerful presence in the French court.

135 Morin, who trained as a physician and for some time practiced medicine, objected to what he considered the ignorant and brutal practices of physicians of his time, including the excessive use of bloodletting. He favored the work of the Swiss physician, chemist, alchemist, philosopher, and astrologer, Paracelsus (c. 1493-1541). Paracelsus based his approaches to medical treatment on observation and experience in place of unquestioning reliance on authority.

136 Louis Des Hayes de Courmenin (1598-1632) was a French diplomat and a member of the Orléans bourgeoisie. His father was reportedly the bailiff and governor of Montargis, and his grandfather was a solicitor. Online reports identify his birthplace as Montargis, in the Loiret department of France, and estimate the year of his birth to be around 1600. They further report that Des Hayes was beheaded on October 12, 1632 for joining a conspiracy against Cardinal Richelieu. It appears from Morin's description of placements in the chart that Des Hayes was born on February 12, 1598 at around 11:30 p.m. Des Hayes carried out several diplomatic missions on behalf of King Louis XIII, including to Denmark, the Levant, and Russia. After these missions, he entered into service of Gaston d'Orleans, Louis XIII's brother, and joined the conspiracy with Duke Montmorency and others against the King and Cardinal Richelieu. When the plot was uncovered, Des Hayes was convicted of treason, and was beheaded on October 12, 1632.

137 The Head of Medusa is the malefic royal fixed star Algol.

138 In his comments on his solar revolution for the year 1605, Morin reports that in that year he received two very dangerous wounds, "because of a famous woman." *Astrologia Gallica*, Book 23, trans. J.H. Holden, Chapter 7. See also Book 23, Chapter 10 for Morin's comments on the lunar revolution under which this incident occurred, Chapter 13 for his comments on the radical directions that accompanied those revolutions, and Chapter 16 on relevant directions taken in the revolution charts.

139 Gustavus Adolphus (1594-1632) was the King of Sweden from 1611 until his death. Under his reign, Sweden became a major European power. He introduced various notable reforms in government, and for his successes as a leader became known as Gustavus the Great. As a result of his successful and influential innovations in tactics and weaponry, he also became known as the father of modern warfare and the Lion of the North. In the Battle of Lutzen, an important battle in the Thirty Years' War, Gustavus' army fought the army of Albrecht von Wallenstein (or, in Morin's spelling, Walstein, also sometimes spelled Waldstein) (1583-1634), a major figure in the Thirty Years' War who fought on behalf of the Holy Roman Empire. Gustavus lead his army's charge into battle, and became lost in smoke behind enemy lines. Though his army won the battle, Gustavus was killed in the fight. Morin often uses Gustavus' nativity as an example chart in *Astrologia Gallica*, writing especially on his death.

140 Translating: *quia haec combinatio quadrabit infortunio Mercurius*. *Quadrabit* is an inflection of *quadro*, which, in this construction, means "to square with"—that is, to agree or be consistent with, to fit or suit. In this astrological context, the word might be misunderstood to say that Mercury squares by aspect the 8th house planets—which, of course, it does not, and cannot. Morin uses an inflection of *quadro* in the same way in Section 2, Chapter 7, and in other places in other volumes of *Astrologia Gallica*. The misfortune of Mercury to which Morin refers explicitly here is the separating square that Mercury receives from Saturn. Mercury's misfortunes also include his fallen condition in Pisces, a condition that does notable harm to the chart as a whole because, as Morin notes, Mercury rules both the Ascendant and the Midheaven. This Mercury, moreover, is disposed to the 8th house by Jupiter, thereby signifying that Mercury, which is a significator of d'Effiat himself (1st ruler) and of his actions and destiny (10th ruler), becomes a cause of his death.

141 Translating *pravis*.

142 Translating *nimium intenditur* as "excessively exaggerated." It could be more literally translated as "excessively aimed at, reached for, directed toward," or as "excessively magnified" or "intended." Indicators of misfortune accumulate when a planet's malefic nature combines with its bad celestial state, especially when it is also determined to unfortunate houses. Unfortunate significations reinforce and build on each other. By virtue of the power of analogy, such reinforcement is more than additive.

143 Translating *benefaciunt* as "acting benefically."

144 By his reference to how important it is to establish the "true method of constructing the celestial figure," Morin refers to the importance of using a true system for erection of the primary houses.

Section II, Chapter III

145 To correct an apparent inadvertent omission, adding *fortunanda* before *vel infortunanda*

146 Morin gives his chart in Book 17, Section 2, Chapter 2. His nativity, which reproduces the degree and minutes on the Ascendant of the chart as he gives it and otherwise closely approximates it, is found in the Appendix of Charts, cast with modern software. Venus is not located by body in the 12th house, but she is in the sign on the 12th house, sits very late in the 11th, and, by Morin's calculations, conjoins the 12th house cusp with an orb of 2°18'. By that conjunction to the 12th cusp, Venus is powerfully determined to the 12th house.

147 Morin further describes this fall from horseback in *Astrologia Gallica*, Book 23, Chapters 7 and 10, where he comments on the solar revolution and lunar revolutions under which it occurred.

148 For more on Louis Tronson and his political fortunes, see Section 2, Chapter 4, pp. 79-80.

149 *Astrologia Gallica*, Book 18, *The Strengths of the Planets*, trans. A. Louis LaBruzza.

150 Léon Bouthillier (1608-1652), Count of Chavigny, was a foreign minister of France under King Louis XIII, and a friend of Morin. Chavigny was engaged in political controversies after the death of Louis XIII, and was arrested and released during the Fronde. The Fronde was a series of French civil wars that occurred between 1648-1653 during the minority of King Louis XIV (1638-1715) in which the French nobility rebelled against royal absolutism, and lost. The word *fronde* refers to the "sling" used in a child's game unlawfully played in the streets of Paris.

151 Correcting *nunquam* to *umquam*.

152 Correcting the glyph for Mars to "Venus."

Section II, Chapter IV

153 *Astrologia Gallica*, Book 15, *The Essential Dignities of the Planets*, trans. J.H. Holden.

154 Here Morin acknowledges that a planet is not properly speaking the "ruler" of another planet. Nevertheless, throughout Book 21 he uses the term *dominus*, "lord, master, owner, ruler," rather than *dispositor*, "disposer, arranger," or, in astrology, "dispositor," to refer to a planet's dispositor. In most cases, it is apparent in the context that Morin is using "ruler" to mean "dispositor." But in some instances his failure to use the proper term may create ambiguity.

155 Translating *Themate*, an inflection of *thema*—literally "theme, topic," and referring to a horoscopic figure or chart.

156 As Morin notes in the preceding paragraph and elsewhere, a sign depends always on its ruler's nature and its celestial state. When he says "only" here, Morin simply excludes the ruler's terrestrial state from the statement, not its nature.

157 Correcting *duodecima* to *decima*.

158 For a qualification of this statement of the effect of the 1st ruler in another house, see Section 2, Chapter 12, items (4) and (5) in the list that ends that chapter.

159 Compare this statement with the statements on a natural malefic in good celestial state in an unfortunate house in Section 2, Chapter 2, pp. 58, 62 and 63-65.

160 By *ergo &c.*—"therefore, &c"— Morin refers to, and implicitly repeats, the conclusion he reached at the close of the preceding paragraph. That is, that a planet can do something through its location in a house without at the same time acting through its rulership in other houses.

161 A quartan fever is a fever that recurs in intervals of four days.

162 Louis Tronson (1576-1642) participated with Charles d'Albert, later Duke of Luynes, in the planning of the arrest of Concino Concini. Following this arrest, and Concini's assassination during it, Tronson became a trusted minister of King Louis XIII. For more on Tronson, including on his participation in the Concini arrest and on his later expulsion from the French court, with Morin's comments on his relevant solar and lunar revolutions and accompanying radical directions, see *Astrologia Gallica*, Book 23, trans. J.H. Holden, Chapters 7, 10 and 13. Tronson was a friend of Morin's, for which see Book 23, Chapters 7 and 13.

163 Translating *scientibus*.

164 King Louis XIII (1601-1643) became King of France and Navarre at the age of eight years, upon the assassination of his father, King Henry IV, and remained king until his death. The king took power upon ending the regency of his mother, Marie de' Medici, in 1617. He relied on strong advisors, the first of whom was Charles d'Albert, who became the Duke of Luynes, and then, upon the death of Luynes, Cardinal Richelieu, who became the king's closest and very powerful advisor. In 1618, early in Louis's reign, the terrible Thirty Years' War that devastated Europe began, and continued through the remainder of his life. Louis' reign was characterized by efforts, led by Cardinal Richelieu, to consolidate power in the king, by conflict with the French Protestant Huguenots, and by war with the powerful Habsburg dynasty, especially the Spanish Habsburgs.

165 Charles d'Albert (1578-1621), later the Duke of Luynes, was a French courtier, and incidentally, the older brother of Leon d'Albert de Luynes, Duke of Luxembourg, whom

Morin served as a physician before his appointment as Regius Professor of Mathematics. Luynes was a favorite and powerful advisor of King Louis XIII, and the most powerful enemy at court of the Queen Mother, Marie de' Medici, and the man who became her favorite, Concino Concini. Luynes, who urged Louis XIII to take power from the Queen Mother and to act against Concini, organized Concini's 1617 arrest, during which Concini was assassinated. In reward, the king gave Luynes the extensive confiscated lands and other possessions of Concini in Italy and France, made him a duke, appointed him to be a Peer of France, and later appointed him to the very powerful position of Constable of France. Luynes died in 1621 from camp fever during a siege to put down a Huguenot rebellion.

166 Concino Concini (1569-1617), Marquis d'Ancre, was a Florentine nobleman who became the most powerful Italian favorite of the Queen Mother, Marie de' Medici during the later years in which she acted as Regent of France. The Queen Mother was also a Florentine, and a member of the very powerful and very wealthy Medici family, During her regency, Concini received ownership of extensive lands and power over several territories, and was appointed to powerful offices. In part simply because of his power, in part because of objections to some of his and the Queen Mother's policies, and in part because he was a foreigner, Concini earned the hatred of many, including especially members of the French nobility and, reportedly, the young King Louis XIII. In 1617, Louis exiled his mother and acted against her favorites. Concini's assassination occurred during this shift in power. In the months following his assassination, the propaganda mill spread rumors and distributed pamphlets in Paris to justify it. As Morin reports, here and in *Astrologia Gallica*, Book 23, trans. J.H. Holden, Chapter 7, Tronson acted with Charles de Luynes in this action against Concini. See also Book 23, trans. J.H. Holden, Chapter 7, p. 34, translator's footnote 1.

167 Henry IV of France (1553-1610) was King of Navarre from 1572, and King of France from 1589-1610, and was the first French monarch from the House of Bourbon. Henry was the husband of Marie de' Medici and the father of Louis XIII, and earned the moniker Good King Henry. He wavered between Protestantism and Catholicism, and, after multiple failed assassination attempts by Protestants and Catholics, was killed in 1610 by a Catholic assassin.

168 Translating *Regi a libellis supplicibus*.

Section II, Chapter V

169 Correcting *duodecimae* to *secundae*.

170 Morin could have made this statement clearer if he had followed the practice of using the proper term "dispositor," rather than the term "ruler," to refer to a planet's dispositor. For, taken in isolation, the statement in the text might be misunderstood to apply to all planets in a house where a planet rules. Yet, taken, as it must be, in the context of basic doctrines of the theory and method Morin states, it applies, of course, only to those planets in a house that the house ruler disposes. So, if more than one planet rules in a house, each of those house rulers in another house acts through the planets that it disposes by sign. But it does not act through planets in the house that another planet, but not the planet in question, disposes. The remainder of the paragraph, including especially the hypotheticals Morin uses to exemplify the doctrine, eliminate any doubt on the matter.

Notes to pages 85–93

171 Correcting *primae* to *octavae*.

172 Referring to the four humors: yellow bile, blood, phlegm and black bile.

173 Note the distinction between "by reason of bodily location and rulership" and "by reason of the combination." The meaning and effect of a house combination changes with the switch in the combining planet's location and its rulership—because location is a more efficacious determination than rulership. In either case, though, the planet does the same thing by rulership as by location, only more weakly by rulership.

174 Translating *transibit in*, which could be translated as "will transform into," "will change to" or "will pass over to."

175 Correcting *decimae* to *duodecimae*.

176 Correcting *secundae* to *duodecimae*.

177 That is, near the Midheaven.

178 Translating *cardinibus*, which could also be translated as "hinges" or "cardinal places," or, more loosely, as "angles." The word is an inflection of *cardo*, "swing, hinge." The Latin term came to mean "that on which everything else turns or depends, the chief point or circumstance." In astronomy, it is "the point about which something else turns, a pole," and "the four cardinal points of the world." Charlton T. Lewis, Charles Short, *A Latin Dictionary*, accessed on 2 June 2023 at https://www.perseus.tufts.edu/hopper/text?doc=Perseus:text:1999.04.0059, at the entry under *cardo*. In *Astrologia Gallica*, Book 18, trans. A. Louis LaBruzza, Section 2, Chapter 14, Morin quantifies and compares the intrinsic strength of the houses, and notes that houses where the planets act more powerfully and effectively are considered to be stronger than other houses.

179 Translating *ut dominus secundæ in duodecima, divitiarum dissipatio, morborum, exilii, aut carceris causâ portenditur*, where *causâ portenditur* could be translated as "is portended from the cause" rather than "is portended as a cause." Although it might seem that illnesses, exile or prison would more likely cause a dissipation of wealth than that a squandering of wealth would cause illnesses, exile or prison, "is portended as a cause" is consistent with the phrase that follows, and with the doctrine that location is a more efficacious determination than rulership.

180 Translating *reducitur*, which could be translated as "is reduced to" or "is brought back to."

181 *Astrologia Gallica*, Book 18 has no Section 8, nor does the reference appear to be a misprint for Chapter 8 of Book 18. Morin comments on primary and secondary houses in *Astrologia Gallica*, Book 17, trans. J.H. Holden, Section 3, Chapters 3 and 4.

182 Correcting *octavae* to *tertiae*.

183 Translating *versetur*, which could be translated as "is situated," or simply "is."

184 Referring to *Astrologia Gallica*, Book 22, *Directions*.

Section II, Chapter VII

185 The Apheta, also known as the Hyleg or the Prorogator of Life, is the planet Ptolemy and others take as the principal significator of the native's life and vitality; it is the "giver of life."

186 To identify the planet with most dignities in a place, in addition to counting dignity by domicile, exaltation and triplicity, Ptolemy and others also count other dignities that Morin rejected. Here, and below in this chapter, Morin omits reference to those rejected dignities.

187 In Morin's nativity, a late degree of Aries rises and Taurus is enclosed in the 1st house. Accordingly, Mars is the domicile ruler of the Ascendant, and the Sun its ruler by exaltation, making them, as rulers of the most powerful point in the house, the principal rulers of the 1st house. Because Taurus is found in the 1st, Venus and the Moon are also rulers of the 1st house, by domicile and exaltation, respectively.

188 Astrologers who wrote in Arabic took from Hellenistic astrologers the practice of judging in a general way the fortune or misfortune of a life from the triplicity rulers of the sect light. In a diurnal chart, the sect light is the Sun; in a nocturnal chart it is the Moon. For an explanation of the use of this technique to judge in broad terms the general prosperity and stability of the life, see C. Brennan, *Hellenistic Astrology*, Chapter 15, pp. 495-510.

189 Morin refers to the fact that different astrologers have used different systems of triplicity rulers. See C. Brennan, *Hellenistic Astrology*, Chapter 8, pp. 266-72.

190 In *Astrologia Gallica*, Book 15, trans. J.H. Holden, Chapter 7, Morin sets out his assignments of the triplicity rulers and the rationale for those assignments. For further comments from Morin on the triplicities and their rulers, see also Book 15, Chapter 9; Book 14, trans. J.H. Holden, Section 1, Chapters 4, 5 and 7, and Section 2, Chapter 1.

191 Abû 'Ali al-Khayyât (c. 770-c. 835 CE), sometimes known in the West as Albohali, was an Arabian astrologer of the early 9th century. Morin refers here to the discussion of two charts in Abû 'Ali's *Kitâb al-Mawâlid* ("On the Judgments of Nativities"), trans. B.N. Dykes, Chapter 7, charts 1 and 2, pp. 243, 244. The first chart, which is a nocturnal chart with Gemini rising, appears in Dorotheus' *Carmen Astrologicum*, trans. D. Pingree, I.24.2, p. 184. The second chart, which is a diurnal chart with Aries rising, appears in Mâshâ'allâh's *Book of Nativities*, trans. B.N. Dykes, "On Nativities," §6, Figure 36, Example 2, p. 404. In a search of planetary sign placements in relevant years, I found among actual celestial configurations none described as the placements in either of these figures. Both are apparently hypothetical. Figures set up as those Abû 'Ali describes appear in the Appendix of Charts.

192 Translating *combinationibus & societatibus*. The former might be translated as "in couples" or simply as "in combinations," and the latter as "in alliances" or "in associations."

193 The *Centiloquy*, or *Centiloquium*, meaning "Hundred Sayings," and also known as *Kitab al-Tamara* or, in Latin, *Liber Fructus* ("The Book of the Fruit"), is a collection of 100 aphorisms based on Ptolemy's *Tetrabiblos*, or *Quadripartite*. Although originally ascribed to Ptolemy, the work is now believed to be a later work whose author is now often given as "Pseudo-Ptolemy." The *Centiloquy* has been an important astrological work over the centuries, and has been several times translated into Arabic, Latin, Hebrew and English. Aphorism 72 provides, in my English translation from the Latin translation of G. Trapezuntius: "As pertains to rearing, take the lords of the ascending triplicity. But for the way of life, take the lords of the triplicity of the sect light."

194 Translating *conversationibus*, which might be translated as "association, familiar intercourse."

Section II, Chapter VIII

195 Translating *casu*, an inflection of *cado*, "to fall, descend, sink, to be overthrown." To refer to a planet "in fall," Morin generally uses inflections of *cado*; to refer to a "fallen" planet or state he generally uses *dejectus*, "cast down, driven out, dispossessed, dejected." Once in Book 21, in Section 1, Chapter 4, p. 28, Morin uses *crateris*, "cratered, caved in," to refer to a planet in a fallen state.

196 Morin identifies several considerations that affect for better or worse the condition of a peregrine planet. According to Morin, in the sign of a friend, a planet that is simply peregrine suffers little diminution in its power to act according to its nature. In the domicile of an enemy, however, it is weakened or corrupted. Similarly, it is worse for a planet to be peregrine in the domicile of a malefic than, it is implied, in the domicile of a benefic. And, unless the combination results in an elemental excess, a peregrine planet in a sign that is of its gender will act more beneficially than in a sign of the opposite gender. See *Astrologia Gallica*, Book 18, trans. A. Louis LaBruzza, Section 1, Chapters 5 and 6. Note also that Morin distinguishes a planet "simply peregrine" from one in a "mixed" peregrine state. A planet simply peregrine is neither in its triplicity nor in its exaltation, but is neither exiled nor fallen. A planet in a mixed peregrine state is outside its triplicity and in exile or fall. See *Astrologia Gallica*, Book 15, trans. J.H. Holden, Chapter 13. In Morin's system of triplicities, a planet is in triplicity in any sign that is of the same elemental nature as a sign where it rules by domicile. So, a planet in domicile is in its triplicity. This system and the distinction between a simply peregrine condition and a mixed peregrine condition draw attention to the importance Morin places on a planet being "in its element" and so in some sense "at home." With thanks to Anthony Louis for drawing my attention to the need to spell out Morin's unique distinction between a planet in a simple versus a mixed peregrine state. For Morin's assignments of planetary friends and enemies, see Book 15, Chapter 14.

197 I understand Morin to say here that, without frequent changes, he would have been intolerant of the tedium of his work, and would have had insufficient patience with it.

198 Morin suggests here that we can understand Mars, and by extension any planet, in exile by considering the nature and dignities of the planets that have dignity in signs of his exile. He does not refer here specifically or solely to Mars in Libra.

Section II, Chapter IX

199 Morin defines a ray of a planet as "only and simply an outpouring of its virtue by some star in a straight line." An aspect, he says, is the coming together of two rays at the center of the Earth. See *Astrologia Gallica*, Book 16, trans. J.H. Holden, Section 1, Chapters 1 and 3. Despite these definitions, Morin nevertheless uses the term "aspect" to refer to a planet's ray sent to an angle or other house cusp, though a house cusp, of course, does not send a ray.

200 The dodectile is one of the two minor aspects that Morin recognized. It is the 30° aspect that is now commonly called the "semi-sextile." See *Astrologia Gallica*, Book 16, trans. J.H. Holden, Section 1, Chapter 4 for Morin's rationale for his recognition of the

six forms of aspect he names here. In Morin's theory, as he says there, the number of the aspects has a similar origin as have the 12 signs and the 12 houses. See *Astrologia Gallica*, Book 14, trans. J.H. Holden, Section 1, Chapters 3 and 4 on the 12-part division of the *Caelum* into the signs, and *Astrologia Gallica*, Book 17, trans. J.H. Holden, Section 1, Chapters 3 and 4 on the 12-part division of the houses.

201 Correcting *beneficis* to *maleficis*.

202 That is, by its aspects to other planets seen as they are locally determined by house location and rulership, and by its aspects to house cusps.

203 Omitting *non* from *non abs re deduci potest*.

204 It is difficult to see how Morin's example here is an instance of the rule he states. The stated rule seems rather to suggest that Mars ruling the 3rd and in the 4th trine the Ascendant would more strongly connect the parents with the native than it would connect the siblings with him—not that it would signify favor from the parents and hatred from the siblings. That is, by its terms the stated rule is one of relative quantity, not different quality. Perhaps Morin assumes jealously or competition between siblings for the parents' favor, which would be a way to perhaps begin to reconcile the example with the stated rule.

Section II, Chapter X

205 See *Astrologia Gallica*, Book 16, trans. J.H. Holden, Section 1, Chapter 10 for Morin's theory on what makes an aspect benefic or malefic.

206 Compare Section 2, Chapter 9, p. 104: "...the partnership of...malefic [aspects] from benefics is middling." And Section 2, Chapter 11, p. 116: "...the square [of Jupiter from his own domicile] is harmless, or only slightly harmful."

207 Correcting *oculo octavi* to *oculo Tauri*, the Eye of the Bull, the malefic royal fixed star Aldebaran.

208 Translating: *susceptis actionibus & honoribus*. With a comma between the first two words, which might be inadvertently missing, the translation would be "undertakings, actions and honors."

209 With this short sentence, Morin refers to the timing of when this combination will come to fruition by direction

210 Translating: *prudenti rapina*, which could be translated as "skilled plunder." Because Jupiter participates, the translation chosen is one that gives the actions a more ethical cast. On the other hand, if Jupiter were in bad, and therefore compromised or corrupted, celestial state, as, for example, fallen in Capricorn, he would be with, and disposed by exaltation to, an exalted, very powerful and highly focused and purposeful Mars. Then "skilled plunder" could be a better translation.

Section II, Chapter XI

211 Translating *ab Ortu in Occasum*, which could be translated as "from East to West."

212 The terms "preceding" and "following" refer to the direction that precedes or follows in the primary motion. A dexter ("right") or preceding aspect, or ray, is sent from the body of the planet in the direction of the primary motion, and against the

direction of the order of the signs. A sinister ("left") or following aspect, or ray, is sent from the body of the planet against the direction of the primary motion and in the direction of the order of the signs. To identify a dexter or sinister aspect, imagine you are in the center of the wheel of a chart looking at a planet on the periphery. The planet's dexter or preceding aspects are sent from the planet's body to your right; its sinister or following aspects are sent from the planet's body to your left.

213 In a single chart, a planet could apply in the primary motion to a dexter sextile to the Midheaven as it departed in the primary motion from a sinister sextile to the Horoscope. To follow the rule Morin states, it may help to imagine or sketch out the set-up with sextiles in a single chart as described here.

214 In the Regiomontanus system of house division, which Morin used, the circles of position are great circles that mark the boundaries of the houses. See note 36, on Regiomontanus houses.

215 Morin apparently refers here to the rule under which a planet that precedes another in the primary motion "dominates" in aspect one that follows it. This statement gives greater power to application than to this form of domination.

216 If one accepts Morin's view that planets apply to house cusps in the primary motion, the rule he proposes on aspects to cusps raises a question he does not address here. That question is whether a planet's application to a cusp in the primary motion prevails, other things being equal, over its own, or another planet's, application in the secondary motion to the degree of the sign on the same or another cusp.

217 Translating *ab Occasu in Ortum*, which could be translated as "from West to East." Morin refers implicitly here to planets in direct motion.

218 Contrary to Morin's statement, it appears that most astrologers have considered dexter interplanetary aspects to be stronger than sinister ones, other things being equal. But the doctrine, mentioned above, according to which a planet that precedes another in the primary motion "dominates" the planet that follows it, lends some credence to Morin's statement.

219 Correcting Mars' glyph to "Venus."

220 As already mentioned, Morin adopted Tycho Brahe's model of the geocentric cosmos. In that model, the Sun and Moon orbit the central and stationary Earth and the five minor planets orbit the Sun.

221 Mars, Jupiter and Saturn are called the "superior" planets because, in the model of the geocentric cosmos, they move in their spheres above the sphere of the Sun. Mercury and Venus are referred to as the "inferior" planets because they move in their spheres below the sphere of the Sun. Compare Morin's comments on the extrinsic strength of a planet in or approaching apogee to one in or approaching perigee. In the geocentric model, the former is closer than the latter to the *Primum Caelum*. Morin suggests that the closer approach to the *Primum Caelum* may add to a planet's extrinsic influential strength. Similarly, the superior planets orbit on spheres closer to the *Primum Caelum* than the inferior planets. By Morin's reasoning, a superior planet's greater proximity to the *Primum Caelum* may add to its intrinsic strength. See *Astrologia Gallica*, Book 18, trans. A. Louis LaBruzza, Section 1, Chapter 10. And see *Astrologia Gallica*, Book 15, trans. J.H. Holden, Chapter 5, where Morin refers to Saturn as the "highest and most

powerful" of the superior planets, implying that greater height gives greater intrinsic power. Height in general is associated with power, as in the power of the houses more elevated above the horizon, especially the 10th quadrant house. See Morin's discussion of the relative strength of the houses, which takes elevation in relationship to the horizon as a key factor in the intrinsic strength of a house. *Astrologia Gallica*, Book 18, trans. A. Louis LaBruzza, Section 2, Chapter 14. Also, the superior planets are "heavier" than the "lighter" inferior ones because, owing to their larger orbits, they take more time to move through the signs. The heaviness of the superior planets is understood to give them, on that account and other things being equal, greater power than the lighter, inferior planets.

222 This statement might be taken to imply by its terms that the ruler of a house has as its accidental significations the essential significations of the opposite house. Morin denied that this doctrine of accidental significations applies to the house rulers. See Section 2, Chapter 5, p. 82.

223 Morin refers here to a partile interplanetary opposition in which one of the planets is in northern celestial latitude and the other in the same degree of southern latitude. In Morin's view, the latitudes of planets, in aspects and especially in directions, are to be taken into account. A diametrical opposition is particularly strong because it is exact by zodiacal degree and by latitude. The line of such an opposition passes straight through the center of the geocentric World.

Section II, Chapter XII

224 The division of planets into benefic and malefic, Morin says, is their most important division, "if not even the ultimate fundamental of all of astrology." *Astrologia Gallica*, Book 13, Section 2, Chapter 3 (my translation). In his discussion there of the meaning of benefic and malefic, he explains that "all the planets are innately or unqualifiedly good; both because being and good are interchangeable, and because in *Genesis*, Chapter 1 it is said...*And God saw that it was good*." In that Chapter 3, Morin further distinguishes benefic and malefic from good and bad as applied to the celestial bodies.

225 On the planets' accidental analogies, see *Astrologia Gallica*, Book 18, trans. A. Louis LaBruzza, Chapter 9 (based on motion); *Astrologia Gallica*, Book 13, trans. J.H. Holden, Section 1, Chapter 3 (based on position with respect to the Sun, and the time of year and day); *Astrologia Gallica*, Book 16, trans. J.H. Holden, Section 2, Chapter 2 (based on the forms of aspects and their applications and separations); and Book 18, Chapter 10 (based on planets' elevation). More generally on planets' essential and accidental analogies, see Book 13, Section 3, Chapter 3.

226 On the effect of a planet's position oriental or occidental of the Sun and Moon, see *Astrologia Gallica*, Book 18, trans. A. Louis LaBruzza, Section 1, Chapter 8.

227 On the bright fixed stars, see *Astrologia Gallica*, Book 13, trans. J.H. Holden, Section 3, Chapter 5.

228 That is, if the ruler of the 8th or 12th is in the 1st.

229 The bracketed insertion states Morin's apparent implied meaning.

230 Translating: *Atque ex sola tali consideratione Planetarum in prima, vel decima, aut earum dominorum.* It should be noted that, of course, Morin's statement here requires consideration of all planets in the 1st and all those in the 10th, and the rulers of both houses. Note that, of course, consideration of a planet requires consideration of all the principal factors that have a bearing on its significations and effects. This striking statement highlights the great and life-determining importance of the 1st and 10th houses. Their cusps, of course, are the most powerful and determining points in those houses, and, therefore, in general, in the chart as a whole.

231 On circumstances that precede and follow an aspect or conjunction, see the eighth numbered item in Section 2, Chapter 11, p. 117.

232 Translating *scientiae arcana*.

233 Determination by location is in general, of course, the most efficacious mode of determination. Morin says that a planet as here described has the weakest influence on 1st house significations among, it is implied, planets located in the 1st house. Yet, still, by virtue of being in the house, that planet will have a strong influence on the significations of the house.

234 See Section 2, Chapter 4, p. 76, Chapter 5, pp. 85-86 and Chapter 15, p. 138, on the 1st ruler in another house.

235 Morin here states an important qualification of the rule he set out about the 1st ruler in another house in Section 2, Chapters 4 and 5, cited in the note immediately above. See also Section 2, Chapter 9, p. 104 on the power of aspects.

236 The rule Morin states here requires reconciliation with other principles and rules he states elsewhere in Book 21. He attributes notable power and importance to the secondary ruler of a house or planet, a power he recognizes without disqualifying a planet in debility. See Section 2, Chapter 4, pp. 74-75 and Chapter 10, p. 110. Morin recognizes also the power of a debilitated dispositor. See the paragraph that begins with "Sixth," above in the current chapter. And he recognizes the power of aspects received in debility. See, e.g., Section 2, Chapter 8, p. 102 and Chapter 11, pp. 112-13. He also attributes considerable power to a planet in domicile or exaltation to influence the significations of the opposite house where a sign of its exile or fall is found. See, e.g., Section 2, Chapter 2, p. 63 and Chapter 8, pp. 100-01. Note also that he does not disqualify as a principal significator of a house a planet that is in exile in the house, a rule that may reasonably be extrapolated to an aspecting or disposing planet. See Section 2, Chapter 14, p. 136. And see Section 2, Chapter 15, pp. 138-39 for a prioritized list of intrinsic and extrinsic determinations.

Section II, Chapter XIII

237 Translating *nati cujus est altera figura*—"the native whose figure is the other one"—as simply "the latter native." The translation follows this approach throughout this chapter, referring to the "first" and "second," or "former" and "latter," native, or sometimes to the "other" native.

238 Translating *susceptis actionibus & dignitatibus*. If a comma was omitted by error, the translation would be "undertakings, actions and dignities."

239 Translating *scientia*.

Section II, Chapter XIV

240 Morin refers here to the technique of chart extraction, or house derivation. That technique allows the extraction of charts, or the derivation of houses, from the native's chart for others who are significant in the native's life. In the technique, the house in the native's chart that is determined to a significant other, or to a category of significant others, becomes the 1st house of the extracted chart, or the derived 1st house. To use the technique, one counts houses for the significant other, or category of others, from the derived 1st house, just as one counts houses for the native from the native's 1st house. In *Astrologia Gallica*, Book 22, trans. J.H. Holden, Section 4, Chapter 6, Morin sets out and discusses the technique. In that chapter, Morin rejects the practice, adopted by some astrologers, of deriving houses from universal significators.

241 Correcting *decimae* to *duodecimae*.

242 At least one other astrologer derived houses for significant others of the native from the relevant house in the native's figure. See Guido Bonatti, *Liber Astronomiae*, Part II, trans. R. Zoller, Second Tractate, Third Part, Chapter V, "On the Significations of the Twelve Houses." There Bonatti sets out with the significations of the twelve houses derived significations of each. Whether or not Bonatti used the technique of house combination in derived houses to which Morin refers here, Morin is correct at least to the extent that numerous astrologers failed, and still fail, to use the foundational and powerful technique of house combination in derived houses.

243 Correcting *decima* to *duodecima*.

244 See *Astrologia Gallica*, Book 22, trans. J.H. Holden, Section 1, Chapters 3 and 6, and Section 5, Chapter 3.

Section II, Chapter XV

245 Charles de Condren (1588-1641) was a French politician, Catholic priest, and friend of Morin's. With a father who wanted him to enter the military, de Condren decided at the age of 11 years, as a result of a spiritual experience, to join the priesthood. He later renounced his substantial inheritance, and became a member of the Congregation of the Oratory of Jesus, an apostolic society founded in the early 17th century in France. For a time he held the position of General of the Oratory, and was the confessor of the founder of the Oratory and of Prince Gaston, King Louis XIII's younger brother.

Section II, Chapter XVI

246 A coronis is a curved line or flourish that writers and transcribers customarily drew at the end of a book or chapter.

247 Salt, sulfur and mercury are the alchemical *Tria Prima*, the "First Three," also called the "Three Primes," a concept Paracelsus (c. 1493-1541) promoted and used in his work. In rough and summary terms, salt is a contractive force, solid stuff and body (*corpus*); sulfur is an expansive force, a combustible substance, and soul (*anima*); mercury is fluid and changeable, and sometimes is said to transcend dichotomies, including those of solid and liquid states, life and death, and Heaven and Earth, and is sometimes said to represent spirit. The *Tria Prima* appear in alchemical diagrams in a triangle that interacts with the dynamic, ever-interacting and ever-transforming square of the four elements.

248 From ancient times, magnets and the magnetic force were a matter of considerable interest among natural philosophers and others engaged in study of the physical World. Yet from the early years of the 17th century in Europe, magnets and magnetism became a matter of increased interest and study. William Harvey (1578-1657), the well known and innovative English physician and natural philosopher, is the author of the influential *De Magnete, Magneticisque Corporibus, et de Magno Magnete Tellure* ("On the Magnet and Magnetic Bodies, and on that Great Magnet, the Earth"), published in 1600. There he introduced a field theory of magnetism, and held that a magnetic soul animates the living Earth. Throughout the 17th century numerous others studied magnets and developed theories to explain magnetism. The phenomenon of magnetism became in 17th century Europe one focal point of the confrontation between, on one hand, Aristotelian, Scholastic or animistic views of nature and, on the other, emerging modern materialistic and mechanistic views.

249 Translating *ineffabile*, which means "unutterable, indescribable, incapable of expression in words."

250 Translating *genere, specie, & numero.*

251 See *Astrologia Gallica*, Book 17, trans. J.H. Holden, Section 1, Chapter 5. And see Morin, *Astrologicarum domorum cabala*, "The Cabal of the Twelve Houses Astrological," trans. G. Wharton.

252 *Joshua* 10:12-14 tells the story that, at Joshua's entreaty, the Lord caused the Sun to stand still over Gibeon so Israel would have light in which to defeat its enemy.

253 *Daniel* 3 tells the story of three Israelites who refused to worship a golden idol at the command of King Nebuchadnezzar. For their refusal, the king ordered them thrown into an extraordinarily hot blazing furnace. The soldiers who threw the three into the fire died from the heat, but those thrown into the fire survived unharmed with the help of an angel who appeared in the flames.

Bibliography

Abû 'Ali al-Khayyât, *Kitâb al-Mawâlid* ("On the Judgments of Nativities"). Translator Benjamin N. Dykes. *Persian Nativities, vol. 1: Mâshâ'allâh & Abû 'Ali*. Minneapolils, MN: The Cazimi Press, 2009.

Abû 'Ali al-Khayyât, *Kitâb al-Mawâlid* ("The Judgments of Nativities"). Translator James H. Holden. Tempe, AZ: American Federation of Astrologers, Inc., 2008.

Angelis, Alexander De, *In Astrologos coniectores* ("Conjectures Against the Astrologers"). Lyon: B. Zannetti, 1604.

Aristotle, *Aristotle's Physics: A Guided Study*. Translator Joe Sachs. New Brunswick: Rutger's University Press, 1995. (Original work published c. 350 B.C.E.).

Bellanti, Lucio (Bellantius), *Responsiones in disputationes Johannis Pici adversus astrologicam veritatem* ("Reply to the Disputations of Giovanni Pico Against the Truth of Astrology"), published with *De astrologica veritate* ("The Truth of Astrology"). Florence: Geertgen, 1499.

Bonatti, Guido, *Liber Astronomiae,* Part II. Translator Robert Zoller. Berkeley Springs, WV: Golden Hind Press, Project Hindsight, Latin Track, Volume VIII, 1994.

Brennan, Chris, *Hellenistic Astrology: The Study of Fate and Fortune*. Denver, CO: Amor Fati Publications, 2017.

Brittain, Patti Tobin, *Planetary Powers: The Morin Method*. Tempe, AZ: American Federation of Astrologers, Inc., 1980 (2nd ed. 2010).

Cardan, Jerome (Cardanus), *De Interrogationibus Libellis* ("The Little Book of Interrogations"), vol. 5; *Opera omnia* (10 vols.), Lyon: Huguetan & Ravaud, 1663; New York and London: Johnson Reprint, 1967, pp. 553-560.

Cardan, Jerome (Cardanus), *Hier. Cardani in Cl. Ptolomaei de Astrorum ludiciis commentaria* ("Commentary on the Quadripartite"). Basel. 2nd edition, 1578.

Dorotheus of Sidon, *Carmen Astrologicum*. Translator David Pingree. Abingdon, MD: Astrology Classics Publishers, 2005.

Firmicus Maternus, Julius, *Mathesis*. Translator Benjamin N. Dykes. Minneapolis, MN: The Cazimi Press, 2023.

Galilei, Galileo, *Siderius nuncius* ("The Starry Messenger"). Venice: T. Baglionum, 1610.

Gartz, Johann (Garcaeus), *Astrologiae methodus, in qua secundum Ptolemaei, exactissima facillimaque Genituras qualescunque iudicandi ratio traditur* ("A method of astrology, in which, according to Ptolemy, the most exact and easiest method of judging Genitures of any kind is handed down"). Basel: Henricpetrina, 1576.

Giuntini, Franciscus (Junctinus), *In duos posteriors Ptolemaei Quadripartiti libros absolutissima commentaria* ("On the two later books of Ptolemy's Quadripartite, the most complete commentaries"), in the second edition of *Speculum Astrologiae* ("The Mirror of Astrology"). Lyon: Phillipus Tinghus, 1581.

Harvey, William, *De Magnete, Magneticisque Corporibus, et de Magno Magnete Tellure* ("On the Magnet and Magnetic Bodies, and on the Great Magnet, the Earth"). London: Peter Short, 1600.

Hemminga, Sixtus ab, *Astrologiae, ratione et experientia refutatae liber* ("Astrology refuted by reason and experience"). Antwerp: Christophori Plantini, 1583.

Holden, James Herschel, *A History of Horoscopic Astrology: From the Babylonian Period to the Modern Age*. Tempe, AZ: American Federation of Astrologers, Inc., 1996.

Holden, Ralph William, *The Elements of House Division*. Romford, England: L.N. Fowler & Co., Ltd., 1977.

Kepler, Johannes, *De stella nova in pede Serpentaris* ("Of the new star in the foot of the Serpent Handler"). Prague: Paul Sessius, 1606.

Kepler, Johannes, *Judicium de trigono igneo* ("Judgment on the fiery triangle"). *Opera omnia*, 10 vols., vol. 1, pp. 439-451. Frankfurt & Erlangen: Heyder & Zimmer, 1858 (original publication 1603).

Kepler, Johannes, *Somnium, seu opus posthumum De astronomia lunari* ("The Dream, or a posthumous work On lunar astronomy"). Frankfurt, at the expense of the heirs of the author, 1634.

Lewis, Charlton T. and Short, Charles, *A Latin Dictionary*, https://www.perseus.tufts.edu/hopper/text?doc=Perseus:text:1999.04.0059.

Mâshâ'allâh, *Book of Nativities*. Translator Benjamin N. Dykes. Minneapolis: The Cazimi Press, 2008.

Mirandola, Giovanni Pico della, *Disputationes adversus astrologiam divinicatrium* ("Disputations against divinatory astrology"). Bologna: Hectoris, 1496.

Morin, Jean Baptiste, *Ad australes et boreales astrologos pro astrologia restituenda epistolae* ("Letters to northern and southern astrologers for the restitution of astrology"). Paris: J. Moreau, 1628.

Morin, Jean Baptiste, *Astrologicarum domorum Cabala detecta a Joanne Baptista Morino* ("The Cabala of the astrological houses discovered by Jean Baptiste Morin"). Paris: J. Moreau, 1623. Translator George Wharton, 1659, in John Gadbury, *The works of that late most excellent philosopher and astronomer, Sir George Wharton, bar. collected into one volume.* London: Johann Rothman, Chiromancia, 1683. "The Cabal of the Twelve Houses Astrological, from Morinus," pp. 189-208; Ann Arbor: Text Creation Partnership, Early English Books. http://name.umdl.umich.edu/A65576.0001.001. Accessed 4 October 2023.

Morin, Jean Baptiste, *Astrologia gallica principiis & rationibus propriis stabilita atque in XXVI libros distribute* ("French astrology established with its own principles and methods and divided into 26 books"). The Hague: Adrian Vlacq, 1661.

Morin, Jean Baptiste, *Astrologia Gallica*, Books Thirteen, Fourteen, Fifteen and Nineteen. Translator James Herschel Holden. Tempe, AZ: American Federation of Astrologers, Inc., 2006.

Morin, Jean Baptiste, *Astrologia Gallica*, Book Sixteen, *The Rays and Aspects of the Planets*. Translator James Herschel Holden. Tempe, AZ: American Federation of Astrologers, Inc., 2008.

Morin, Jean Baptiste, *Astrologia Gallica*, Book Seventeen, *The Astrological Houses*. Translator James Herschel Holden. Tempe, AZ: American Federation of Astrologers, Inc., 2008.

Morin, Jean Baptiste, *Astrologia Gallica*, Book Eighteen, *The Strengths of the Planets*. Translator Anthony Louis LaBruzza, from the Spanish translation of Pepita Sanchis Llacer. Tempe, AZ: American Federation of Astrologers, Inc., 2004.

Morin, Jean Baptiste, *Astrologia Gallica*, Book Twenty-One, *The Morinus System of Horoscope Interpretation*. Translator Richard S. Baldwin. Tempe, AZ: American Federation of Astrologers, Inc., 1974.

Morin, Jean Baptiste, *Astrologia Gallica*, Book Twenty-Two, *Directions*. Translator, James Herschel Holden. Tempe, AZ: American Federation of Astrologers, Inc., 1994 (2nd ed. 2005).

Morin, Jean Baptiste, *Astrologia Gallica*, Book Twenty-Three, *Revolutions*. Translator, James Herschel Holden. Tempe, AZ: American Federation of Astrologers, Inc., 2002 (2nd ed. 2003).

Morin, Jean Baptiste, *Astrologia Gallica*, Book Twenty-Four, *Progressions and Transits*. Translator James Herschel Holden. Tempe, AZ: American Federation of Astrologers, Inc., 2004.

Morin, Jean Baptiste, *Astrologia Gallica*, Book Twenty-Five, *The Universal Constitutions of the* Caelum. Translator James Herschel Holden. Tempe, AZ: American Federation of Astrologers, Inc., 2008.

Morin, Jean Baptiste, *Astrologia Gallica*, Book Twenty-Six, *Astrological Interrogations and Elections*. Translator James Herschel Holden. Tempe, AZ: American Federation of Astrologers, Inc., 2010.

Morin, Jean Baptiste, *Astronomia iam a fundamentis integre et exacte restitute* ("Astronomy now completely and exactly restored from the foundations"). Paris: At the place of the author, 1640.

Morin, Jean Baptiste, *Astrosynthesis: The Rational System of Horoscope Interpretation according to Morin de Villefranche*. Translator Lucy Little. New York: Zoltan Mason Emerald Books, 1974. (A translation of Henri Selva's French paraphrase of an abridgment of Book 21.)

Morin, Jean Baptiste, "Jean Baptiste Morin's Comments on House Division in his *Remarques Astrologiques*." Translator James Herschel Holden, Journal of Research of the A.F.A. 6, Nos. 1 & 2 (1991), pp. 19-35. (Available at https://forumonastrology.com/foa/newmain.html. Accessed 4 October 2023.)

Morin, Jean Baptiste, *La Théorie des Déterminantions Astrologiques de Morin de Villefrance conduisant à une Méthode rationelle our l'Interprétation du Thême Astrologique* ("The theory of astrological determinations of Morin de Villefranche leading to a rational method for the interpretation of the astrological figure"). Translator and editor Henri Selva. Paris: Bodin, 1897. (This work, which has been several times republished, is a French paraphrase of an abridgment of Book 21 of Morin's *Astrologia Gallica*.)

Morin, Jean Baptiste, *Ma Vie Devant les Astres* ("My Life Before the Stars"). Translator Jean Hieroz. Nice: Éditions Cahiers Astrologiques, 1943. (A collection of Morin's comments on his life from *Astrologia Gallica* translated into French.)

Morin, Jean Baptiste, *Remarques astrologiques de Jean-Baptiste Morin sur le Commentaire du* Centiloque *de Ptolémée ou la seconde partie de l'*Uranie *de Messire Nicolas de Bourdin, marquis de Villennes, etc.* ("Astrological Remarks of Jean-Baptiste Morin on the Commentary on the *Centiloquy of Ptolemy or the second part of The Urania by Mr. Nicolas de Bourdin, Marquis de Villennes, etc."*). Editor Jacques Halbronn. Paris: Retz, 1976 (original publication: Paris: P. Ménard, 1657). (This edition includes an introduction, notes and a bibliography of Morin's publications.)

Origanus, David (David Tost), *Astrologia Naturalis Sive Tractatus de Effectibus Astrorum Absolutissimus* ("Natural Astrology Or the Most Absolute Treatise on the Effects of the Stars"). Marseilles: Giovanni Baptista, 1645.

Pseudo-Ptolemy, *Centiloquy*, Translator Georgius Trapezuntius. Cologne: Gymnich, 1544.

Ptolemy, Claudius, *Tetrabiblos*. Editor & translator F.E. Robbins. Cambridge, MA & London: The Loeb Classical Library, Harvard University Press and Wm. Heinemann Ltd., 1940 (2nd ed. 1980).

Schwickert, Friedrich "Sinbad" and Weiss, Adolf, *Conerstones of Astrology*. (No translator identified.) Dallas: Sangreal Foundation, Inc., 1972. Reportedly a translation of Weiss' Spanish translation of Schwickert and Weiss's *Bausteine der Astrologie*, vol. 2, *Dei astrologische Synthese* ("Astrological Synthesis").

Wharton, George, "Something farther touching the Doctrine of Eclipses, Chiefly, from Morinus," *The works of that late most excellent philosopher and astronomer, Sir George Wharton, bar. collected into one volume.* Editor John Gadbury. London: Johann Rothman, Chiromancia, 1683, pp. 104-110. Ann Arbor: Text Creation Partnership, Early English Books. http://name.umdl.umich.edu/A65576.0001.001.Accessed 4 October 2023.

Wharton, George, "Teaching how Astrology may be restored; from Morinus," *The works of that late most excellent philosopher and astronomer, Sir George Wharton, bar. collected into one volume.* Editor John Gadbury. London: Johann Rothman, Chiromancia, 1683, pp. 184-189. Ann Arbor: Text Creation Partnership, Early English Books. http://name.umdl.umich.edu/A65576.0001.001. Accessed 4 October 2023.

Index of Persons

Albohali (Abû 'Ali al-Khayyât)
  example figures, see Appendix of Charts
  judges fortune and misfortune from the triplicity rulers of the sect light, 95–97
Aristotle
  power of the inferior world is governed from the superior regions, 49
  sublunary things need celestial ones, 34
  Sun and man beget man, 30, 49
Bellantius, Lucio, 26
  re accidents of children in the figures of parents, 133
  re principal significator, 56, 135–37
  re universal cause, 36
  rejects a planet in a house as principal significator because it may be in exile or fall, 135
  rejects the sign in a house as principal significator because he supposes a sign does not act in itself, 135
  supposes the force of planets varies through the houses rather than through the signs, 135-36
  supposes the force of the planets is impressed upon the *primum mobile* and remains there, 22
Cardanus, Jerome
  Aphorism 166 re planets in triplicity, 98
  Book of Interrogations, 40
  Book of Revolutions, 15
  Commentary, 2, 3
  refers to universal significators as significators according to substance, 1, 14, 135
  ridicules misuse of the Moon's universal significations, 15–16
  takes judgment of the father from the celestial state of the Sun or Saturn, character from the Moon and her dispositor, and inborn talent from Mercury and his dispositor, 16, 18
  wants the stars to be only causes and not signs, 40
De Angelis, Alexander
  supposes the whole *Caelum* concurs in any and all sublunary effects, 45, 50
de Condren, Charles
  had a Jovial nature from Sagittarius rising, 138
  nativity, see Appendix of Charts
Des Hayes, Louis
  nativity, see Appendix of Charts

Index of Persons

re benefic badly conditioned in an unfortunate house, 61

Chavigny, Count of
nativity, see Appendix of Charts
re two malefics strong in a fortunate house, 71

Concini, Concino, Marquis d'Ancre, 79

d'Effiat, Henri
benefic with a malefic (and a 12th ruler) in the 8th, 61
malefic in domicile in an unfortunate house, 58
many planets in 8th prefigured remarkable 8th house accidents, 69
Mars is most efficacious in d'Effiat's 8th from his analogy and rulership, 69
much to attend to re the causes of his violent death, 62
nativity, see Appendix of Charts

Firmicus Maternus, re what planets do in the domicile of another planet, 29

Garcaeus, Johannes, *Book of the Judgment of Genitures*, re planet in the 1st house as the principal significator of character, 56

Gaston, Prince
efficacy of dignity of exaltation in another house, 94
exalted malefic in an unfortunate house, 58
malefics well conditioned in an unfortunate house, 62
nativity, see Appendix of Charts
two malefics strong in a fortunate house, 71

Gustavus Adolphus, King of Sweden
benefic and malefic rays of a malefic in unfortunate celestial and terrestrial state, 107
benefic ray of a malefic, 106
direction of the Midheaven to the square of Saturn in exile in the 8th, 116
Horoscope ruler Jupiter applying to the opposition of Saturn exiled in the 8th and struck by the square of Mars, 108
malefic well conditioned in an unfortunate house, 62
nativity, see Appendix of Charts

Hemminga, Sixtus ab, supposes the whole *Caelum* concurs in any and all sublunary effects, 45

Henri Bourbon, King of France and Navarre, 79

Junctinus, Francisco, *Comment*, re planet in the 1st house as the principal significator of character, 56

Kepler, Johannes, 23-26, 38-40
attributes to animals, plants and Earth itself a divine faculty that senses intelligible celestial configurations, 23
Book on the Fiery Triangle, 23, 24
contradicts himself when he says the celestial constitution is imprinted on the animal faculty and rouses a person to action but denies that a causal power pours from the *Caelum*, 39
dream about the Moon, 24
faculty he posits is alien to the dignity of intellect and reason, 39

    fails to prove that a divine faculty senses celestial objects and moves sublunary things to action, 25–26

    incongruously denies that the outpouring of real virtue accounts for the conformity of nature with the celestial figure, 26

    locates the whole force of a celestial configuration in sublunary nature, 23

    Of the new star, 24

    says that planets' aspects only move the faculties of sublunary things as objects move the senses, 38

Louis XIII, King, 69, 79

Luynes, Lord of, 79

Montmorency, Duke
    nativity, see Appendix of Charts
    re malefic badly conditioned in an unfortunate house, 59, 63

Morin, J.B.
    10th ruler Saturn in 12th, 87
    11th ruler in 12th often turned friends to enemies, 87
    benefic 8th ruler in 12th with Saturn, 62
    benefic Jupiter's trine to Mars and conjunction with Saturn did not remove all malignity, 121
    efficacy of dignity of exaltation, 94
    father in Morin's nativity, and harm from the mother, 17
    from 10th ruler Saturn in 12th Morin left the profession of medicine, 87
    illness from directions to Saturn in the 12th and to his square were unrelated to the houses Saturn rules, 79
    in Morin's 12th Jupiter is most efficacious from rulership and Saturn from analogy, 69
    Jupiter in domicile and Venus exalted in 12th gave favorable 12th house effects but unfavorable 6th house ones, 100–101
    many planets in 12th prefigures many remarkable 12th house accidents, 68–69
    Mercurial nature from Mercury's partile sextile to the Horoscope, 138
    nativity, see Appendix of Charts
    Richelieu as his hidden enemy, 17, 69

Origanus, David,
    wants Mars and Saturn in Aries to be effectively warm to the same degree, 12
    re planet in the 1st house as the principal significator of character, 56

Pico della Mirandola
    supposes it is believed the whole *Caelum* concurs in any and all sublunary effects, 45, 50
    writing against astrology, 22, 36, 133, 135

Ptolemy, Claudius, 19, 42, 77, 130
    judges of particular persons or things from universal significators, 2, 14, 18
    Quadripartite, 3, 14, 56, 93
    rejects the ancient method of determination, though he is frequently compelled to use it, 2
    relies on universal significators, and gives many significations to one significator, 15

wants judgment of the father to be from the celestial state of the Sun or Saturn, and while the Sun is in Leo must suppose that all children born will have a fortunate father, 16

was deceived by accidental significations of 6th and 11th, 100

Rantzau, Heinrich, re what planets do in the domicile of another planet, 29

Richelieu, Cardinal

12th ruler Venus near the Midheaven within her orb of virtue, 87

benefic badly conditioned in an unfortunate house, 61

direction to malefic ray of a benefic in unfavorable celestial state in an unfortunate house, 106

Mars in 1st and (1st ruler) Venus in 10th in fixed signs, from which he always had a mind for wars and maintained power, 123

Martial nature from Mars in the 1st, 138

Morin's hidden enemy, 17, 69

nativity, see Appendix of Charts

Stofler, Johannes, re what planets do in the domicile of another planet, 29

Tronson, Louis

causes that denied siblings foretold death of older siblings, 55

honors from directions of the Midheaven to Moon in the 10th, and of the Moon, were unrelated to her rulership in the 9th, 80

Jupiter in 10th and ruler of other houses prefigured honors but they did not happen through houses he ruled, 79

many planets in 10th prefigured remarkable 10th house accidents, 69

nativity, see Appendix of Charts

planets acted first by location in 3rd and in consequence combined their signification by location with those by rulership in 2nd and 4th, 80–81

several planets in the same house and their ruler outside it, 71

Subject Index

Morin's translated text is indexed here; the translator's introduction and notes are not. This index is to provide page references to topics, and is intended to provide a partial summary and partial guide to theories, doctrines and rules Morin states and his reasoning in support of them.

A

Analogy
    1st ruler with the Sun, 2nd ruler with Jupiter or 8th ruler with Mars, 89
    accidental analogy of direction and speed of motion, 119
    analogy in accord with or contrary to determinations, 18, 19, 57, 70, 77, 123
    benefic planet in 10th with or trine Sun or in 2nd trine Jupiter, 66
    by analogy a planet does not signify one thing more than another, but does refer to qualities of things, 15
    contrary analogy of Venus in 12th or Saturn in 10th, 123
    exaltation is analogous to honors, 60
    Jupiter in 2nd, Sun in 10th or 1st, Saturn in 12th, Mars in 7th or Venus in 7th or 5th, 123
    malefic planet in 8th with, square or opposite Mars, or in 12th square Saturn, 66
    natural analogy is essential and universal, and indifferent to particular sublunary things, 16
    of a planet that accords with its dispositor's house location, 84
    of a planet to a house it rules or aspects, 122
    of a planet to which planets in or ruling a house apply, 18
    of a planet engaged with a planet in or ruling a house, 30, 89
    of well conditioned benefics in congruent places, 96
    particular determinations work in full measure when they concur with analogy, 17
    planets act particularly through their determinations, not through their analogy, 78
    planets are universal significators of things with which they have an analogy, 1
    planets especially promote or signify those things with which they have an analogy, 16
    planets have an essential analogy with the various classes of sublunary things, 15
    planets share their analogies with diverse earthly things, 16
    planets' analogical virtue is the same as their influential or essential virtue, 15
    universal determination through analogy often concurs with the particular one through the houses, 17

Apheta, election of, 93

Subject Index

Aspects
- 1st ruler Jupiter in 2nd opposite Saturn in 8th, 108–9
- are determined with respect to particular things in two ways, 104
- are opposition, quincunx, trine, square, sextile and dodectile, 103
- aspect acts in itself but does so by virtue of the planet from which it flows, 37
- aspects act or a planet acts through its aspects, 104
- benefic in 10th applying by body to an exalted Saturn, 71
- between a planet and its dispositor, 95
- by aspect a planet always influenes by reason of its nature and celestial state but not always by its location and rulership at the same time, 107
- by its rays other than by body a planet acts only through the eleven parts of the *Primum Caelum* determined from the planet's body, 103
- by their aspects planets influence threefold, 107
- by their aspects planets may remarkably or moderately increase, diminish or corrupt the power of other significators, 109
- concordant aspect between a planet and its dispositor when they agree with each other in nature and determination, 122
- conjunction is not properly speaking an aspect but is only the beginning of the aspects, 105
- conjunction is *per se* indifferent to the quality of its effect, 105
- connection with another planet in strong, weak or intermediate state, 120
- force of action in the aspects depends on the formal virtue of the aspecting planet, 104
- general statements about aspects' effects, 105
- into a house from its ruler, 96. 106
- Jupiter and Mars well conditioned and conjoined in 10th or 2nd, 109
- kind of effect of a planet by body or aspect is known through its essential significations and its places in the figure, 109
- may be between planets or to house cusps, 104
- minor aspects rarely act unless partile, 110
- mutually determine each other to the houses of their location, 108-09
- places in the *Caelum* determined to a planet's aspects act according to a threefold consideration, 103
- planet in a house can be determined again by the nature and analogy of another planet through conjunction or aspect, 66
- planets act in accord with the houses where their aspects fall or to which the planets are determined, 103
- planets can act more strongly by aspect than by rulership, 104
- planets in mutual aspect act together as partners, 29, 103–4, 119
- planets that aspect the same significator act as partners, 114
- power of aspects, especially in directions, is known by experience, 103
- ray of a planet's body is called a conjunction, 103
- same aspect signifies diverse things, 109
- terrestrial state of a planet in aspect is twofold, 107
- through its aspects a planet acts universally in diverse ways, 103

Aspects compared
- application or approach and separation or departure, 108, 111, 112, 115
- applying vs. separating is a greater distinction than dexter vs. sinister, 111, 112
- aspects between planets as they move in secondary motion are compared, 112

197

Morin's Book 21

aspects of different kinds from a single planet are compared in their *per se* and accidental strength, 114
aspects of the same are kind compared with respect to beneficence and maleficence, 116
aspects of two planets to the same significator are compared in five ways, 114–15
both planets in an aspect are taken into account as partners, 114
consider the strength of the following aspect, 117
degree of the prevailing planet's victory requires proportionate attention to the houses where its aspects fall, 114
dexter aspects to house cusps are more efficacious than sinister ones, 111
dexter or preceding and sinister or following, 111
direct planet that applies to a cusp by primary motion departs by secondary motion from the part of the *Caelum* on it, 111
efficacy of an aspecting planet by reason of house location vs. rulership, 104
house cusp itself vs. part of the *Caelum* on it, 111
in application force is directed toward the aspect but in departure it is slackened, 111
planet determined in more or more efficacious ways to the house of the aspect or to its contrary prevails by terrestrial state, 113
planet in stronger celestial state prevails by that measure over the other, 113
planet nearer the significator is stronger, especially if it attains union first, 115
planet that applies to another prevails by that measure over the other, 113–14
planets are moved to the house cusps by the primary motion, 111
planets in mutual aspect are compared in four ways to determine which prevails, 112–14
preceding planet is not stronger than the one following unless it also applies to the latter, 111
prevailing planet in an aspect predominates by a little or by much, 114
Sun and Moon prevail in dignity over the others, and the Sun over the Moon, 113
same kind of aspect from the same planet is compared to itself as the placement of the planets varies by sign and house location, 112
sinister interplanetary aspects are considered to be *per se* more efficacious than dexter ones, 112
stronger aspects frustrate and suppress the force of weaker ones, 110
superior planets prevail in dignity over inferior ones, 113
to Horoscope or Midheaven vs. to their rulers, 28
two aspects of different kinds are compared in strength in two ways, 114-15
when one planet applies to another the latter also is effective, 108
with respect to the planets' house rulerships, 117

Aspects compared for beneficence and maleficence
application of a fortunate or unfortunate ray, 120
aspects of Jupiter and of Saturn from domicile, exile or an intermediate state, 116
badly conditioned planet applies to a badly or well conditioned planet, 122
badly conditioned planet in or ruling the 1st or 10th applies to a badly or well conditioned one, 122
benefic and malefic rays of a well or badly conditioned planet, 107
benefic or malefic aspects from benefics or malefics, 104

Subject Index

benefic or malefic rays of a benefic in malefic celestial and terrestrial state, 106

benefic or malefic rays of a benefic or malefic in fortunate or unfortunate houses, 106

benefic rays of a malefic in unfortunate celestial and terrestrial state, 106–7

benefit of any planet flows through the trine, sextile and dodectile, 105

by their aspects planets confer benefit or misfortune or remove it, 108

by its aspects to planets or cusps, or by directions, a planet makes their significations fortunate or unfortunate, 108

conditions under which Jupiter is most beneficial for life, 115

conjunction of benefic planets is in general beneficial and of malefics unfortunate, 105

departing from a benefic or malefic aspect or planet to a benefic or malefic one, 117

each planet by its aspects benefits and causes misfortune at the same time, 105

efficacy of benefic or malefic aspect forms compared, 105

favorable aspect of a benefic received in dignity vs. unfavorable aspect of a malefic received in exile, 102

Jupiter in 1st trine the Midheaven, plus ruling the Midheaven, plus trine Sun in 10th, 107–8

malefic aspect of a malefic into a house it rules, 106

malefics in unfavorable connection to a luminary or to rulers of the Horoscope or Midheaven, 77

Mars in the 2nd ruling the 8th almost always kills, 106

misfortune flows from the opposition, square and quincunx, 105

Moon departing from Saturn and applying to no other, 17

mutually received in domicile, 96

opposition of Saturn in Leo and Sun in Aquarius is the worst and the trine of Jupiter in Pisces and the Moon in Cancer is best, 117

partile or diametrical opposition between Mars and Saturn, 116

planet benefic by nature badly conditioned by sign in the malefic ray of a malefic, 107

planet malefic by nature and sign in the malefic aspect of a malefic by nature or determination vs. in the benefic aspect of a benefic, 107

planet's location congruent with the benefit or misfortune of the house it aspects, 107

same aspect can be at the same time beneficial for one thing and unfortunate for another, 107

same kind of aspect from the same planet in fortunate vs. unfortunate celestial state, 115

Saturn or Mars afflicting planets in or ruling the 1st or 10th or 8th or 12th, especially the Sun or Moon, 116

some aspects are suitable to benefit and others are maleficent, 105

square or opposition of Saturn or Mars in unfavorable celestial state and determined to unfortunate houses, 116

trine or sextile of benefics in favorable celestial state determined to and aspecting fortunate houses, 116

Astrologers

abused the analogical virtue of the planets, 15

Adam and Noah, 2, 3

all used the four major forms of aspect, 110

aphorisms of, 2, 29, 30

Arabs predicted much from triplicity rulers, 95

Arabs, Greeks and Latins, 139

attended to Mercury and his dispositor for inborn talent without regard to his particular determinations, 19

deceived by accidental significations of 6th and 11th, 100
deceived by frequent concurrence of analogies with particular determinations, 17
did not recognize determination of the celestial bodies as the primary cause of effects, 3, 139
disregarded multiple significations of each aspect, 109
Egyptians, Chaldeans and Arabs, 1, 2
election of rulers based on the power of dignities, 93–94
err re elemental natures of planets in signs, 12
err when they direct universal significators, 1, 14
err when they say the square and opposition of benefics are of no harm, 106
err when they take particular things from universal significators, 14–15
extracted figures for others, 130
fail to count derived houses from the other's derived 1st, 131
fictions or figments of, 1, 2, 3, 139
good contained in their books is here restored, 139
great error of misuse of planets' analogies now exposed, 20
Greeks, 2, 139
have assumed that universal significators signify particular sublunary things, 14
have been principally occupied with universal significators, 1
intermingle the true method with fictions, 2
judged from fictions alien to nature, 1
looked at four significators of things, 135
method of determination unknown to, 31
offer many examples of use of triplicity rulers of the sect light, 97
re power of dignity by domicile, exaltation and triplicity, 95
tables on aspects omit distinctions among similar aspects, 112
taught by experience, 93
truth compellingly directed them to locations and rulerships of planets in houses, 139
uncertainty among them about triplicity rulers, 95
went astray in belief that celestial state particularizes, 18

Astrologia Gallica
Book 2, 104; Book 7, 7, 21, 33; Book 8, 8; Book 9, 10; Book 10, 45; Book 12, 25, 42, 140, 143; Book 13, 1, 10, 15, 16, 52, 141; Book 14, 8, 12, 21, 22, 51, 103, 141; Book 15, 73, 95, 97; Book 16, 22; Book 17, 8, 9; Book 18, 70, 77, 88; Book 19, The Elements of Astrology, 10, 12, 15, 25, 50, 58, 61, 78, 112; Book 20, 8, 32, 34, 35, 36, 73

Author of nature, 7, 10

B

Book of Interrogations. See Cardanus, Jerome in the Index of Persons

Book of Revolutions. See Cardanus, Jerome in the Index of Persons

Book on the Fiery Triangle. See Kepler, Johannes in the Index of Persons

C

Cause
a universal cause is indifferent to its accidental effects and determinable to them, 7
cause concurring with its inferiors is universal, 33
cause of a cause is a cause of what is later caused, 39
celestial bodies act as particular causes when they produce physical effects without the concurrence of inferior agents, 7

celestial bodies act as universal causes when they produce physical effects with inferior agents, 7
false definitions of universal and particular causes have crept into astrology, 33
first and second causes, 22
inferior and particular causes yield to superior and universal ones, 43
innumerable and diverse simultaneous effects do not make a cause formally universal, 34, 36
is that which produces an effect, 37
planets are the cause of the cause of accidents, 42
Primum Caelum seen as a whole is the first and most universal physical cause, 33
sign seen in its material nature as part of the *Primum Caelum* is a universal cause, 33
signs and planets act as universal causes when they concur with an inferior cause and act as particular causes when they simply pour out their virtue or act as partners, *33–36*
the same virtue causes different effects in different things and different circumstances, 10

Celestial bodies
are indifferent with respect to individual sublunary things, 1, 78
contain in their eminent virtue the powers and effects of sublunary bodies, 34
formal effects are present in them from their essence, 7
formal vs. accidental effects of, 7
gender polarity of, 17
have something peculiar to themselves that cannot be conferred by sublunary causes, 34
influence sublunary things only through the houses, 2
particular effects they produce without an inferior agent are present in their essence, 7
particular effects they produce with inferior agents are accidental to them, 7
suffer no mixture from the primary houses, 11
were essentially determined to their formal effects by the Author of nature, 7

Celestial bodies and divine will, *140–43*
as God concurs in all that the celestial bodies cause so the *Primum Caelum* concurs in all the planets cause, 141
both act sometimes as universal causes and sometimes as particular ones, 143
cause at the same time whatever can be caused, 141
cause diverse things in diverse subjects and in the same one, 142
celestial bodies are as God's vicars in nature, 140
celestial bodies more perfectly imitate God's way of acting than any other physical cause, 140, 143
concur in all natural effects, 141
God has impressed the imprints of his omnipotence and wisdom on the celestial bodies, 140
God subjects to his will and the celestial bodies subject to their influential rule all that they cause, 143
power of action of both is something simple and ineffable, 141
sublunary bodies are subject to their power, 141

Celestial state. *See also* Planets in domicile; Planets, Dignities and debilities of
badly conditioned planet in any house, 58
badly conditioned planet's influx is corrupted, 31, 58, 59, 99, 100, 116, 119
badly conditioned planet's influx is weakened or corrupted, 30, 64
benefics in favorable or unfavorable celestial state, 31, 57-60, 60-62, 63-65, 69, 70-71, 73, 84, 85-87, 88,

95-96, 99, 100-01, 104, 106-09, 113, 115, 116, 119-22, 123, 124, 136, 137
by their mutual aspects planets help or weaken or corrupt each other, 30
compare Sun in Leo trine Jupiter in the absence of malefics with Sun in Aquarius square or opposite malefics, 31
conditions a planet universally, 99
congruence with a planet's own nature, 58
dispositor's celestial state, 57
does not particularize, 16, 18, 30
effect of malefics' greater efficacy by celestial state, 58
factors of favorable and of unfavorable celestial state, 57
feral planet, 120
maleficence or beneficence, and efficacy, of malefics in favorable or unfavorable celestial state, 27, 31, 53, 54, 57-59, 60, 62-65, 70-71, 77, 84, 88, 92, 99-100, 106-09, 113-17, 119-22, 123, 124, 128, 129, 134, 136
malefic in unfavorable connection with the Sun or Moon, or the Horoscope or Midheaven or their rulers, 121
malefics' connection with benefics will not remove all malignity, 121
Mars in favorable or unfavorable celestial state in the 11th, 53
moderate condition, 27, 59, 60, 62, 63, 99
most fundamental factors of celestial state, 31
persists while sublunary effects change, 16, 19
planet well or badly conditioned in several ways, 59
planets are more efficacious the more congruent their celestial state is with their nature, 58
realizations accord with nature and celestial state, 57
Saturn will always harm but more so when he is in unfavorable celestial state, 115-16

well conditioned planet in any house, 101–2

Centiloquy
Aphorism 47 on combination of planets in two nativities, 126, 129
Aphorism 5 on averting effects of the stars, 41
Aphorism 72 on rearing of children and way of life, 98

Chart combinations
Aphorism 47 of the Centiloquy can often be false, 129
discernment in these judgment is in making possible and congruent combinations and defining their effects, 128–29
effects of these combinations happen as much to the older as to the younger native, 129
is looked at as much by signs as by planets, 126
occur also through aspects between planets in the two figures, 129
planet of one figure in any house or with any planet of the other, 128
planet of one figure in the 1st of the other, 127–28
planets in one figure are seen in the houses of the other or with planets in the other, 127
sign in 1st of one figure in 1st of the other, 126
sign in 2nd, 3rd, 4th &c of one figure in 1st or another house of the other, 127

Commentary. See Cardanus, Jerome in the Index of Persons

D

Determination, Accidental
celestial bodies act only as they are determined to particular things, 139
determination of the celestial bodies is the primary cause of their effects, 139
primary houses actively determine the celestial bodies but those bodies

Subject Index

passively determine the essential significations of the houses, 138

sublunary bodies actively determine celestial bodies and celestial bodies passively determine sublunary things, 21, 28

sublunary things determine celestial causes, 1

universal mode of action springs from the particular and the universal is determined by particulars, 59

Determination, Accidental of planets and fixed stars, *29–30*

planets and fixed stars are efficient causes that are accidentally determined in various ways, 29

planets and the signs they occupy mutually determine each other, like two men steering the same ship, 29

planets are accidentally determined by the receiving subject and by the houses, 30

planets are determined by coming together with other planets and fixed stars, 29

two of these accidental determination are universal and two are particular, 29–30

when two stars come together by body or aspect they act as partners that mutually determine each other, 29

Determination, Accidental of the *Primum Caelum*, 21–28

by planets and fixed stars in their motion under the *primum mobile*, 21–22

by the nature of the planets through the signs at the beginning of the World, 21

difficult to define the means by which the virtue of the planets and fixed stars remains in their natal place, 22

force of the planets does not remain in the *Caelum* through an impression, 22–23

in two ways universally in two ways particularly, 28

particularly by sublunary receivers and by the houses, 27

radical places of the planets remain in the *Caelum* by virtue of a determination, 26

to the nature of the planets and fixed stars at a birth remains for as long as the native lives, 73

Determination, Formal of planets and fixed stars, to their proper natures and formal virtues, 10

Determination, Formal of the *Primum Caelum*, to the virtue most universal and proper to itself, 7–8

Determination, Local

benefic or malefic planet and its dispositor determined to benefit or misfortune, 121-22

by connection with house rulers, 17, 18

by dignity (rulership) is threefold, 30

by house location is the most efficacious mode, 49, 56

by location or rulership, 1, 16–17, 18, 49, 53, 88, 116, 122

by location, rulership or aspect, 2, 19, 45, 46, 52, 115, 118, 121, 136

by rulership or aspect, 19, 122, 124

determination by rulership or aspect can be stronger than by location, 122

essential significations of each house are determined intrinsically and extrinsically, 138

four modes of local determination, 1, 2, 30

houses particularly determine the *Caelum*, 27

intrinsic and extrinsic determination each occurs in nine ways, 138–39

intrinsic and extrinsic determination are simple or composite, 139

intrinsic and extrinsic determinations prioritized according to strength, 138-39

Jupiter well conditioned in the 7th will accidentally signify wealth from

marriage, in the 10th wealth from the profession, 137
most fundamental factors of, 31
of a planet connected to planets in or ruling a house, 30–31
particular significations require particular determinations, 2, 18, 19
particularizes a planet's significations and effects, 31
planet determined to the same or congruent kind of effect in several ways, 122
planet may signify more efficaciously the house it opposes than does the ruler of that house outside it, 104
planet with multiple or strong determinations to a house, 19
planet's determination, but not its virtue, varies as it is moved from house to house, 137
planets can act more strongly by aspect than by rulership, 104
particular effects depend on the receiving subject and the planet's terrestrial state, 30
presence of a planet is more efficacious than rulership of an absent one, 55, 56, 65, 67, 75, 76, 86
terrestrial state is determination in the celestial figure, 78
with respect to the four angles does not particularize, 19

Determination, Method of
ancient method must be completely restored, 3
became impure and corrupted, 2
is a method of divination, 2
is ancient, 2
is the primary foundation of judicial astrology, 3
whole natural science of judging or predicting consists of this method of determination, 3

Directions
demonstrate that the planets determine the *Primum Caelum* to their nature and condition, 73
error to direct universal significators, 1, 14
fortunate or unfortunate effects of, 108
of the Horoscope or Midheaven vs. of their rulers, 28
of universal significators, 136

Directions, revolutions and transits, show the efficacy of the accidental determinations of the *Caelum*, 22

Dispositors
effect when a planet and its dispositor agree with each other in nature and determination, 122
if a planet is in a foreign domicile consider its dispositor, 119
of a planet in its exaltation, 94–95
planet acts by reason of its dispositor's celestial state and house location, 84
planet acts in dependence on the ruler of the sign it occupies, 74
planet connected to its dispositor, 120-121
planet in a sign acts with the sign's domicile and exaltation ruler, 95
planet's aspect with its dispositor, 95
properly speaking no planet rules another planet, 74
secondary ruler of a house or planet, 74-75, 110

Dodecatemoria, 9, 33

E

Earth, 8, 9, 16, 19, 21, 22, 23, 24, 25, 26, 30, 35, 37, 38, 39, 61, 88, 95, 99, 113, 120, 141, 142

Eclipse, 49, 131
election of the ruler of, 93

Ecliptic, 8, 54

Elements
at World's end the elements will melt in fire, 21
fire, 8, 21, 26, 143
the four elements, 140

Elemental qualities
heat, 7, 26

Kepler says planets act only to illuminate
and heat, 23
of Saturn, 12-13
Primum Caelum eminently contains the
elemental qualities, 9
Saturn's harmful elemental qualities
come out excessively in Capricorn
but mix in due proportion in
Aquarius, 13
Sun is a particular cause of heat and
illumination, 7, 35
Sun was essentially determined to
illuminate and heat, 10
Sun's illumination and heat are formally
elemental, 8
would still pour from the planets in the
absence of the *Primum Caelum*, 7-9
Elemental nature, 12-13
acts especially on temperament and on
universal constitutions of the air,
12, 97
duplex domiciles of minor planets have
contrary elemental natures, 12
elemental qualities of the celestial or
influential nature of the minor
planets and their formal elemental
qualities, 13
elemental vs. celestial or influential
nature, 8
is both formal, extrinsic or manifest and
eminent, intrinsic or latent, 13
planets' elemental nature is not altered
by the signs they occupy, 12
Primum Caelum was accidentally
determined to its elemental nature,
21
signs act elementally in accord with
the nature to which they were
determined at the beginning of the
World, 12-13
Equator
houses are divided along the equator, 8
is the circle proper to the *Primum
Caelum*, 8

F

Fate and self-determination, *40–44*

about some things extrinsic to him the
native freely determines with his
actions, 42
by their actions sublunary bodies
become particular causes of their
own effects, 21
for the very reason that the celestial
constitution at birth is a cause it can
be resisted, 41
no one should be frightened by the fatal
subjection to the natal figure, 42
it is arduous and beyond nature to resist
natural inclinations, 43
most things follow the stars because a
person is often ignorant of self and
of what is to be, 43
predictions are only conjectural, 43
stars do not signify opposition to their
force by foresight and divinely
illumined reason, 42
Fixed stars
accidentally determine the *Primum
Caelum*, 21
act as universal and particular causes, 35
are determined by the houses, 51
bright stars produce remarkable and
unexpected effects, 121
Eye of the Bull, 29, 61, 106
Head of Medusa, 61
Heart of the Scorpion, 29
Pleiades, 61

H

Horoscope, 3, 9, 12, 19, 23, 27, 28, 34, 53,
54, 56, 58, 74, 79, 80, 84, 94, 101, 102,
104, 106, 111, 113, 114, 115, 121, 124-
25, 127, 135
beginning of the 1st space vs. degree of
the sign on it, 54, 111
directions of, 54, 79, 106
life is judged from the Horoscope and
its ruler, 3
malefics in and sending malefic rays to
the ruler, 58
particular signs in, 27, 34, 54
planet in as principal significator of
character, 56

primary significator of life, 106
sign on it signifies the native more efficaciously than its ruler or a planet in it, 28

Horoscope ruler, 2, 3, 17, 18, 19, 30, 42, 53, 61, 62, 74, 75, 77, 80, 84, 85, 90, 94, 98, 100, 102, 104, 107, 108, 114, 116, 121, 124-25, 138
analogy of a planet to which it applies, 18
analogy of a planet with it, 30
aspects to it, 17
in unfavorable condition, 74, 100

House combinations
accord with the nature and state of the combining planet and the condition of the native, 83
analogy of a planet that accords with the house location of its dispositor, 84
combine things similar or contrary to the significations of the combined houses, 83
combining planet badly conditioned in or ruling fortunate houses or in an unfortunate house, 88
combining planet in the privots, 87
congruence of the combining planet and its state with significations of the combined houses, 87
determination by rulership contrary to that by location, 66
dispositor's celestial state and location in another house, 84–85
house with the greater analogy to its ruler takes precedence among the houses a planet rules, 92
important to know whether the ruler of one house in another always combines the houses, 78
is the subject that occurs most frequently in all of judicial astrology, 73
multiple houses combined, 108
must be possible if they are to occur, 83
nature and state of the combining planet, 83, 86

nature, analogies, and celestial and terrestrial state of the combining planet, 88
of houses with congruent or contrary significations, 87
planet can act through its determination by body without acting at the same time through its determination by rulership, 78-79
planet in a house can be determined again by the determinations of another planet through conjunction or aspect, 66
planet influences all three houses in the triplicity of houses it occupies, 83
planet located in a house but ruler of another combines the significations of the houses, 65
planet may act first by location and in consequence combine its signification by location with those by rulership, 80
planet outside its sign causes one thing by reason of its house location and another by reason of its rulership, 78
planet that rules over several houses combines those houses, 92
planets are determined by the houses to act in accord with their location, rulership and both together, 83
possible combinations will be made at some time, 80, 82
presence of a planet is more efficacious than rulership of an absent one, 20, 65, 75, 76, 86
ruler of a house in another acts by reason of planets in the house it rules, 84
ruler of a house in another combines those houses in accord with possible combinations and the planet's state, 80
ruler of a house in another sometimes combines its effects through location with those through rulership, 80
ruler of one house in another prefigures possible combinations in accord

with its nature, analogy and celestial state, 77
ruler of two houses outside those houses, 88
several planets in the same house and their dispositor outside that house, 71
take a principal place in judicial foresight, 82
those other than 1st house combinations are judged according to a threefold consideration, 86
through house rulership of two planets that come together, 89
when a planet is significator of one accident by rulership and another by body sometimes one or the other and sometimes both occur, 83–84

House combinations, 1st house exception, 76, 85-86
1st house exception implied, 86
1st house significations are caused and signified more efficaciously and certainly by rulership alone than are the rest by bodily location even added to rulership, 76
1st house significations are the first of all and the foundation of the rest, 76
1st house signifies the native himself, 85
1st ruler in another house combines the native's life, health, character &c with the significations of the other house, 85
1st ruler in another house determines life, character, and inborn talent in accord with the significations of the house in which it is, 76
1st ruler in the 1st house vs. in another house, 138
aspect to the Horoscope or a planet in the 1st from the 1st ruler in another house, 124
if the 1st ruler is in another house or the ruler of another house in the 1st the combination will be reciprocal, 85

House combinations with 1st, Particular
1st house planet conjunct or aspecting the 10th ruler or aspecting a planet in the 10th, 66; 1st house planet conjunct, square or opposite 8th ruler, 66; 1st ruler in 10th vs. 10th ruler in 1st, 85; 1st ruler in 10th, 9th or 5th, 138; 1st ruler in 12th or 8th or the contrary, 123; 1st ruler in 6th, 84; 1st ruler in 8th, 66; 1st ruler in 8th vs. 8th ruler in 1st, 85; 1st ruler in 9th with 7th ruler vs. in 7th with 9th ruler, 76; 1st ruler Jupiter in 2nd opposite Saturn in 8th, 109; 1st ruler Sun in 10th vs. in 8th, 75; 1st ruler with 12th or 8th ruler vs. with 10th or 11th ruler, 89; 1st ruler with 12th ruler Sun, 31; 1st ruler with 8th ruler, partile, applying or mutually applying, or departing, 117; house in which the 1st and 8th rulers meet, and their dispositor and aspects to them, 117; dispositor of Mercury in 1st, 84; Horoscope directed to 12th ruler in 1st vs. to 10th ruler in 1st, 80; 1st and 8th rulers mutually departing, 117; 1st ruler applying to 8th ruler, 117; ruler of 1st and 8th in 7th, 88; same planet rules 1st and 10th, 92; same planet rules 1st and 12th or 8th, 123

House combinations, Particular
2nd ruler in 4th, 7th or 10th vs. in 12th, 87; 2nd ruler in 7th vs. 7th ruler in 2nd, 86; 2nd ruler with 10th ruler or 8th ruler with 12th ruler, 89; 4th and 11th ruler Mars in 7th trine the Sun in 10th, 108; 4th ruler in 5th, 83; 4th ruler Moon in 7th, 20; 6th ruler in 7th, 83; 7th or 10th ruler well or badly conditioned in 2nd, 65–66; 7th ruler in 2nd, 106; 7th ruler in 8th, 83; 8th house planet that rules over two other houses, 90; 8th house signification of death combined, 89; 10th ruler in 11th vs. 11th ruler in 10th, 87; 10th ruler in 12th or 8th or the contrary, 123; 10th ruler in 12th vs. 12th ruler in 10th, 86–87, 87; 10th ruler in 8th, 81; 10th ruler Sun in 11th, 69; 11th ruler in 12th vs. 12th ruler in 11th, 76, 87; 12th house planet applies to 8th ruler, 71; 12th ruler vs. 10th ruler in 7th, 53; benefics in 2nd trine benefic

207

dispositor in 10th vs. malefics in 12th square or opposed to malefic dispositor in 6th or 8th, 122; dispositor of Sun in 10th, 84; Jupiter in 12th as ruler of 1st and dispositor of the Sun in 4th, 85; ruler of another house in 8th vs. 8th ruler in another house, 89–90; same planet rules 10th and 12th or 8th, 123; same planet rules 7th and 8th, 92; Venus in 3rd and her dispositor in 1st as ruler of 12th, 85

House rulers
    act as an efficient cause of the essential significations of the house, 74
    domicile rulership, other things equal, overcomes that by exaltation or triplicity rulership, 95, 97
    factors that determine precedence among house rulers, 91–92
    house ruled by a single planet, especially in its domicile and in that house, 91
    if Libra is in the 1st character is judged from Venus and Saturn and their state, 94
    of the cusp takes precedence though others are not to be neglected, 91
    ruler by domicile and by exaltation are both always to be observed, 95
    ruler of a house in the house, 77
    ruler of a house prefigures the same as a planet located in the house only more weakly, 77
    ruler of a sign in a house rules the house, 74
    rulers of the same house contrary by nature, state or mutual aspect, 91
    secondary ruler of a house, 74–75, 110
    signify the same thing as if they were in those houses, 52
    to assess any house consider the planet whose exaltation is there, 94
    when several planets rule a house a mixture, a division and sometimes a contrariety occur, 91

House, Several planets in
    all benefics or all malefics or both benefics and malefics, 68
    all planets in a house jointly govern its essential significations, 68
    benefic and malefic here means such by nature, celestial state or determination, 71
    benefic follows a malefic or a malefic follows a benefic in a fortunate or unfortunate house, 71
    consider other planets as they help or hinder the most powerful one and judge from the combination of influences, 68
    each conjoined planet acts separately and with the others, 68, 69
    factors of relative efficacy, 69–70
    identify the planet most powerful for granting, denying, removing or making fortunate or unfortunate significations of the house, 68
    malefic follows a malefic in an unfortunate house, 71
    many planets in a house prefigures something remarkable about its essential significations, 68
    of multiple strong planets determine the strongest and combine them in due proportion, 70
    render judgment from the combination of the mixed influences, 68
    two benefics or two malefics in a house, 70
    two planets in the same house can be combined in nine principal ways, 71–72
    two strong malefics in a fortunate house, 71

House, Single planet in or ruling
    after effects in a house of a planet's nature and state its other determinations are examined, 65
    after its nature note a planet's celestial state, 56
    analogy or contrary analogy of, 57, 58, 61
    congruence of a planet's nature and state with significations of the houses it influences, 59

Subject Index

benefic or malefic well or badly
conditioned in a fortunate or
unfortunate house, 64–65
benefic well conditioned in an
unfortunate house, 63
benefic well, badly or moderately
conditioned in a fortunate house,
59–60
benefic well, badly or moderately
conditioned in an unfortunate house,
60–62
celestial state of malefics in an
unfortunate house, 58
evaluate the planet's nature, analogies,
and concordant or discordant celestial
state, 57
in domicile in the house, 56, 77
located in a fortunate or unfortunate
house it rules, 65
malefic badly, well or moderately
conditioned in a fortunate house, 60
malefic in domicile in unfortunate
houses, 77
malefic peregrine or badly conditioned
in the Horoscope or Midheaven, 58
malefic well conditioned in fortunate or
unfortunate houses, 58
malefic well, badly or moderately
conditioned in an unfortunate house,
62–63
malefics determined to misfortune or
benefics to benefit, or the contrary,
64
may confer, deny, hinder, or remove
accidents of the house, or affect them
fortunately or unfortunately, 56
presence of a planet is more efficacious
than rulership of an absent one, 56,
67
principally acts on and governs the
accidents of that house, 56
what is said about a single planet in a
house applies also to the ruler of a
house, 67

Houses
a determinative kind of virtue is in the
houses, 51
all particular influence comes through
the houses, 8
are divided along the equator, 8
are empty space, 9
are not effective but only determinative,
9, 54
are not intrinsically active but only
determinative, 9, 11, 51, 54
are properly said to determine or signify
only with respect to things, 51–54
circle of position, 111
cusp is the most efficacious point, 69,
77, 91
fortunate houses identified, 59
houses neither remove nor alter
beneficence or malignity of planets
but only determine it, 58
no active virtue is in the houses, 137
planet's nature is not varied by diverse
placements among the houses but
simply determined, 61
planets in angular, cadent or succedent
houses, 123
primary houses, 9, 11, 51, 88, 131, 138
secondary houses, 51, 88
things extrinsic to the native are found
in houses other than 1st, 45
unfortunate houses identified, 58, 61

Houses, Accidental significations
are the essential significations of the
opposite house, 63, 82, 100
effect of a malefic by reason of its
opposition, 63
house rulers are not determined to
accidental significations of a house,
82
of 2nd, 6th and 8th, 63; of 6th and 11th,
100; of 6th by opposition to 12th, 84;
of 8th by opposition to 2nd, 96
of a benefic well conditioned in an
unfortunate house, 63
malefics in 8th in favorable aspect with
benefics, 96
planet in domicile in the 6th prefigures
unfortunately for significations of the
12th, 100

planet in domicile or exalted in a house is exiled or fallen in the opposite one, 100
planet strong by state strongly signifies the opposite house and if weak, weakly, 82
planet's adverse action on significations of the opposite house, 83

Houses, Derived and their combinations 10th is 8th with respect to 3rd and 12th is 8th with respect to 5th, 134; 3rd ruler in 8th, 132; 3rd ruler in 8th vs. in 10th, 89; 5th ruler in 12th, 134; 8th and 10th with respect to the 1st are death and honors only of the native, 131, 134; 8th house is the 8th only with respect to the 1st, 88
accidents of persons who affect the native are in the native's geniture, 51
celestial influence is determined by the houses not absolutely or indifferently but insofar as it refers to the native, 130–31
combinations of derived houses function like combinations taken from the 1st, 134–35
essential significations of each house are first and *per se* accidents of the native, 130, 132
planets signify re the native and his accidents and about things or persons houses signify, 55
reckoning of houses is not the same for the native as for others, 88
universal vs. particular figures, 131–32

Houses, Derived significations, cause of, *132–34*
an admirable divine providence connects or permits connection of genitures that agree in common effects, 132–34
Bellantius supposes earlier figures are a universal cause with respect to later figures, 132
is not in the nativity of either figure alone, 133
one who is to be murdered will not lack an assailant and one who is to marry unfortunately will not lack a suitable wife, 133–34

Houses, Particular
1st house, 2, 17, 19, 27, 28, 31, 45, 51, 52, 53, 54, 56, 58, 59, 61, 66, 76, 80-81, 82, 83, 84, 85, 86, 88, 89, 90, 94, 106, 107, 108, 111, 112, 116, 117, 120, 122, 123, 124-25, 126-27, 129, 130, 132, 134, 143; 2nd house, 51, 57, 59, 60, 63, 65-66, 71, 79, 80, 86, 87, 89, 90, 96, 106, 108, 109, 122, 123, 128, 135-37; 3rd house, 55, 59, 79, 80-81, 82, 88-89, 104, 114, 128, 131, 132, 134; 4th house, 17, 20, 59, 80-81, 82, 83, 85, 87, 94, 96, 104, 108, 131, 135; 5th house, 79, 83, 100, 123, 131, 134, 138; 6th house, 59, 63, 82, 83, 84, 96, 100, 122; 7th house, 18, 19-20, 52-53, 57, 58, 59, 61, 62, 65-66, 71, 76, 81, 82, 83, 86, 87, 88, 90, 92, 94, 106, 108, 117, 123, 125, 128, 130, 131, 137; 8th house, 42, 51, 58, 59, 60, 61-62, 63, 66, 69, 71, 75, 77, 81, 82, 83, 85, 88-90, 92, 96, 100, 104, 106-07, 108, 113, 114, 115-16, 117, 122, 123, 128, 130, 131-32, 134; 9th house, 59, 76, 80, 83, 87, 96, 138; 10th house, 17, 51, 52, 53, 57, 58, 59, 60, 62, 66, 69, 70, 71, 75, 76, 77, 79, 80, 82, 84, 85, 86, 87, 88, 89, 90, 93, 96, 100, 108, 109; 112, 114, 116, 122, 123, 128, 131, 134, 137, 138, 11th house, 53, 59, 69, 71, 76, 87, 89, 90, 93, 96, 100, 108, 114; 12th house, 17, 31, 53, 57, 58, 60, 61, 62, 63, 64, 68, 69, 71, 75-76, 77, 78, 80, 81, 82, 84, 85, 86-87, 89-90, 100, 107, 115, 116, 117, 122, 123, 130, 134
1st house signifies with respect to things intrinsic to the native, 45
7th participates to some degree in misfortune, 61
Saturn feral in the 1st signifies a hermit or monk, 120

Houses, Planets' seven states in relation to, *124–25*

Houses, Realizations in

celestial bodies act on accidents of the houses by granting, denying, removing or affecting fortunately or unfortunately what has been granted, 54–55

nature and state of planets in or ruling a house signify whether the native will have something and, if so, its quality and quantity, 52-55, 60, 68, 84-85

prediction of particular effects requires that the receiving subject and the terrestrial state of the relevant Planets be taken into account, 30

planets confer, deny, hinder, remove, or affect fortunately or unfortunately accidents of the houses, 55, 56

removing what is granted pertains to its success and stability, 55

J

Judgment
above all note in each house whether the causes of granting, denying or removing are powerful and distinguish them from each other, 55

action of celestial bodies is both perceptible and imperceptible, 110

although judgment is difficult for human capacities it is not impossible because the effect follows the nature and state of the most powerful planet, 101

effects are to be judged only from particular and stronger causes, 110

even at first sight of a figure a true judgment is composed from the proper and more principal causes of an accident, 110

from celestial state and determinations of planets in the 1st or 10th and the house rulers a judgment can be made at the outset whether the geniture is fortunate or unfortunate, 122–23

house combinations take a principal place in judicial foresight, 82

in almost all figures the causes of effects are evident from the planets' bodily location, rulership, and aspects, 94

is composed from the nature, then celestial state and finally the other local determinations of a planet in a house, 56

is to be pronounced according to the strongest planet, 110

it is error to base judgment on undetermined significators, 1

many things are to be attended to about every planet, 101

notwithstanding the weakness of human discernment it should not err at least about the most notable things, 118

of the greatest importance in judgments is to know whether possible house combinations always occur, 78

only that part of the *Caelum* determined to the relevant house concurs in particular effects, 45, 50–51

principal concealed treasures of, 18, 31, 66, 126

principal considerations for judgment on the significations of each house, 18, 117–18

requires circumspection lest the astrologer dishonor himself and the art, 110

the whole *Caelum* concurs with the effect of a person seen as a totality, 45

Judgment, Planets' seven states in relation to the houses, *124–25*

Judgment, Seven considerations to assess each aspect, *123–24*

Judgment, Ten considerations to assess each planet, *119–23*

L

Lunations, 131, 133

M

Magnetic force, 140

Midheaven, 27, 28, 53, 58, 76-77, 80, 87,

104, 107, 108, 111, 116, 121, 127
cusp itself vs. degree of the sign on the cusp, 77
directions of, 116
malefics in and sending malefic rays to the ruler, 58
planet on the Midheaven, 77
ruler in unfavorable condition, 100
sign on it is more efficacious than its ruler or a planet in it, 28
Midheaven ruler, 2, 61, 62, 75, 80, 81, 87, 92, 100, 121

O

Of the new star. See Kepler, Johannes in the Index of Persons

P

Part of Fortune, 106

Planets
  act as partners with other planets and fixed stars through disposition and aspects, 29, 35, 56, 104, 107, 114
  act as partners with other planets in the government of the World, 35
  act as partners with other planets that aspect the same significator, 114
  act as partners with the signs they occupy or rule, 29, 34, 36, 73, 104, 107, 136-37,
  act by reason of their nature and celestial state, 74
  act only according to their nature, celestial state and local determinations, 122
  act universally and particularly, 8, 30, 75
  are essentially determined to things with which they have an analogy, 16
  are the Governors of the World, 35
  beneficial things are caused by a planet's benefic nature or fortunate celestial state, 64
  benefit caused by malefics is ever mixed with misfortune, 71
  cause only that to which they are determined, 50
  celestial or influential nature distinct from elemental nature, 12
  celestial vs. elemental effects, 8
  depend as a partner on the sign they occupy and do not act without it, 73
  depend as partners in action on the sign they occupy and on their connections with other stars, 107
  each has an intrinsic and unqualified essential virtue that acts universally and is determined by particular receivers, 101-2
  each is active intrinsically and from its own formal virtue independently of the sign over which it rules, 78
  each planet produces different kinds of effects of the same essential nature in different houses, 11
  formal or essential determination of, 14
  from benefics more is to be hoped and less is to be feared and from malefics the contrary, other things being equal, 119
  from nature and celestial state a mixture of virtues arises in which nature prevails, 31
  in fixed or moveable signs, 123
  misfortune is caused by a planet's malefic nature or celestial state or by the exaggeration of a malefic influence, 63-64
  must necessarily act with some sign, 29
  nature and celestial state are universal, 31
  nature and formal virtue is difficult to discern, 10
  planet and the sign it occupies mix their forces yet each acts separately, 74
  primary planets, 8, 113
  secondary or proper motion, 54, 111, 112
  stars cannot influence particularly without the concurrence of the *Primum Caelum*, 9
  Sun and Moon determined to fortunate or unfortunate houses, 122

Sun illuminates other planets and excels them, 36
superior and inferior, 113
their influential or essential virtue is universal and indifferent, 15
universal virtue is known from a planet's nature and its helping or hindering celestial state, 31
were essentially determined to their proper natures and formal virtues, 10
with other planets have a composite influx, 11
with the mixture of its nature and its celestial state a planet acts on the native as determined in the figure, 31

Planets in domicile. *See also* Celestial state; Planets, Dignities and debilities of
act in this respect purely and independently, 119
are undivided in their power, independent, strong and in itself benefic, 77
nature is unmixed with another, 11
signify about the stability of things or about stable things, 98
their influential nature or virtue is doubled, 13, 27

Planets, Dignities and debilities of. *See also* Celestial state; Planets in domicile
by accident a planet simply peregrine can be in a better and more effective state than one essentially well conditioned, 99
effects of planets in the various essential dignities and debilities, 93, 98, 99, 119
in an adverse sign planets' forces are hindered and distorted, 27
in exile or fall a planet is in a sign contrary to its nature, 99
peregrine and simply peregrine, 57, 58, 59, 70, 99, 116, 119, 120
planet acts on the significations of the houses by reason of its dignities of exaltation and triplicity, 97
planet in a non-hostile sign has middling influxes, 27
planet is said to be well or badly conditioned in the sign it occupies and retains that condition, 73
planet outside the house of its exile does not act by reason of its exile in that house, 102
planet simply peregrine is in a middle state between essentially well conditioned and badly conditioned, 99
planet's dignity or debility in another's sign reveals something about that planet's nature, 101
power by domicile, exaltation and triplicity, 93, 95
power of dignity of exaltation in another house, 94
Saturn in exile or fall in 12th, 8th or 10th, 100
when a planet is in the domicile of another the two planets combine their virtues, 29

Primum Caelum, 7, 9, 34, 35, 141, 142
among physical causes is the one most like God, 141
as the first physical cause is determinable both universally and particularly, 22
concurs in all the effects of secondary or inferior causes, 33
eminently contains the elemental qualities, 9
first physical cause, 8, 21, 73, 126, 141
first unique cause of celestial effects and first common cause of elemental ones, 9
formal determination of, 10
is determined to kinds of substantive effects by the receiving subject, 30
is the first cause and is determinable in every way, 26
is unalterable, 22
Primary motion, 54, 137
Primum mobile, 9, 21, 22, 24, 111

Q

Quadripartite. See Ptolemy, Claudius in the Index of Persons

R

Receiver of celestial influence
    a person receives an impression from the *Caelum*, 28
    a planet's virtue is received in the manner of the receiver, 50
    only things congruous with the condition of the native are accustomed to happen, 83
    son of a king is different from the son of a peasant, 30
    sublunary bodies receive from celestial bodies, 21
    sublunary subjects determine substantive effects of planets and the *Caelum*, 30
    sublunary things determine planets' influence to kinds of accidents congruent with themselves, 30
    virtue of the celestial figure is continuously imprinted on sublunary things and is received in the mode of the receiver, 141

S

Salt, sulfur and mercury, the three chemical properties of bodies, 140

Secondary ruler
    of a house or planet, 75, 110

Sign and cause
    a cause may lack concurrence or be hindered entirely by preventative grace, 44
    a sensible sign is diagnostic, prognostic, or recollective, 37
    a sensible sign presents itself to a sense and reveals something to the understanding that is unknown to the senses, 37
    celestial bodies are both signs and causes, 40, 51–52
    celestial bodies signify things only as they cause what they are said to signify, 52
    celestial causes are said to signify only from their effects, 49
    celestial configuration at birth is an actual and potential cause, 43
    celestial constitution at birth contains the power of the accidents to be produced at congruent times through directions, transits, and revolutions, 41
    celestial constitution at birth is the cause of that of which it is a diagnostic and prognostic sign, 41
    celestial figure at birth is a recollective, diagnostic, and prognostic sign, 40-41
    celestial figure at birth is a recollective, diagnostic and prognostic sign and a cause of the present and future, 43
    celestial figure is an actual cause of that of which it is a diagnostic sign and a potential one of that of which it is a prognostic sign, 41
    force of the seed affected by the celestial influx at the moment of conception is a cause, 43
    from the constitution of the *Caelum* at birth the propensities, character, and the whole fated subjection are imprinted like a seal on the native, 40
    if the celestial constitution were not an efficient cause some other cause would be needed to bring about the exact conformity to it, 41
    if the stars do what they signify the planets that are significators of accidents must cause them by directions or revolutions, 41
    in *Genesis*, Chapter 10, the Sun and Moon are causes of days, years and seasons, and signs of other effects, 38
    infant is born in a state of the *Caelum* and a location most congruent with

his temperament and constitution, 40
infant's temperament and bodily constitution precede birth, 40
Jeremiah, Chapter 10 refers to idols of the Babylonians, not to celestial bodies, 38

Significators
abuse of universal significators, *14–20*
Jupiter is not a significator of wealth if he has no connection to the 2nd house, 137
particular significations require particular determinations, 17
principal significator, 56, 80, *135–37*
principal significator identified and others prioritized, 137
signification is what is signified by an efficient cause, 54
universal significators are mistaken for particular ones, 17
universal significators signify the same throughout the whole World and for all sublunary things, 18, 31, 49, 75
universal, general or essential significators, 1

Stability, 55, 59, 60, 71, 98, 123

T

Terrestrial state. *See* Determination, Local

Transits
demonstrate that the planets determine the *Primum Caelum* to their nature and condition, 73
transit through the Horoscope vs. rising by the primary motion, 54
transiting planets act according to the natures of, and their own relation to, the places where they occur, 73

Triplicities
a change in any sign belongs in a certain way to the whole triplicity of that sign, 97
diurnal and nocturnal triplicity rulers are distinguished, and primary and secondary rulers are assigned, 98
judgment from the ruler of the sign is more certain than from the triplicity ruler, 97
minimal powers are to be attributed to the triplicity rulers, 97
planets in diverse triplicities vs. in a single triplicity, 98
power of the aspects is far more efficacious than that of the triplicity rulers alone, 97
signs act in accord with the nature and state of their rulers, 97
signs of the same triplicity agree in elemental nature and differ in formal virtue, 97
triplicity ruler of a sign is a more remote cause and one on which the sign does not essentially depend, 97
triplicity rulers are more effective with respect to temperament and constitutions of the air, 97
true things are predicted from erroneous triplicity rulers only when true causes concur, 95
virtues are certainly in the triplicity rulers and judgment can be had from them, 97

Triplicity rulers of the sect light, 95–97
nothing is predicted from the triplicity rulers of the sect light that could not be more strongly and evidently predicted by location, rulership and aspects, 95–96

W

World, 12, 13, 18, 21, 31, 35, 36, 57, 58, 63, 73, 74, 75, 94, 103, 131
annual revolutions of, 133
regions of, 8
what happens in the inferior region is caused by the superior ones, 49

Z

Zodiacal signs
act elementally in accord with their determination and influentially in

accord with their rulers' natures, 12–13
act in accord with the nature of their ruler and against the nature of the planet that would be exiled in the sign, 101–2
actively influence alone and with the planets, 9
are mobile through the primary houses, 9
are of the same nature as their rulers, 11, 12, 18, 29, 35, 52
are parts of the *Primum Caelum* that were determined from the planets, 9
depend on the nature and celestial state of their ruler, 74
influence with the planets as first and second causes of the same effect, 9
intercepted sign, 56
repeat the natures of the planets, 11
Saturn's domiciles both have a Saturnine influential nature and have contrary elemental natures, 13
sign acts always by reason of its ruler's nature and celestial state but not always by reason of its terrestrial state, 81
sign depends in its action on the nature and formal virtue of its ruler, 73–74
sign depends on its ruler's celestial state in its universal action and on its ruler's terrestrial state in its particular action, 75
sign in a house acts on the significations of the house in dependence on its ruler and in accordance with its ruler's nature and celestial and terrestrial state, 78
sign is a part of the *Primum Caelum* determined to the nature of some planet, 73
signify in accord with planets in domicile, exaltation and triplicity there, 28
signify more and more efficaciously than the planets, 28

www.ingramcontent.com/pod-product-compliance
Lightning Source LLC
Chambersburg PA
CBHW062018220426
43662CB00010B/1376